SUBHAS ANANDAN

THE BEST I COULD

SUBHAS ANANDAN

THE BEST I COULD

Marshall Cavendish
Editions

© 2009 Subhas Anandan and Marshall Cavendish International (Asia) Private Limited

First printed 2009.
Reprinted 2009 (three times), 2010, 2011, 2012, 2014

This edition published 2015.

Editor: Lee Mei Lin
Designer: Benson Tan

Published by Marshall Cavendish Editions
An imprint of Marshall Cavendish International
1 New Industrial Road, Singapore 536196

Other Marshall Cavendish Offices:
Marshall Cavendish Corporation. 99 White Plains Road, Tarrytown NY 10591-9001, USA • Marshall Cavendish International (Thailand) Co Ltd. 253 Asoke, 12th Flr, Sukhumvit 21 Road, Klongtoey Nua, Wattana, Bangkok 10110, Thailand • Marshall Cavendish (Malaysia) Sdn Bhd, Times Subang, Lot 46, Subang Hi-Tech Industrial Park, Batu Tiga, 40000 Shah Alam, Selangor Darul Ehsan, Malaysia

Marshall Cavendish is a trademark of Times Publishing Limited

National Library Board Singapore Cataloguing in Publication Data
Anandan, Subhas, 1947-2015.
Subhas Anandan : the best I could. – Singapore : Marshall Cavendish Editions, c2009.
p. cm.
ISBN : 978-981-4677-81-3 (pbk.)
1. Anandan, Subhas, 1947-2015. 2. Lawyers – Singapore – Biography. 3. Trials (Murder) – Singapore. I. Title.
KPP11
340.092 -- dc22   OCN262489315

Printed in Singapore by Fabulous Printers Pte Ltd

To my son, Sujesh,
who indirectly gave me the idea of writing this book,
and to my wife, Vimi,
who made it possible by typing out my rambling thoughts,
crystallising my ideas and clarifying my writing.
I thank them both for always allowing me to focus
on doing the best I can in my profession.

To my late brother, Surash,
who left me without saying goodbye
on October 31, 2000.

CONTENTS

REFLECTIONS

ACKNOWLEDGEMENTS

I started my law firm, Subhas Anandan, Advocate & Solicitor, with $500 given to me by my elder sister, Subhashini, who was then working as a medical officer. When I told her that I needed $500 to start it, she was surprised I could start a law firm with just that amount. I told her that the money was to open a current account so I could issue cheques. My sister, who is a very generous person, offered me more money. But I refused with a caveat—I told her that if I needed more funds, I would call on her. True to form, I did call on her generosity many times and she did not turn me down once. I don't think that I have repaid all the money I borrowed from her yet.

On my first day of practice, my younger sister, Sugadha, who was then a relief teacher (she is now a reading specialist in the Ministry of Education with a Master's degree in English), gave me a poster which read something like: Aim High, Aim Far, Aim for the Sky, Aim for the Stars. I stared at the poster and wondered at the audacity of my sister to think I could reach the stars. I was just hoping to make ends meet. Today, when I hit the headlines, I think of that poster and my younger sister. She had the courage to dream for me.

My younger brother, Sudheesan, who was then working in the Ministry of Defence did not say anything. He is the sort who will not interfere but you can be sure he will be there for you through thick and thin. I owe him my undying gratitude for all he did for me when I was in prison in 1976. He played football for Singapore and was the captain of the National Youth Team but this fact is not known to many.

My late younger brother, Surash, was then a well-known footballer in the early 1970s. He played for Singapore and made a name for himself. His only goal against West Germany in Tokyo was, at that time, the talking point in many a sporting function. He was one of my biggest fans as I was his. During my days in prison, I was known as his brother and I was so proud of him when prisoners came to talk to me about him.

My father was more a friend than a father. I recall when my own son was three years old, he was asked by some friends how he related to me and his answer was: "My father is, firstly, my best friend. Secondly he is my partner, and thirdly, he is my father, and sometimes he is my enemy." I am glad I passed on my relationship with my father to my son.

To my mother, I was everything. She openly showed her bias and to the credit of my siblings, they took this without any grudges. To some extent, they were all quietly spoiling me as well when I was growing up. In fact, they are still spoiling me even at this age. In many ways, my mother was also everything to me. She did say that I made her cry the most but I also made her laugh the most. She was the only person who could make me do what I didn't want to do.

When I was studying for my 'A' level and university exams, she used to sit with me to keep me company. Quite often when my friends felt I needed a break, they would come by around midnight with fried chicken and all sorts of other goodies. They would provide entertainment for half an hour before they left me with my studies again. My mother did not know at the time that the chicken was probably stolen from some neighbour. She used to say that part of my law degree belonged to her while my friends said that they were entitled to part of my earnings for the sacrifices they made.

The death of my father was a blow to me. I was not able to deal with it for some time. I had started to earn good money and I wanted to share my good fortune with him. I could only do it for a short time. I remember the pride and joy on his face when he got into my first Mercedes 280S. When I switched on the air-conditioner, he told me to switch it off. I asked him if he was feeling cold. He said that he was not but using the air-conditioner would increase the usage of petrol. I laughed and told him that I could afford it.

At the slightest excuse, he would ask me to give him a lift to meet his friends and sometimes he even requested me to drive one friend to visit another. I realised he just wanted to show off his son's car.

My mother's demise was more acceptable. She witnessed my marriage and had a few years with my son. When my wife Vimi confirmed her pregnancy, she rang my mother up to give her the good news. As usual my mother was lamenting about her ill health and wondering why she was still alive. She was in one of her depressive moods. On hearing the good news, she was delighted and even today, everybody feels that the birth of my son extended her life by another five years.

When she died, in some ways, we were glad because she was suffering a lot of pain and it was terrible to see her controlling her pain to make us feel better. She is the bravest lady I know. She took many a blow and came back stronger. I attribute this to her great faith in her God.

Apart from my family, there are many people who shaped my life and my character. It is practically impossible to name all of them and if I have inadvertently left out some names, please forgive me.

I grew up in the British Naval Base. My childhood friends were many and they had a good influence on me. Friends like Ah Teng, Ah Tee, Chee San, Poh Leong, Ah Soo, Chee Kok, Ramli, Ismail, Mohd Noor, Narainasamy, Ah Sai, Sai Chee, the late Lai Beng, Sivalingam (otherwise known as Mark, who first taught me how to drive) and many others. With these friends, I learnt the meaning of loyalty and realised that true friendship knows no boundaries.

In Naval Base School, I had other friends like Yusof (the last I heard he was in trouble and had run away from Singapore), Resman, Teck Boo, Hin Kiew (whose football wizardry was remarkable) and many others. Teachers like Mr Ngoh Cheong Hock, Mr Gabriel Pillai, Mr Oliver Seet, Mr Haridas and many other teachers also helped to shape me.

I would also like to acknowledge my brother-in-law, Bhas, and my wife's brother-in-law, Nala, for all the medical care they gave me unflinchingly and, of course, for free. My sister-in-law, Nan, for being one of the first to be at my bedside whenever I was in hospital, my sisters-in-law, Syon and Justina, and my niece Sunita for always being there.

To Philip Ong, who ignored his busy work schedule in Shanghai to be at my bedside on the eve of my heart by-pass operation. He was, and always has been, a pillar of strength to me and my family.

My secretary, Sandra Cheng, for assisting my wife in liaising with the publishers. Thusita de Silva for his help to me in writing this book.

Last, but not least, to the late Justice M Karthigesu and Mrs Rathi Karthigesu I owe a debt for all that they have done for me.

Subhas Anandan
October 2008

FOREWORD

Strong friendships have been a very integral part in my brother's life. Growing up in the British Naval Base workers' quarters, he had the good fortune of having good friends in the different phases of his life. In his Naval Base school days, in Raffles Institution and the University of Singapore, Subhas had good friends that stood by him when he needed them. The friendships one makes growing up tend to mould the person one becomes. His growing up experiences with his friends, together with the love, support and guidance of our parents, have crystallised the adult Subhas. In his practise of the law, he had many successes and disappointments, but there were two very distinct phases in his life, and the law he loves passionately, that reveal the character of the man.

In the early years of his law practice, Subhas was framed by rogue police officers and incarcerated in Queenstown Remand Prison under the Criminal Law (Temporary Provisions) Act. Many people then deemed that his life was over. However, that was the period when special friends stood by him and worked tirelessly to get him released. Friends and neighbours, although frightened that they would also become targets of the rogue police conspiracy, still came out in large numbers to support the mass signature campaign to the Home Minister for his release. More than 5,000 signatories joined us in his release petition. Many others gave affidavits to support the contention that Subhas was framed and declared that they would go to court to testify if needed. Indefinite detention is a cruel sentence.

In the darkest hour of our misery, Subhas realised many things. Friendship is a crucible—friends are tested in crises. Most of his friends remained friends. Some, beyond our expectations, eased away, the fear of collateral damage haunting them. A few, to our despair, anguish and pain, gloated. But most of his tested and trusted friends stood by him and his family. They warmed our hearts and gave us courage and hope.

When Subhas was released early, he focused on his law practice. He and his partner, Mr M P D Nair, restructured their firm and took on many cases. In his practise of the law, Subhas showed compassion and empathy for the underdog. Many of the cases in this book testify to this. He has been there for people accused of heinous crimes who pleaded for help to clear their names. For many of them, Subhas the defence lawyer became their only friend. His practice blossomed and reputation as an excellent criminal lawyer grew.

The second milestone that shaped his life and his practise of the law was the death of our younger brother Surash, a chief steward in SIA. Surash died tragically in the infamous SQ006 flight that failed to take off from Taipei airport and crashed and burned on the runway on October 31, 2000. His colleagues who survived told us that Surash remained in the burning aircraft helping the passengers under his care to escape. Many survived, but Surash and others were caught in a blinding flash fire and perished. They found Surash close to his friend and colleague, Alfred, who also stayed back to help and made the ultimate sacrifice as well.

In many ways, Subhas reminds me of Surash. Both have the same fierce determination to complete their professional responsibilities.

"Not on my watch. The best I could." These were beacons to them. Like Surash, Subhas also cares for his friends and the people who come to him for help. Both of them had many friends but Surash was the more realistic one. He reminded us that all you need at the end are six friends to be your pallbearers in the Mount Vernon crematorium. Surash had more than a thousand friends in his final send-off.

Subhas is very different now. Many of his life experiences have tempered him, and the criminal cases he shares with us in this book reveal the tough, aggressive, brash, gentle, generous and kind nature of the man. He has always loved being a court-room lawyer, enjoying the cut and thrust of logic, evidence, and setting precedents. He now shares his vast expertise with many young lawyers, teaching and mentoring them. My son, Sunil, his legal assistant, is grateful to his uncle for the guidance and training. Both of them share a deep love of the law.

Friends there were many and many more will come into my brother's life. He knows those who will stick by him regardless of the slings and arrows of misfortune. He is patient, listens well, and has become more compassionate and tolerant. His dry sense of humour and that rare smile that can light up a room is still there.

Our parents taught us well. They always reiterated, "Never forget the good that people have done for you and do your best to help them whenever you can." The practise of law enables Subhas to continue doing this. All of us, his family and his friends in Sembawang and other parts of Singapore, wish him well and pray for his good health, happiness and prosperity.

Sudheesan Anandan
October 2008, Singapore

PREFACE

I have been asked many times why my son is not studying law as though it's a given that he must read law. Some blame me for not encouraging him to be a lawyer while others accuse me of being indifferent. To me, it doesn't really matter if he is a lawyer, a doctor or a salesman. He should grow up to be a good human being. A person who will have time and compassion for those who are less fortunate than him. I want him to have a life where he has time to stop and smell the flowers. I want his life to be a journey of surprises and discovery, and not one where he is in a constant rush. Let him be anything he wants to be as long as he is happy. He should lead his life according to standards he sets for himself and he should not live to please others. He should have the discipline to resist evil and the same discipline not to overindulge. He knows my weaknesses and my strengths, and with that knowledge, he should be able to build his own strengths and discard what is not good for him. I have, to the best of my ability, taught him to differentiate between good from bad. You don't need to be a lawyer to know that.

There is a long-standing TV programme in Singapore called 'Crimewatch'. I remember watching it 10 years ago with my son who was then eight years old. Many of the cases shown in the programme were cases for which I was the defence counsel. Often, I would tell him, "Hey, that was papa's case."

One day, during the showing of a particular case, I got very angry because the police had taken credit for something they did not do. It was such an exaggeration and the police overplayed their importance. I told my wife Vimi: "You know, this is nonsense. Actually it's quite shameful. What they are showing in this programme is nothing like what really happened. I think I should write to the papers to say that they are pulling wool over the public's eyes." The police did a good job in many cases but sometimes their exaggerations were a bit too much.

Vimi didn't think I should send a letter. "Why don't you leave it as it is?" she said. "Don't go and antagonise these police people. Don't you remember why you went to Queenstown Prison? It's because you antagonised some of these people that you got into trouble. So, just leave them alone, please."

My son had been quiet during my rant but he suddenly interrupted us. "Papa, all these people in these cases are your clients?" he asked earnestly.

"Yes, my son, most of them are," I replied with pride in my voice, hoping my young son would be proud of his father and that I could inspire him into a legal career.

"Papa, don't you have any good clients?" he exclaimed and walked away in disgust. I just looked at Vimi and we both burst out laughing.

But his innocent question lingered in my mind for many days after that. How do you tell a boy that everyone charged with an offence is not necessarily guilty? How do you tell him that the defence counsel has an important role to play? How do you tell him that people who are charged with crimes are not necessarily bad people? Some of them commit their crimes on impulse, or perhaps when they are in a state of utter despair, drowning in their own disappointments and frustrations.

How could I tell my son that, sometimes, people hit out at society because they have lost all hope? I couldn't explain these thoughts to my son but I shared them with my wife.

She said, "Yes, I understand that you have to do what you have to do."

"You know, Vimi, in my years of practice, I've seen all sorts of people. I've seen the best in men and the worst in men."

When I was young, my father told me that he wanted all his children to receive a university education. That was his target for all of us, which we met. I personally argued with him about it because I was sick of studying by the time I reached the age when I could go to university. But I did and forged this career for myself. It made him very proud. A few years ago, my son indicated to me that he didn't want to read law and, naturally, I had to ask him for his reasons.

"I don't have an interest in that subject, papa. I hope you don't mind," he replied.

"Of course I don't mind. I've never insisted that you must read law and I will encourage and support you in whatever you choose to do."

When I asked him what he wanted to do, he replied, "Banking and finance."

I said, "Okay, that's fine." My wife listened to our conversation but didn't say anything. She asked me later if I was disappointed and I told her that I honestly wasn't. As I have stated, my son has to make his own choices in life. I will support him in whatever he does.

It wasn't like that for me initially. In 1963, I was sent to India to study medicine because my mother wanted me to be a doctor. I lost one whole year of my life trying to please my mother. I knew from the first few classes I attended that I wasn't suited to study medicine. I was very homesick too. I came back after only three months in Loyola

College, Madras, and enrolled in Raffles Institution. I had to wait a long time to start school because the school year was already in full swing. I wouldn't want my son to be in a position where he is doing something he doesn't want to do just to please me or my wife.

Right now, he's chasing his own dream, studying banking and financial services at Ngee Ann Polytechnic. He chose to go to the polytechnic despite qualifying for a place in a junior college because he wanted to start doing the subjects that he liked straight away. He said there was no point in doing history or geography or physics or chemistry when he could embark on banking and finance at Ngee Ann. It made sense to me. But lately, he has shown some interest in the law which I'm secretly pleased about. He will read the case files that I bring home from the office and sometimes even discuss aspects of those cases with me. I find his input valuable also because he provides me with an insight into how his generation thinks about crime and punishment. In fact, he has enlightened me on many issues. I must say that, even after almost four decades of working as a lawyer, crime and punishment is something which I find very hard to define. Many books and papers have been written, but to me it's a subject that bears different definitions for different people. Like my career as a lawyer, crime and punishment has evolved since I first started. It's like a living being I have walked side by side with all these years, our respective paths sometimes crossing but never for too long.

Not long ago, as I was addressing the Court of Appeal in a case of the prosecution's appeal against the sentence of three years given to a person who had killed his pregnant wife, I was trying very hard to argue why the sentence was not manifestly inadequate. I was throwing arguments about how there must be rehabilitation. The Court of Appeal, comprising Justice of Appeal Andrew Pang, Justice of Appeal

V K Rajah and Justice Tay Yong Kwang listened very attentively. I was stopped at one stage by the presiding judge, Andrew Pang. He said: "You know, Mr Anandan, we agree with you on rehabilitation and the need to rehabilitate offenders, especially those who suffer from mental disorders, but don't you think that this court also has the responsibility to look after the interest of the community?"

I agreed. "Of course, you have the responsibility to look after the community."

"Don't you think we should balance the rights of the accused person and the rights of the community and society in general, and make sure that the rights of the accused person do not supersede the rights of the community?" Justice Pang asked.

Again, I agreed. "Yes, Your Honour, it's a very fine balancing act and I am glad that I don't have to do it. The responsibility is yours." It was the first time I saw Justice Pang showing one of his rare smiles. Justice Rajah was smiling too. Naturally, they reserved judgment on the appeal and subsequently raised the prison sentence from three to five years. I thought it was fair, especially as the prosecution was asking for 10 years.

One of the questions that people often ask me is how I deal with my cases and the accused persons. I always tell them that preparation for a case is not an easy task, especially when it is a capital case. In capital cases, you are burdened with a very heavy responsibility because the life of the accused is at stake. You simply cannot afford to make mistakes. If you do, there is a possibility that your client will hang. The situation puts you under a lot of stress and the pressure is unrelenting. You have to do the best you can to keep your client away from the gallows.

In the last few years, I have been lucky in the sense that I have my nephew, Sunil, to help me. He does most of the ground work of running around and most of the preparation. He has a passion for criminal law and does his research very well. We also have our own interns and other legal associates who will do research and prepare documents and briefs, which I read and correct if necessary. Whatever others do for you on a case, you still have to countercheck and amend. Sometimes, you have to rehash the whole thing because if something goes wrong in your case, ultimately only you will be held responsible.

Interviewing and taking instructions from the accused person is a very difficult task. In all capital cases, the accused persons are in prison and instructions can only be taken from them there. Practically every Saturday morning, Sunil and I spend our time in one prison or another because that's just about the only time we have to interview clients who are being held there. We are both in court virtually non-stop from Mondays to Fridays, but we do make trips to prison during weekdays when we don't have to appear in court. For accused persons who are out on bail, instructions can be taken in our office at Raffles Place, which is definitely a more conducive environment. We can even do it over a cup of coffee. I can tell you that it's certainly more relaxing as you know that the punishment will not be as harsh as in capital cases. No one's life is in your hands.

When you are seeing the accused for the first time, there are always difficulties. They don't know you and they have no reason yet to trust you. It's very difficult to build trust and confidence in a prison. In the early days of my practice, it was especially difficult because no one knew me. But as I became a little more popular, prisoners started to know about me and it was easier to talk to them. Still, it is no cakewalk. As a lawyer you have to ensure that the accused person is telling you the truth and, to do that, sometimes you have to cross-examine him, just as you would do a witness in court. When you think that the accused is not telling you the whole story, you have to scream and shout at him, or threaten to discharge yourself, or tell him that you know he is a liar. It saps a lot of energy out of you because you have to make judgement calls on people you don't know at all. Only after two or three sessions with the accused person will you get the truth, or at least very close to the truth. Without these sessions, it is very difficult to defend an accused person because you can be caught by surprise by what the prosecution presents in court. In our system where ambush tactics are still allowed, the prosecution sometimes takes full advantage and catches you flat-footed in court. It's definitely not a pleasant feeling for any lawyer when that happens.

As you go through the facts of a case with the accused person, you warn him of the dangerous minefields he could face under cross-examination but you should not coach him on what to say. You can tell him what kind of questions to expect and to reply truthfully. You cannot ask him to lie because that is unethical. It is also a dangerous tactic. You can be caught out because if a client is pressured under cross-examination, he can always turn around and say, "My lawyer instructed me to say this, so why are you shouting at me?" That would be the end for you as it could land you in a lot of trouble. In your mind, you must always remember that your client can be your worst enemy.

As I will bring up later in the book, another source of problems you have in most cases is the relatives and friends of the accused person. They can be a real pain in the neck. Often, they feel that since they have paid you some money, all of them can call you at half hourly intervals to find out what's happening with the case. Uncle will call, aunty will call, cousin will call. I have to say, too, that this is more of a problem with my Indian clients. Of course some of these calls are out of genuine concern for the accused person, but in many instances, you get the feeling that they are doing it because they think it's their right. So, what we do is that when we visit the accused person, we tell him to inform his relatives and friends to stop bothering us because it interrupts our work. When they hear that we are not able to do our jobs properly defending the accused person, they usually back off. That's how we deal with this particular type of problem. But having said that, we must always remember that as practising lawyers, relatives and friends are part and parcel of the deal. We try hard to be diplomatic in our dealings with them.

In fact, some of these relatives and friends can be very helpful. They can give us information which the accused person has forgotten or not given because he thinks it casts him in an unfavourable light. Yes, relatives and friends can be a nuisance at times, but they are always available to help you out. For example, they will personally bring a witness to the office to allow us to record a statement. We can understand the agony and the stress that parents and siblings go through especially when their son or brother faces a capital case. So, you have to give them some leeway, you have to empathise. However much you feel like screaming at them or telling them to get out of the office when they get so irritating that it affects your work, you have to choose to control that feeling, smile at them and offer them a cup of coffee instead. You have to take deep breaths, remain calm and assure them that you are doing your best for their loved one. In capital cases, everyone wants you to give a kind of guarantee that the accused person will not hang or, in other cases, that they will not go to jail. But when the accused person goes to jail or gets sentenced to death, the family and friends will pounce on you because they think you have reneged on your promise. They will scream at you and abuse you in public. In their frustration, they will even report you to the Law Society.

Lawyers should never make promises or give guarantees. I will usually give an assurance that I will do my best for the accused person. I'll tell the family that we have a whole team who will be involved in the accused person's defence and who will do their best. But the outcome of a trial cannot be guaranteed because that's the nature of the law. And I will go on record here to say that any lawyer who gives you a guarantee is a snake-oil merchant and only interested in your money. How can anyone make such a commitment when the system is so unpredictable? Anything can happen in a trial. Usually, when we give the family our assurance that we will do our best, that is enough. If they insist on a guarantee, I will always tell them that I would like to discharge myself from the case.

For the most part of my years as a lawyer, my wife has been by my side. She worked with me when I was running a small firm in the 1970s—we weren't married then. She was in charge of conveyancing. She knows what happens in a legal firm, and is well aware of all the trials and tribulations I go through with the courts, accused persons, their families and friends. When I get frustrated, she's the calming influence. Vimi stopped work when she was pregnant with my son and never went back to work after that. She devoted herself to being a good mother and a good wife. She not only drives me around but also takes care of all issues pertaining to our household. This includes the task of dispensing the 15 types of medication I require on a daily basis because of my health. Her dedication to my health gives me the peace of mind to attend strictly to my passion—my work. At the end of each day, I will tell her almost everything I did that day. I often tap on her for opinions to give a new perspective to handling a case in question. Vimi is my multi-tasking princess—she's my nurse, my driver, my financial controller, my best friend, my partner.

When she married me, she knew about my health condition. I suffered my first heart attack in December 1978. I collapsed on a field while playing football for graduates of the University of Singapore against undergraduates. I was rushed to Toa Payoh Hospital by my good friend, Choo Ker Yong. The ECG showed that I was having a massive heart attack and I was immediately warded in the ICU. I spent my 31st birthday in the ICU, struggling for my life. Partly because it was my birthday, everyone came to see me. There were too many visitors. Towards the end of the visiting hour, my elder sister, who was a doctor there, noticed a visible slur in my speech and she quickly got rid of the visitors, but the harm had already been done. All that excitement had triggered a stroke. I was paralysed on the right side and lost my ability to speak. I was diagnosed with a blood clot on the left side of my brain. With the stroke, my heart weakened and the graph showed that my heartbeat was coming dangerously close to a flat line. I believe many of my relatives and friends had given up hope. Some of my friends later confessed to me that they were praying for me to die. They didn't want me to survive half paralysed and dumb. Most of them prayed for me to recover fully. Vimi was outside the ward, praying along with the rest.

While I was fighting for my life in the hospital, my elder sister took leave and stayed with me every day. My other family members were also always there and whenever I opened my eyes, I would see one of them sitting beside me. It gave me a great sense of comfort and confidence that I would recover. My late brother, Surash, would sit outside the ward, reading a book and waiting for me to summon him. When I recovered and could walk to the corridor, I used to stand

and stare at him as he concentrated on his book. After some time he would realise that I was standing beside him and he would put his book down and ask me, with a smile, "How Joe? How are you today?" We sometimes played Scrabble and only later did I realise that he had sat outside the ward throughout the night. We also shared the specially brewed soup made by my then future mother-in-law to speed up my recovery.

The doctors considered my full recovery nothing less than a miracle. I went back to work a few months later. Vimi and the other girls, especially Jacqueline Chow and Lina Lim, looked after me.

Many people thought I would give up my practice after that heart attack. I never even contemplated it. Some of my rivals in the profession started spreading rumours, telling people that I had lost my legal mojo after my heart attack and that I didn't have the stamina to continue. The more I heard those vicious rumours (some even spread by my own friends), the more disillusioned I became. I went back to smoking, a habit which I had given up for a few months after my heart attack. But I continued to practise with a vengeance to show everybody I was still capable of good work.

Many readers will wonder why I chose to feature the cases that appear in this book. They were selected for various reasons: some because of their high profile nature, some for their complexity and some because of their simplicity. But most of all, they were chosen because they somehow brought out the best in me. All these cases also had a profound effect on me and even now I have flashbacks of good and bad memories of them. I hope readers will enjoy my simple narration of the facts and my feelings. I have written for the man in the street, not for law students and lawyers to analyse.

At the time of writing, I was already briefed to act for three accused persons charged with murder and drug trafficking. The briefs look very interesting. In one of them, the accused is a Chinese national charged for the murder of her brother-in-law. I was asked to defend her by the Chinese embassy. Cases keep coming in, some more interesting than others.

When I was released from prison in November 1976, I said that I would write a book about my experience in prison. *The New Nation*, a newspaper that is now defunct, headlined on the front page: "Subhas to tell his own story". David Marshall, after reading the article, called me and warned me to be careful. He said that it was easy to fall into a trap and be charged for breach of some prison regulations. I, too, had reconsidered the position as I realised that I could not say many things because my friends were still incarcerated and I would, in some ways, be breaking their confidence in me. The title of that book was to be "It's Easy To Cry". I started it but never finished writing it. In some ways, this book is a substitute. And who knows—there may even be a sequel depending on whether my wife is prepared to go through the whole rigmarole once again.

THE MOULDING YEARS

The Base

Prefect

Raffles Institution

University Days

First Murder Trial

Becoming a Criminal Lawyer

Temple

Prison

Prison Intermediary

ONE

THE BASE

The floor was icy cold and I could feel the chill creeping through my body as I lay on the floor of a solitary confinement cell in Queenstown Remand Prison. I tried to inform the prison officer that I suffer from claustrophobia and this made him even more determined that I should spend the night alone in the musty, cold, dark and narrow cell. I suspected that he was silently enjoying my predicament. What I feared most was becoming a reality. I started to perspire in the cold as I felt the walls of the cell closing in on me. Suddenly I was afraid and my imagination ran wild. The fear that I felt was strange to me, for the only two things that I feared in the past were the tears in my mother's eyes and the anger on my father's face. Without wanting to boast, I feared nothing else then. I remember reading somewhere that the only way to overcome this feeling of fear was to think of happy times. So I said to myself, "Concentrate". Slowly, I let my mind wander to happier times in the past.

I was running with my friends along sloping green fields dissected by winding roads that barely allowed two cars to pass each other. This was the British Naval Base in Sembawang in the north of Singapore. It was a glorious place in those days. We played in parks, cycled on trails and swam at the natural beaches opening to the sparklingly blue waters of the Straits of Johor. Across the straits, we could see the coastline of

Johor. Our neighbourhood was shady and breezy, with huge, almost crouching trees that were older than all of us put together. The Base was simply a paradise for a child. Some of the colonial bungalows I recall from those days are still around today, near the junction of Sembawang Road and Admiralty Road East. The roads still bear the names of British soldiers like Canberra and Wellington.

The Base was a self-contained village and classified as a protected area. There was a swimming pool, a few grocery shops, a barber shop and a drinking hole. The only place we have today that's similar is Seletar Camp but that's being redeveloped into an aerospace hub. Residents at the Base were issued with special entry passes to ensure that no outsiders could enter without the knowledge of the police officers who worked there. My childhood memories of those police officers are not positive. The junior officers were mostly local. They were often drunk on duty, ill-disciplined and easily bribed. A cup of tea or even 10 cents was usually enough to sway them to our point of view.

My father worked as a recorder for the British Royal Navy. I realised later this was a glorified term for a clerk. It was a senior position though, which made my father a high ranking individual in our local community. The fathers of all my friends also worked in the Base, serving their British masters in innocuous ways which all seemed very important at the time. Our quarters, provided for by the British, were austere but comfortable. I lived with my parents and four siblings in Block 9, Room 9. It was one of 16 units in the block and we knew every family that lived there.

Each unit had two bedrooms, a kitchen and a bathroom with a toilet attached. Electricity was free as was the piped water. Our home was at the corner of the block, enclosed in the front by a large L-shaped corridor. Just as what some residents of corner HDB units do today, my parents turned the front portion of the corridor into our living room and a study. My brother, Sudheesan, and I shared the other side of the corridor as a makeshift bedroom. We had much more space than most of the other units. P N Sivaji, who would later become the coach of the Singapore football team and his brother, P N Balji, who is a prominent media man in Singapore, grew up in the unit directly below us. They lived there with their parents and three sisters.

I started my primary school education when I was six years old. I don't know many people who can remember their earliest days in school but I recall mine vividly. The name of my school was Admiralty Asian School. It was housed within the boundaries of the Base and catered for the children of employees of the Base. I say "housed" loosely because the school was essentially a dilapidated old building made of wood and canvas. Some of the classrooms had floors of sand. It was exciting when it rained heavily. Water would pour into the classrooms through cracks in the canvas, showering students who sat under them and splashing mud onto our socks. I remember we could sit anywhere in the classroom and, obviously, there was never a rush to sit near the canvas, especially during rainy days or if dark clouds hovering overhead threatened rain during school hours.

My early education in the Base was fun. When I first started, there were students as old as nine and ten years in my class. As it was a private school, age was not an issue when you were put into a class. The monitors were chosen by the teachers according to size. The bigger you were, the better your chances of being selected. My class had two monitors, one to look out for the boys and one for the girls. I recall they happened to be a brother and sister team. They were much taller and heavier than the rest of us. Even at that age, they knew how to abuse their positions. They would terrorise the rest of us with their clique of friends.

My best friend at that time was a boy called Shashideran, who was Malayalee like me. After months of being bullied by the two monitors, we decided we would not take it any more. One day, during our recess period, we cornered the male monitor in a secluded part of the school grounds and beat him up. His sister came to his rescue but we beat her up too. We were too young to know about being gentlemanly and not hitting girls. When their friends came to help them, many of our classmates joined Shashi and I in the fight. It was eventually stopped by some older students.

When we returned to class after recess, all hell broke loose. Our form teacher, Mrs Foo, was fuming mad. When the monitors were asked about the incident, they pointed without hesitation at Shashi and I as the main instigators. The boy's shirt was torn and he had bruises on his body, topped off by a beautiful black eye. The image of that black eye shines brightly in my memory even today. His sister's blouse was also torn and she too had bruises though they weren't as bad. Mrs Foo beckoned Shashi and I to the front of the class. When she asked us if it was true that we had inflicted the injuries, I didn't lie. I said yes. She stared at me for some time. Then she asked me if I was a hooligan. That was a new word to me and I wondered for a moment what the right answer was. As I had said yes to her first question, I decided to be consistent and say yes again. As soon as I said it, Mrs Foo slapped me. I didn't have time to duck. I don't think teachers are allowed to slap students these days, but when I was younger, it was not an issue. Teachers could hit us on the knuckles with rulers, pull our ears and grab our hair without compunction. It was all part of the character-building process. My face stung with pain and I knew I had given the wrong answer. She turned to Shashi and asked him whether he was a hooligan. Without hesitation, he said yes too and received an even harder slap. As Shashi was fair-skinned, his face soon turned red. Later I asked Shashi why he answered yes, knowing that I got slapped for that same answer. He told me he hadn't realised that. Shashi was a great kid, if not particularly bright. I bumped into him a few years ago. He was driving a taxi for a living and looking very well. We laughed over the incident. However, I must say that Mrs Foo was a fair lady. She made her own inquiries into why the monitors had been assaulted and discovered their bullying nature. They were removed from their positions and we spent the rest of the year with no monitors. That was the end of the indiscriminate bullying.

I did well in primary school, gaining a double promotion from Standard I to Standard III. I was almost given a second double promotion from Standard III to Standard V, but it was vetoed by the Principal, Mr Thambapillay. He said I was too young to be in Standard V. By the time I reached Standard V, our school was transferred to the Naval Base School, and Admiralty Asian School ceased to exist. From then on, we were in a properly run school under the Ministry of Education.

While my primary school days were fun, I think I spent the happiest times of my life in Naval Base School. At the time, it was the only government, English-medium school in Singapore with pupils from Primary 1 to Secondary 4. It was also a co-ed school with morning and afternoon sessions. Children from the greater Sembawang area went to the school, creating a rich mix of students from different backgrounds. Some of them came from families who were so poor that they found it difficult to pay school fees. They often didn't have enough money to buy even the cheapest items in the school tuckshop. I remember some of them living in attap huts in the Sembawang area. Conditions were squalid in those days, with families living in small partitioned rooms within each hut. A common kitchen served all the families. The toilet facilities comprised an outhouse which nightsoil carriers cleared each day. Many residents still used well water to bathe but there were PUB standpipes serving villages. I don't think they had electricity, telephones or street lights. The roads were muddy tracks that would become rivers of flowing mud when it rained heavily. Kerosene lamps were the brightest source of light and these usually lit up the common verandahs of the attap huts. Inside their partitioned rooms, residents had to make do with candles. I felt lucky to be living in the relative comfort of Block 9. The circumstances from which the poorer students came drove some of them to work extremely hard at school so they could escape the poverty trap. Many succeeded, going on to become lawyers like me, and doctors and engineers. Some went into business. But the same poverty also drove others to crime. Many of my friends joined the triads of the time, with some becoming powerful leaders in them. Some of those who had chosen crime went to jail while others just vanished from Singapore.

Along the way, there were some wonderful teachers who genuinely cared about us. Names like Oliver Seet and Gabriel Pillai ring from my past. They were the kind of teachers who went the extra mile for us and inspired us to think about our futures. Former young 'hooligans' like me will forever be grateful to them. Unfortunately, we had many more teachers who were not particularly interested in teaching us. They just went through the motions. Some openly told us we didn't have to aim high in our exams but to just do well enough to find employment within the Base. Perhaps they felt that it was noble to follow in our fathers' footsteps, but I've always felt they should have given us more to aim for. They should have allowed us to dream. When the bell rang at the end of each school day, some of these teachers raced off in their

Volkswagens or Morris Minors or motorbikes.

I was at Naval Base School throughout my secondary school education. From a personal viewpoint, Secondary 1 and 2 were terrible years academically. I only just managed to pass those years and was usually propping up the rest of the class in our tests. It didn't help that my disciplinary record was also among the worst in my class. We got into trouble for a range of things, including fighting, truancy and playing jokes on our teachers and other students. In Secondary 2, I was nearly expelled for hitting a prefect who I felt was dishonest. My instincts about him were later proven to be correct. Mr Pillai, who knew my family, came to my rescue. He gave a guarantee to the school principal that I would behave. It was an incredibly risky thing for him to do. Looking back, I think that represented a key crossroads in my life. I had to change my ways or I was out of school. My deepest fears relating to my parents reverberated around that misdeed. Mr Pillai's faith in me also had an impact. I decided to change my ways insofar as a young boy can make such a momentous decision. It was helpful that many of my cohorts in misbehaviour had by then left school to start work. It made it easier to concentrate on my studies as there were fewer people to distract me. I started to be more attentive in class and stopped playing truant. I took exams seriously, actually making an effort to study for them. The teachers were happy with my progress and their mantra of "Must try harder" gradually became one of "Has shown good progress".

My turnaround from being a chronic troublemaker in school was complete when at the end of Secondary 3, I was nominated by the teachers to be a prefect. It was a terribly embarrassing moment for someone like me who had shown scant respect for authority, apart from my parents, for much of my life. I decided to accept the nomination only because my childhood friend, David Cheng Lai Beng, who had also been nominated, said it would look good in our testimonials if we were prefects. I can remember vividly the first day of the new school year walking through the gates of Naval Base School wearing my prefect's badge. I was jeered. Things soon got worse as Lai Beng left school after only about a month to become an apprentice at the Base. I was alone with my prefect's badge.

TWO

PREFECT

I think I was born to be a prefect. I remember minute details of my duties. The disciplinary master would send me to admonish the most notorious characters in school. In fact, my proficiency as a prefect got me appointed as assistant head boy of the school. I was really flying in those days. I was also elected house captain and chairman of the drama society, and I won school colours for athletics, hockey and soccer. I participated in all these sports at combined schools events too. These activities certainly helped mould my character, and I still look back at my youthful achievements with tremendous pride.

Though my star shone brightly in the second half of my secondary school years, I didn't forget the friends I used to get into trouble with. We remained supremely loyal to each other even though we didn't see each other as often as before. I recall once getting into serious trouble with my friends Lai Beng and Thee Kow while waiting for my 'O' level results. Lai Beng lived in Block 26 in the Base which faced some bachelors' quarters. There was a Malayalee man who would always stand at his balcony in his underwear, knowing full well that women lived in Lai Beng's block. Since he was Malayalee, it was decided by my friends that I should tell him to put on his trousers whenever he was at the balcony. One day, seeing him at the balcony, I called out to him and politely suggested this to him. He didn't take it well.

"It's none of your business," he said gruffly.

"It's very rude," I replied earnestly. "There are ladies around."

"Who are you to tell me what to wear in my own house? Just get out of here," he screamed.

After quickly putting on a pair of trousers, the Malayalee man came running downstairs brandishing a knife. In a flash, Lai Beng and Thee Kow were by my side. He probably expected us to run away, but I stood my ground and hit him instead. The next thing we knew, the man's roommates came charging down and a scuffle broke out. We were initially outnumbered but help was at hand. Former national footballer Quah Kim Lye, his friends and other boys from the neighbouring blocks came to back us up. The Malayalee man was given the beating we all felt he deserved. In the meantime, somebody had called the police. When they came, the Malayalee man pointed at me, Lai Beng and Thee Kow as the main assailants. We were arrested on the spot and taken to the police station in a police car. The Malayalee man, somewhat bruised and battered, was allowed to cycle to the station at his leisure.

We were kept in the police lockup for a long time. Lai Beng was the most worried among the three of us. He was scared about losing his fledgling job in the Base. Since we were students, Thee Kow (who is now a teacher) and I weren't too worried. We knew we had done the right thing by confronting the Malayalee man about his indecency. We tried to distract Lai Beng by singing Elvis Presley's songs. I suppose we got carried away. A police officer came to tell us to shut up as a white police officer had arrived at the station to handle our case. White police officers were always the most senior officers in the Base in those days, and it was claimed that they came from Scotland Yard.

An hour later, we were taken to see the white police officer. He asked whether we needed an interpreter. In my best English, I said, "No, thank you, sir." He appeared to be very impressed by my grasp of his native tongue as I explained to him what the Malayalee man had a habit of doing at his balcony. I was only 15 years old and my two friends were 16, but we knew that what the man did was wrong. The officer agreed with us and gave the man a telling-off. As he had the authority to do so, he also told the man to find alternative accommodation. Lai Beng, Thee Kow and I escaped with only a warning. To Lai Beng's relief, the white officer assumed all three of us were students.

The memory of this particular incident came back to me a few years ago when I learnt that Lai Beng had died suddenly of a heart attack. The morning he died, his daughter rang me at home. In between her sobs, she asked me about my health. She knew I had a heart problem. After her call, I had to sit down and steady myself as I thought about my old friend. His wake was surreal. It had always been his wish to have Elvis Presley's songs at his funeral. As each song played, I had to choke back the tears because I could see Lai Beng miming those songs himself. When I saw him lying in his coffin, I was overcome by a sense of helplessness. His wife, Swee Neo, who is a sibling in the Quah footballing family, came to me and held my hands. Because we had all been through so much together she, more than anyone, could understand how I felt.

The Malayalee man incident made Lai Beng, Thee Kow and me heroes in our neighbourhood. Women thanked us for taking a stand against the "horrible half-naked Malayalee man" as they described him, while the men told us they should have done something about it themselves long before we did. I was on a high by the time I got home and was not prepared for the reaction of my parents. My mother was in tears, saying I had brought shame to my family by being put in jail.

My father wanted to disown me and scolded my mother for spoiling me. The next two days were unbearable because I had to deal with my parents' disappointment.

Then our exam results were released. Now, parents tend to forgive their children for any indiscretion if they do well in their examinations. I was the only one in the Base who achieved a First Grade, and it made me a celebrity again in our neighbourhood. My father was waiting for me when I came home and that was the one time in my life I remember him hugging me.

"What do you think of my son now?" he asked my mother proudly.

She laughed happily. "Just two days ago, you wanted to disown him. Now, he's your son."

The enormity of my academic achievement did not really strike me until Mr Thomas Joy came to our house that night to congratulate me. He was the person who taught me the English alphabet when I was a child. When I saw the tears and pride in his eyes, I was glad I had studied for the exams.

You should not underestimate my Naval Base School experience because, deep inside, I know that the school, along with my parents and close friends, moulded my character. For example, I remember I was the only one from the school selected to play cricket for Bukit Timah District. The rest of the cricket team comprised players from Anglo-Chinese School. Most of them went on to play cricket for Singapore. I suppose to make it look as though the team was not a monopoly of ACS boys, they made me their wicketkeeper. I wasn't particularly interested in playing cricket for the district, but my cricket master, Mr Van Schoenbeck, thought it was a great honour that I had been chosen to play. It was the first time a Naval Base School student had been selected. He made sure that I went for all the games whether I liked it or not.

At that time, I was already assistant head boy at school and I had no choice but to obey the instructions. The games were played in several different schools in different parts of Singapore. In one game, Bukit Timah District was to play against City District in Monk's Hill Secondary School.

Mr Schoenbeck asked, "So you're going for the game at Monk's Hill?"

"Yes, sir."

He explained to me the logistics of making it to the game and back home. "It will cost you 25 cents to take a bus to Rex Theatre. From there, another bus ride to Monk's Hill will cost you 5 cents. So for a return ride, you will need 60 cents. A drink will cost 20 cents. Here's a dollar. In total you should only spend 80 cents out of it and I expect change of 20 cents tomorrow. It has to go into the kitty for someone else who may need it."

It was a very long journey from the Base to Monk's Hill Secondary School. It took me more than an hour to reach my destination. Distances are obviously the same today but somehow those bus trips seemed endless. I suppose it's because the buses just trudged along at low speeds and made countless stops along the way.

As I was changing into my cricket gear, my teammates started to arrive. Most of them were chauffeur-driven in big cars like Mercedes Benzes and Jaguars. Some even drove their own cars. It seemed to me like they lived in a different world. After the game, I didn't hang around. I quickly removed my wicketkeeper's paraphernalia—the pads, the gloves and the box—and hopped onto a bus on

Bukit Timah Road heading for the Rex Theatre. I spent my 20 cents on a drink there. Then I made my long journey back to Sembawang. Mr Schoenbeck was waiting for me with anticipation as I got off the bus near our school.

He asked, "So how? Did Bukit Timah District win?"

I assured him. "As long as the ACS boys are in the team, Bukit Timah District will definitely win. They're really good players. There's nothing much to do and I don't think I should go for the next game."

"No such thing. You're going to complete the season," he insisted.

Mr Schoenbeck was a Eurasian of Dutch origin who spoke with an unusual accent. Everyone knew him as a kind man. Although he was not rich, there were occasions when he would give money to students out of his own pocket. I was reluctant to continue playing as I didn't enjoy watching my teammates driving up or being driven up in fancy cars. But I persevered as I didn't want to disappoint Mr Schoenbeck. It also spurred me on to fulfil a dream of one day owning a Benz or a Jaguar myself. I have fulfilled this dream. It is a passion of mine to drive big capacity cars like the Mercedes Benz, Jaguar or BMW.

Naval Base School taught me what it is to be loyal, and about loyalty to your school and loyalty to your friends. Rich or poor, a different race or creed, as long as we were wearing the uniform and the badge of Naval Base School, we stuck together. It didn't matter what kind of trouble we were getting into. This is why I always say that the uniform you wear—a school uniform, a sports kit or whatever—you must always be loyal to it. It doesn't matter whether your teammate is in the wrong or not. You should stand by him against the world. But in the dressing room, you can tell him off if you have to.

I tell this now to the young lawyers at KhattarWong. If you have a problem and you are upset about a situation, try to sort it out within the firm. Talk to me, talk to the partners, but don't ever take the problem outside the firm, like in the Bar Room, and share it with members of other firms. You do that and you are out. I talk to them this way as though I have the power to sack them but that's how I feel. To give credit to the partners of KhattarWong, they have assured me that, as a respected consultant, I can take such liberties in addressing younger lawyers.

THREE

RAFFLES INSTITUTION

My elder sister was studying medicine in New Delhi by the time I completed my 'O' level exams and my mother wanted me to be a doctor too. The problem was that I didn't qualify for the pre-medicine classes in Singapore because of an F9 in chemistry. The grade was inevitable considering I did many of my extra-curricular activities by cutting chemistry classes. I didn't get into trouble for doing that because my chemistry teacher, a very attractive Malayalee lady, was very indulgent with me. The rare days when I did attend her class, she would ask me to run errands such as changing $10 or $50 notes for her. I would always tell her that the canteen owner would only give me change if I bought something from him. The usual response from her was to ask me to buy a drink for myself. This became a joke as everyone in the class knew that I was hustling her for a drink. Later, we realised that she knew exactly what was going on.

I was accepted at Loyola College in Madras (now Chennai) as a pre-university medical student. It didn't matter to the college that I had failed chemistry. What mattered was that I had a First Grade for my 'O' level results. After the first few lessons, I realised that I was not meant to be a doctor. I was also very homesick. I missed my mother very much and missed her cooking even more. I wrote to my father to say that I was very unhappy and as expected, he asked me to take a flight back home. Once back in Singapore, my father said that I had to continue my studies. So, I enrolled at Raffles Institution as it was the nearest pre-university school with the most convenient bus route from my home.

While we often hear the likes of Lee Kuan Yew and Goh Chok Tong extolling the virtues of RI as old boys of the school, I didn't like it very much. My memories are dominated by the hot and sweaty bus journeys I had to endure. We didn't have air-conditioned buses in those days. I had to wake up at 5.00 am every day to ensure that I caught the first bus out of Sembawang by 6.00 am. At that time, the school was located on Bras Basah Road. In all, I had to catch three buses and reached school by 7.20 am.

Apart from the long travel time, I didn't like the way the Raffles boys and teachers behaved. Many of the teachers thought they were God's gift to Singapore's education system as RI was considered the best school in Singapore. I also found my fellow students overly competitive, arrogant and conceited. I suppose that's an inevitable outcome when you are constantly told by your family and friends that you are the best or that you have to be the best.

On my first day at RI, there were many 'outsiders' like me in class. A teacher walked in and said: "I am the hockey master for Raffles Institution and all those who have played hockey for their former schools, put your hands up." I saw many hands up in the air around me. Although I had played hockey for Naval Base School, I kept my hands on the desk. I didn't want to play hockey or any other sport because of the distance I had to travel each day to school. If I were to play these games, I would have to stay in school for an extra three to four hours before a game. It would have been late in the evening by the time I got home, if I was lucky to catch my buses on time. I also just wanted to concentrate on my studies as I felt that I had wasted one year of my life with the failed experiment in Loyola.

I thought I'd be left alone after not putting my hand up, but the hockey master recognised me. He had umpired in the district final between Naval Base School and Jurong Secondary School in 1962. You wouldn't know it looking at me now, but I was noted as a fast, nippy right-winger and the solitary goal that won the final came from the right side. I ran all the way from our own half and centred the ball for the centre forward to score.

The teacher asked me, "Haven't you played hockey before for your school?"

"Yes I have," I replied.

"Then why didn't you put your hand up?"

I told him I didn't want to play hockey anymore. Instead of asking me why I was opting not to play, he shouted at me, "Which stupid school gave you this stupid attitude?"

I didn't mind being scolded or being called stupid, but I objected very much to someone calling Naval Base School a stupid school. So I told him quietly, "Don't call my former school stupid."

There was absolute silence in the class. He left his books on the table and came marching towards me. For a moment, I thought he was going to hit me and I wish he had because I would have punched him in his face. He said, "What do you want? Tell me, what is it that you want?"

"I don't want anything from you, sir. I just don't want you to call my school stupid."

"Well then, get out of my class."

I left the class, went to the school library and waited. I thought that would be my punishment, but things did not end there. The hockey master reported me to the senior master, Mr K P John (who later became a client of my firm for a property transaction). I was called in by Mr John to explain what happened in class. I told him the story and about why I didn't think I could play hockey for the school. He listened patiently. When I had finished, he told me I should not have responded to a teacher in the way I did as it showed a lack of respect. Mr John said he admired my loyalty to my former school and hoped I would show the same loyalty to RI in the years to come.

He also said that the hockey master was my history teacher and that I had to apologise to him. If I didn't, the teacher wanted me out of the class. I was quite prepared not to do history, and I told Mr John that I would manage without history. The senior master said it didn't work that way. "You have to apologise. If you don't, this matter will blow up into a bigger one and it's not going to be good for you. So, you think about it and apologise to him tomorrow," he said.

At home later that day, I explained to my mother what had happened in school. "Maybe I'm not meant to study at Raffles. I should go to some other school or maybe I should do some other course in the polytechnic," I said. At that time, I think only Singapore Polytechnic was in operation and it wasn't that well established yet.

My mother would have nothing of that. "You've wasted enough time. Raffles is a very good school and you're lucky to be there. Don't give any excuses. You will go to school tomorrow," she ordered. My father remained quiet but was giving me the stare that always made me feel uneasy. It was one that said: "Look, you've wasted enough of my money. Get on with it." I knew what I had to do.

The next day in class, I apologised to the hockey master for being rude. I can honestly say it was one of the most insincere apologies I have ever made. Sometimes you have to do things that you don't like to do and that was one of those times. Instead of accepting my apology with grace, this is what he told me: "Don't worry, Subhas. Even if you want to play hockey for the school or for that matter any other game, your standard will not be that good because the standard of RI is very high."

I was quietly amused because by then I had represented Combined Schools in both hockey and soccer. I was a Combined Schools athlete too. The standard of Combined Schools must definitely be better than RI. This is a fact. Unfortunately, my encounter with the hockey master had repercussions. He made sure the other teachers knew about my behaviour that first day in school. Every teacher who came to teach in my class, except for my form mistress, found some reason to pick on me. The geography teacher was especially harsh. I thought about what my mother said and tolerated everything.

Things began to change after I attended a school house meeting, my first one ever at the school. I was in Hullet House. The house master, Mr Hernon, recognised me as he had taught me in Secondary 1 at Naval Base School. He put his arm around my shoulders like I was an old friend and said, "Hey, you rascal, I'm so happy to see you here." He remembered that I played football and asked me to play for Hullet House. Since the next game was on a Saturday morning and I wouldn't have to wait after school for the game, I agreed. I can't remember which house we played against, but the school's football master, Mr Siddhu, was the referee. After the game, Mr Siddhu asked me why I hadn't attended the school selection trials.

The devil in me couldn't resist and I replied, "I didn't come because the hockey master said that the standards in RI are so high that I would not have been picked to play for any team in the school."

"It doesn't matter what he said. Would you like to play for RI?"

"I don't mind but the problem is I stay so far away. If there's a game on, I cannot go home and return for the game on time. I would have to hang around in school and by the time the game ends, I will be so late getting home because I have to take three buses."

Mr Siddhu smiled. "Don't worry, Subhas. We will try to make arrangements comfortable for you. You can take a taxi." I looked at him and wondered how I was going to afford that but he continued: "I will pay for it so you won't be so tired to study when you get home. I would really be happy if you played for RI." As he came across to me as a genuine person, I said I would.

That was how I became a member of the RI football team. I was vice-captain in our second year and, for once, RI shone in soccer. We reached the finals of the inter-schools competition but lost to St Patrick's School after a replay. I also ran cross-country and broke the course record in my first run for Hullet House. I subsequently came in second in the inter-schools cross-country. The hockey master who said I wasn't good enough never acknowledged my sporting achievements.

Talking about my sporting experiences in RI, I have to mention a tradition in the school that I took part in. RI always played an annual football match with Johor English College. In 1965, I was in my second year at RI and also vice-captain of the football team. The captain was Mansoor Marican, but he was captain in name only. He was a pleasant person but on the field, I would normally take command. He was too soft to make tough decisions.

RI was always slaughtered by Johor English College. That year, though, we had finished second to St Patrick's School and we felt for once that we had a team that could beat Johor. The football standard at RI had never been that high. Everybody was excited about the game.

But out of the blue, we received some bad news and it had to do with me. Mr Pestana, the athletics master, told me I had to run in a cross-country race for City District on the same day that the football match was scheduled to be played. Gopal Singh had come in first in RI's main cross-country race, with me a very close second. I told Gopal jokingly, "Look out for my brother next year. He'll beat you hands down!" Sure enough, Sudheesh won hands down the following year.

Gopal and I were chosen to run the cross-country race. I had no choice but to seek the assistance of Mr Siddhu. "Sir, can I get out of this? Whether I go or not, City District is going to win because they have enough runners. Can you speak with Mr Pestana and get me out of it so that I can play football?" So, Mr Siddhu went to see Mr Pestana about my request. Mr Pestana explained to him: "This game that you're going to play against Johor English College is a friendly game though it may be an annual affair. But this race is an official race and it's an inter-district final. City District must win and they are depending on RI. There's no way I am going to release Subhas from running."

Mr Siddhu understood the importance of the race. "Looks as though Pestana is right," he told me. "You have to run at MacRitchie. The run is at 3.00 pm and the game is around 4.00 pm at our RI field. Can you run and return to school to play?"

I shrugged. "I'm fit and I think I can do that but I need somebody to fetch me from MacRitchie because if I have to catch the bus, I might be too late."

"No problem," Mr Siddhu replied. "I'll ask Lam Peng Kwee to fetch you from MacRitchie and bring you back to school to play. You won't be able to stay for the prize-giving ceremony after the run." Peng Kwee was a reserve player in the RI football team who drove a car.

"Fair enough."

It's the strangest thing because as I was thinking about whether or not to include the events surrounding the Johor English College game in this book, Lam Peng Kwee came to see me at KhattarWong. He didn't have an appointment and told the receptionist that he was just an old friend who was in the neighbourhood and wanted to say hello. I hurried to meet him when I heard he was in the office. Peng Kwee is now settled down in Texas, USA, and I was so glad to see him after such a long time. I couldn't recall when I last saw him. We hugged and I insisted on buying him at least a cup of coffee. He said, "I heard from your girls that you're very busy." I assured him that I always had time for an old friend who dropped by unexpectedly. We talked and reminisced about our RI days and we even talked about the Johor English College game. His visit inspired me to include that particular experience in this book.

Anyway, City District won the inter-district cross-country by a good margin. I enjoyed running at MacRitchie as you could feel nature brush against your face as you careened at full speed down the winding footpath that cut through the trees and undergrowth. It always felt wet because of the tropical forest and often you had to jump over puddles of muddy water. The route opened suddenly out to Lornie Road and the glare from the road would hurt your eyes for a while until they adjusted to the brighter light. Passing cars would sometimes honk at you, as if to urge you to go faster. Lamp-posts were markers that would tell you if you were closing in on the runners in front of you or if someone behind was narrowing his distance to you.

Just like the Forrest Gump character in the movie, I did not stay to receive the trophy on behalf of City District and ran straight to Peng Kwee's car. I did say goodbye to Mr Pestana though. "Good luck. Hurry up now. I think you can just make it," he called out.

I was still sweating from the run as Peng Kwee's car surged down Thomson Road towards Bras Basah Road. I put on my socks and boots in the car. I didn't have to change my shorts because they were the same ones used by the football team. I was filled with excitement and so was Peng Kwee. When we got to the school, I heard that the game had just started. Mr Siddhu, who was anxiously looking out for us, threw a football jersey at me and shouted, "Put it on and get in there." I put the RI jersey on and went in to play. The adrenaline was rushing through me and I didn't feel tired at all.

At half time, the score was 1-1. While we were taking our drinks during half time, our principal, Mr E W Jesudason, came up to me with the principal of Johor English College. Mr Jesudason was a kind man though a tough disciplinarian. He was one of the most colourful principals in Singapore and is credited with writing the Institution Anthem of RI. He was fuming mad and reprimanded me in front of everybody. "I don't care whether you are the star of RI or not. I can't stand people like you who have no discipline. You think you are a superstar and that you can come late for a game? What is wrong with your football master? Holding on to your jersey, giving it to you and spoiling you? Who do you think you are? I don't care what your football master says, I'll be dealing with you personally later. This is breach of discipline of the highest order." Throughout his rant, I remained silent. Everyone was silent as he walked off in a huff. I think even the players from Johor English College were feeling a little embarrassed for me. I quietly finished my drink.

The game ended in a draw. Johor English College did not find us easy meat like they usually did. We played a very good game. After shaking hands with our opponents, I immediately went to

Mr Siddhu and said: "I'm really very, very tired. I have to go home."

He understood. "Yes, please do that. You don't have to stay for the reception." I packed my things and, as usual, he gave me money to take a taxi home.

That was a Friday evening. During the reception, Mr Jesudason apparently approached Mr Siddhu and complained: "How can you allow this to happen?" Mr Siddhu explained to him exactly what I did, rushing back after a cross-country race. Feeling rather bad, Mr Jesudason remarked, "Oh my goodness, I was scolding him and he did not tell me about this."

On Monday, after a good rest over the weekend, I went to school as usual. One of the prefects informed me that the principal wanted to see me. I went to his office and he said, "Ah, Subhas, come in. Mr Siddhu explained to me what had happened. Why didn't you explain to me what you had done when I was scolding you? Why were you just keeping quiet? Why didn't you tell me something?"

I looked at him. "You really want to know the reason, sir? I didn't want the principal and students of the other school to see that you were making an ass of yourself."

At first he looked at me angrily, then he burst out laughing and said, "You know, Subhas, that is the Rafflesian spirit. You didn't want to embarrass your principal." He proudly shared this incident at the next school assembly.

On one of the occasions when I had to go for cardiac rehabilitation after my heart attack in late 1978, I saw Mr Jesudason sitting on a wheelchair, accompanied by his wife. I was shocked. "Oh my God, he was such an active person. He was a boxer and a black belt judo exponent," I thought. I saw him sitting there looking so helpless.

I went up to him and asked, "Mr Jesudason, do you remember me?"

He stared at my face for a while. "I remember you. I can't remember your name. You were the one who played football."

"Yes, I'm Subhas. Sir, what are you doing here?"

"Never mind about what I am doing here. At this age, what are you doing here?" he asked.

I told him that I had suffered a massive heart attack and was advised by my cardiologist to attend rehabilitation classes. He said, "You were such a fine sportsman. What have you done to yourself?"

"Well, sir, when you start working, your routine changes and inevitably there is a lifestyle change."

"Yes, everybody wants to make money and they forget the greater issues in life. I hope you recover and will be back to your normal self again." He took my hand and pulled it towards him. "May God bless you," he said. I thanked him and said goodbye to him and his wife, who was standing behind him and smiling at me.

Not long after that, on a return from one of my business trips to Manila, I was told that Mr Jesudason had died of heart failure. Although I was not close to him, I was quite sad to hear the news. He was one of those who made life in RI a little bit more pleasant for me with all his amusing, sometimes even political, comments. I remember him as a tough man who didn't treat the sons of ministers and presidents differently from other students. His stint as an RI principal lasted only from 1963 to 1966 and I feel fortunate that my time in RI coincided with his tenure as a principal.

FOUR

UNIVERSITY DAYS

After RI, I wasn't too keen to go on to university as I felt that I had studied more than enough. With my 'A' level certificate, I could have joined the police force. Two of my close friends had done that. My father insisted that I get a university degree though, and he didn't really care what I read. I still remember his words: "Son, when I die, I will be leaving you nothing except the education I give you. I am not rich, but I will make all of you university graduates."

I noted the steely determination in his voice even as I argued with him. If my father had relented, I suppose I'd be a retired policeman by now. I told my father that it would be difficult to travel all the way to Bukit Timah Road where the university campus was located. The journey to RI had taken about 90 minutes, and I couldn't contemplate another long period with the same travel time. I demanded a car even though I didn't have a driving licence yet. My father just kept quiet and reminded me to send in my university application forms.

It was a choice between business administration and law. Since I had no business acumen, I picked law and was accepted by the University of Singapore. When I showed my father the acceptance letter, he just smiled. A few days later, he bought me a car—a brand new Austin 1100. The registration number was SM 8788. I learnt he had withdrawn money from his CPF to buy it.

The next day, I hung two 'L' plates on the bumpers of the car and drove it around with my friend Ah Teng who had a licence. We were driving along very comfortably, radio blaring, until we turned into Mandai Road. We then ran head-on into a Malaysia-registered Peugeot. It was unbelievable. We weren't travelling that fast. But Mandai Road used to be one of those long and winding roads where you can sometimes veer onto the wrong side of the road at the bends if you're not careful.

As a driver with zero experience, I guess an accident was on the cards. Both cars were badly damaged and we went to Mandai police station to make a report. The occupants of the other car were an old lady and a very young and attractive girl who I learnt was the lady's granddaughter. The old lady kept abusing me and blaming me for the accident. I remained silent. What else could I do? The young woman was embarrassed and told me that her grandmother was upset as their car was less than three months' old. I sniggered and showed her the inside of my car. The plastic covers were still on the seats. When I told her my car was less than 24 hours old, she burst out laughing.

Despite the circumstances, I was taken by her and we exchanged telephone numbers. I had to give her Ah Teng's number as we didn't have a telephone at home in those days. The old lady saw what we were doing and her granddaughter explained that we needed each other's phone numbers to exchange insurance details later. Her grandmother continued to glare at me throughout the whole episode. I dated the young woman, Shanti, on a few occasions but it didn't work out. Ah Teng always said I deliberately caused the accident to befriend her.

After we were done at the police station, I was too scared to drive the damaged Austin home. So we went instead to Ah Teng's house, left the car there and took his car to my place. Both of us were extremely worried about my father's reaction. As usual, he was sitting at the corridor reading the Malayalam newspapers. When he saw me, he smiled. "Did you both enjoy driving the car?" he asked. We kept quiet. He studied my face and turned serious. "What is it, son? Why are you looking so worried?"

I told him that we had met with an accident and the car was damaged. I braced myself for a tongue lashing, but he only asked if Ah Teng and I were injured. Neither of us was. He laughed and said: "Son, it's only a car. What is important is that the both of you are not hurt." I will never forget that response. That's the sort of example my father set for me, and it's always been a hard act to follow.

The car was taken for repairs and I was told in no uncertain terms by everyone who cared for me to enrol in a driving school. But when you have had such an embarrassing accident, it tends to stick with you for years. People would jokingly refer to it all the time when the issue of driving or the topic of cars came up in our social or family gatherings. The ribbing got worse because, after taking a few lessons with Lambert Driving School, the instructor refused to give me any more lessons. He said I was a dangerous driver who drove as though there were no other cars on the road. The few lessons that I took had, however, given me confidence. Another good friend, Mark, took over the responsibility of teaching me to drive. After the accident, Ah Teng lost the nerve to teach me. I finally passed my driving test on my third attempt.

I started reading law at Singapore University in May, 1966. Before the course started, new students had to attend an interview with the sub-dean of the Law faculty, Mr Tommy Koh. At my interview, I met a former classmate from RI. She had also come for the same interview. When it was over, we foolishly decided to go to the Union House for a drink. As soon as we sat down and ordered our drinks, we knew we had made a big mistake. We were surrounded by senior students who were waiting for innocent 'freshies' to rag. They called it 'orientation' as ragging freshmen was illegal. Whatever name they put on it, it was bullying. You were asked to do very silly things to be humiliated. For instance, you had to stoop when you walked past a so-called senior gentleman who was shorter than you. Ragging officially started when the term began, but if you happened to be caught in the premises before the term started, your 'orientation' would begin immediately.

My friend and I didn't know what a foolish move we had made when we sat down and ordered our drinks. The drinks came and before we could start drinking, one person in the group of seniors, Chan Kian Hin, who was obviously their leader (and later became my good friend), told us to leave the drinks on the table and to stand up. It was barked out like an order which shocked us. I refused to stand up and because of that, my friend remained seated too. The seniors became very agitated and started shouting at me. They repeatedly asked me to stand up but I continued to refuse. They left my friend alone. There were about eight of them and they all sat down at the table. Kian Hin said I was outnumbered and that none of the group wanted to get physical but if they had to, they would. I remained quiet but refused to stand up. Then one of them tried to lift me and I grabbed my bottle of 7-Up. When they saw me reach for the bottle, some of them panicked and moved away. Kian Hin then asked me why I was going for the bottle. I told him very calmly that I was going to crack his head with it and then stab at least two of them before they got me. I could sense they were scared. A few other senior students who knew me intervened. They said I had no business being in Union House as I was not even a union member and told me to get out. They told my friend she could stay if she wanted to. She rejected their offer and walked out with me. Much later, when I was courting the same girl, she told me she was very surprised by the way I acted that day. She said she was trembling inside but I looked so cool and unafraid. She then asked me whether I would have done what I had threatened to do. I told her I would. She laughed and said she thought I enjoyed the whole incident.

I was a marked man from that day onwards. When term started and ragging officially began, every senior gentleman was after my blood. I had to be tamed. As far as the seniors were concerned, it would be a disaster if I wasn't. They waited at every corner to confront me, but I refused to buckle. None of the freshies was allowed to be with me. They were threatened and so I walked alone with no friends. I refused to be ragged and humiliated by a bunch of morons who took great pride and satisfaction in humiliating a fellow student. Most of these raggers found courage only when they were in a group. On the occasions when I met any of them alone, they scurried away like the cowards they were. That one month of orientation was hell for me. I had no friends and everywhere I went, I saw hostile faces.

We were coming to the end of the orientation period when I was told secretly by some students that I should watch out for the seniors. They were plotting something against me. I normally sat alone outside Union House near the pond. Sure enough, one day, a group of students led by Karpal Singh (who is now an opposition member of parliament with the Democratic Action Party in Malaysia) confronted me at my table. I realised all the students were from the nearby Dunearn Road Hostel.

Karpal Singh asked me, "Are you a gangster?" I just kept quiet. He told me that silence under the Evidence Act meant yes. I remained quiet wondering what the Evidence Act was about. He then asked me what number I played, meaning what gang I belonged to. I kept quiet. "I am asking very politely, so I expect an answer. Tell me what number you play?" he said.

I told him that if he wanted to speak in that type of language, this was not the right place. Karpal Singh said that as far as he was concerned, it was the right place. I looked at him for some time and said that since he had chosen the place, it was only fair that I chose the time. He nodded his head. I said that I was sick and tired of what was happening to me and that at 7.00 pm that day, I would be at the same place and he was welcome to ask me what number I played. I also told him that this was a serious business and not to take it lightly as people could get hurt. He asked me what I meant by that and I replied that he would find out at 7.00 pm. I had decided that enough was enough. I was prepared to leave the campus and forget about law but before leaving, I was going to teach these senior gentlemen a thing or two. I gathered my things and left. I had a few calls to make.

I called Ah Teng first and told him I needed help. He immediately understood what I meant as I had been complaining to my friends about the ragging. I had told them many times that I felt like leaving university. My friends, who were proud of me as I was the only one from the group who was in university, refused to accept that. I made a few more calls to rally my friends. Ah Teng and Mark knew the campus very well as they dropped me off and picked me up from university on most days. They didn't want me to face any danger from the seniors, especially outside the campus.

At about 6.30 pm, I walked into Union House by myself. I could sense the excitement. Most students knew of the confrontation that morning and everybody was waiting to see what was going to happen. From where I was sitting, I could see Dunearn Road Hostel. At that time, Bukit Timah Road and Dunearn Road were both two-lane roads separated by the canal that still runs between them today. There were no underpasses as there are now. In fact, it was even before the time when overhead bridges crossed Adam Road. (They have since been removed.) There was a grocery shop called Palaniamma's in the row of shophouses at the Adam Road/Bukit Timah Road junction and a few houses lined up on the Adam Road/Dunearn Road junction, in front of what later became the Adam Road hawker centre. Then, part of the hawker centre site was still a jungle. It often flooded when it rained heavily, sometimes making the roads impassable to vehicles but, that evening, the weather was fine.

I saw some students walking across the field towards Union House. I recognised some of them as the ones who had confronted me in the morning. Karpal Singh was not with them. It was still early. His friends came and sat a few tables away. I continued drinking my black coffee and puffed on a cigarette as though I had no problems at all. In my mind, this would be my last day in campus because I was sure there was going to be a big fight. People were going to be hurt. I was a bit sad that it had come to this, but I was also excited about what was going to happen.

At about 6.45 pm, I saw five cars moving in a convoy along Dunearn Road. My friends had arrived. Two cars parked along Dunearn Road just outside the entrance of the hostel. The other three cars proceeded towards the direction of Union House. I smiled to myself. Ah Teng and Mark had done their homework carefully. At about 6.55 pm, the three cars arrived at the entrance of Union House and my friends got out of the cars. It was obvious that they were not empty handed. They came into the building shouting my name and I walked towards them. Mark came along with many of my childhood friends like Ah Soo, Ramli, Sam (who is now the president of our temple) and others. I remember Ah Teng asking, "Where are the bastards?"

The next thing I knew people were scampering out of Union House. The students who were not involved stayed put, looking worried but not wanting to miss anything. The Dunearn Road Hostel boys were the first to bolt. They ran across the field towards their hostel. My friends who were waiting in the two cars parked outside got out and chased them. The students did not expect that to happen. Some of them ran along Dunearn Road while others just raised their hands in surrender and sat on the pavement. My friends did not harm them. They were not bullies. In the meantime, I walked around Union House asking those senior gentlemen and ladies who were still around whether they wanted to rag me. All of them said no. My friends told them to pass the word around that I was to be left alone and if they had to come around again, people would get hurt. I got into one of the cars and left. We caught up with the other two cars and headed for Sembawang. My friends told me what a let-down it had been and that I had wasted their time.

One could get the impression from this incident that I was an important member of a gang. This is not true. Sembawang was a tough neighbourhood to grow up in. I had many friends inside and outside the Base. We were mostly around the same age and shared the same interests like playing football and listening to the popular music of the day. The Beatles and Elvis Presley were huge then. It was one big family and we were there for each other. I may have been the pride and joy of not only my parents but also the friends I grew up with. I was the first student from the Base to ever go to Raffles Institution to do the 'A' levels. I was also the first from the Base to study law. My friends wanted to see me succeed academically. I was doing what they could not do and they accepted it. There was no jealousy or envy. They were prepared to do anything to help me and definitely didn't want a bunch of students to destroy my future. That's how deep our friendship was. The day after the incident, I went to university as usual. Everybody left me alone. Some of my friends who were scared to be seen with me came over to say hello. They were not frightened any more.

Soon, orientation month was over and everybody continued with the business of studying. Eventually, the seniors forgave me. I played football for the university for four years. I also played for the combined universities of Hong Kong, Malaysia and Singapore. I was president of the Non-Hostelites Organisation which represented all the students who did not stay in the hostels. It was the second largest organisation after the Students' Union. I was also secretary-general of the Socialists' Club (a club which Mr Lee Kuan Yew once described as a pro-communist club) and an executive committee member of the Law Society of the university.

During my time, the intake of law students was high and anyone who qualified was probably accepted. But in the years that followed, many were told to leave or had to repeat a year. There was no re-exam for students in the law faculty. In my third year, we were joined by some repeat students. One of them was Lau Tow Weng. He was from Malacca and we became good friends. Lau, Isaac Selvanathan, Tommy Choo, Christian Ayadurai and a few others who often joined us at Union House made up one of my cliques.

One day, while we were having our usual coffee in Union House, the subject of Karpal Singh popped up. I stated that he was a coward who did not turn up when he was supposed to during the orientation incident, about two years earlier. Lau looked at me and said that I didn't know the full story. Karpal and his friends had returned to Dunearn

Road Hostel that morning and reported what happened. They said that I had challenged them to go back to Union House at 7.00 pm. Some of the students were worried and consulted a security officer, Martin, at the library. Martin was supposed to be a high ranking member of a triad. He told the students that I was very dangerous and that they should not fool around with me. Later on, when I was doing my pupilage, Martin came to me for help on a case which I will recount later in the book.

After hearing Martin's advice, the students went back to the hostel and told Karpal and his friends not to turn up at 7.00 pm as they might get hurt. Karpal said he had to go. It didn't matter if he was going to get hurt or killed because his reputation was at stake. At about 6.45 pm, his friends burst into his room, overpowered him, tied him up and locked him in the room. They made sure he was released only after we had left. Lau told me that Karpal was a brave man. I had no reason to doubt Lau and my impression of Karpal changed.

Many years later, the Workers' Party chairman, Wong Hong Toy, was charged with contempt of court. I was asked by J B Jeyaretnam to defend him. I was not familiar with the law and was quite nervous to appear alone. On the other side was Attorney-General Tan Book Teik, who was assisted by Glenn Knight. In desperation, on the eve of the hearing, I called Karpal Singh in Penang. When he took the phone, I told him who I was and he laughed. "You are the Sembawang kid, aren't you?"

"Yes," I replied.

I told him I needed his help and explained the problem. I said that the Workers' Party could only pay for his air ticket and hotel room expenses. They were unable to pay his fees. He said that it was not a problem and asked when the case was scheduled for hearing.

"Tomorrow," I said.

"What, tomorrow!" he exclaimed and scolded me. He said he had many things going on in Penang. He was also by then a member of parliament. I apologised and said that I was only given the approval to call him that same morning. He was still very angry and grumbled about me being irresponsible, but he said he would call me back. I didn't think he would and began to get ready for the case. However, at about 3.00 pm, Karpal Singh called me. He said that he would be coming to Singapore with his wife and gave details of his flight. I was so relieved. I was at the airport to receive him and his wife, a lovely woman. I took them to the Pavilion Inter-Continental Hotel (now The Regent Hotel) and checked them in. After that, we left to see J B Jeyaretnam at his flat. We worked on the case until around 4.00 am. We argued the case before Justice Sinnadurai. Karpal was at his best, giving the Attorney-General and Glenn Knight a run for their money. Judgment was reserved. That night, I took Karpal and his wife to dinner with my then girlfriend, who later became my wife. J B Jeyaretnam couldn't join us. It was a wonderful dinner. In a way it was good that Jeyaretnam was not there as we were reminiscing about Union House and all the mad things we did.

The next day I went to the hotel, paid the bill and invited Karpal and his wife for lunch. I also bought some gifts for them. Jeyaretnam again said he could not join us. I was very disappointed. Maybe it showed in my face. Karpal said, "Subhas, why are you so glum today?" I did not reply and he asked, "Is it because Jeyaretnam is not here?" Again I kept quiet. He looked at me and said: "You know, I didn't come down to Singapore to see Jeyaretnam or his party members. I came down because you asked for help and you know the Union House spirit that binds us will not allow me to let you down." He then grabbed my shoulder and asked me not to be so moody. I laughed and I realised that this was really a great man. I was glad he was unable to keep his appointment with me that day in Union House.

Ladyhill Hotel was a favourite haunt of university students during my time. It was a walking distance from campus and the stroll down the Nassim area amid the leafy environment and the massive colonial houses could be romantic, especially at night. It reminded me a bit of Sembawang. Ladyhill Hotel was also near the Soviet Union embassy.

One night, we were invited for cocktails at the embassy. We often received such invitations as we were supposed to be in solidarity with them as socialists. After cocktails, we took a stroll to Ladyhill Hotel to talk about the events of the night. I remember there were four of us—Conrad Jeyaraj, Sim Yong Chan, Sunny Chew and myself. I can't remember why another person in the group, Francis Yeo, wasn't with us. As usual, we discussed politics.

Then Conrad started making his corny jokes and we decided to throw him into the hotel's swimming pool in his full formal suit. Many of the guests thought it was funny, but some members of the staff thought otherwise. The manager of the coffeehouse demanded that we leave immediately because we had bothered the guests. He was not prepared to listen to us. 'Leave immediately or be thrown out' was his ultimatum. He was flanked by the hotel's bouncers and we had no choice but to leave. We headed back to Union House to summon help. Students from Raffles Hall, Dunearn Road Hostel and some medical students led by the always-ready Adam Liew gathered at Union House. There were about 70 to 80 students, most of them in pyjamas. Some Sikh students deliberately removed their turbans and let their hair loose. We marched to Ladyhill Hotel. At about midnight, all of us jumped into the pool. We created quite a din. Bedroom lights came on and guests were peering out of their balconies or windows to see what the ruckus was about. The same manager who had chased us away earlier saw me and asked me what was happening.

"Are you blind? Can't you see what is happening?" I replied after taking a deep drag on my cigarette.

He didn't know what to do. I told him we were university students and he shouldn't have behaved so arrogantly earlier. I also said that we would be calling the journalists and his hotel would have great publicity the next day. I advised him to call the police if he wanted to. When he tried to speak again, I told him I'd rather not speak to the help and to let me speak to the general manager of the hotel.

Ten minutes later, I was told that the general manager would like to see me. She was an attractive Swedish lady and introduced herself only as Mrs Philip Seow. With two of my friends, we explained to her what had happened with her staff member earlier that evening. She apologised for his behaviour but I said that that the apology was insufficient. We sought some compensation from the hotel, perhaps some alcoholic drinks to warm everyone up. She smiled and said no. As we were students, she was prepared to give us hot chocolate and cookies. So we had a small party by the hotel's pool, drinking hot chocolate and eating cookies and cakes under the moonlight. It turned out to be one of those fantastic, surreal moments in your life that you never forget.

To me and my friends, university life was not just about lectures, tutorials and hours spent in the library. It was about moments like the one at the Ladyhill Hotel. We did so many more things which would seem amazing to students in Singapore's universities today. You have to realise the backdrop during those times. Singapore had recently been handed its independence from Malaysia and there were pockets of turbulence all across the island. The relatively new Lee Kuan Yew-led government was more worried about the threat of racial riots than what university students like us got into, such as taking part in demonstrations outside embassies.

I personally led a demonstration outside the American embassy to protest against the horrible incident which took place on March 16, 1968 in My Lai, Vietnam, when US marines indiscriminately killed old men, women and children. Students gathered outside the embassy which was located along Hill Street, opposite the Singapore Chinese Chamber of Commerce building. Before the demonstration, we sent Violet Oon and Linda Neo to scout the area. They came back and reported that there were police everywhere. It didn't stop us. The students arrived at the embassy in a convoy of cars that had proceeded gravely and full of intent down North Bridge Road. The union bus was also used to carry banners condemning the United States. When we arrived, we saw US marines guarding the embassy. It appeared as though they were expecting us. We demanded an audience with the ambassador. We were told he was not in and that we could see the first secretary instead. Francis Khoo (now in exile in London), Peter Chen (who, if I am not mistaken, was our ambassador to Russia a few years ago) and I went inside to hand over our petition as well as challenge the absent ambassador to a debate.

As soon as we entered the embassy, the doors were shut. The din from the street outside vanished and we were completely cut off from our fellow protesters. We saw marine soldiers walking around on the grounds carrying guns. They were all more than 1.8 m tall and each of them must have weighed more than 100 kg. We were quite afraid and more than a little bit intimidated. The first secretary was a calm and polite person. He took our petition and said that he would pass it on to the ambassador together with our demand to engage in a debate. He then requested that we tell the students outside to disperse.

When we went out, we saw that a huge crowd had joined the students. It looked as though the students were outnumbered by the outsiders. To add to the drama that was unfolding, Conrad Jeyaraj decided to burn the American flag. Since he could not reach the flag flying at the embassy, he decided to torch the flag that we brought along. It was given to us by Jackie Sam, a senior *Straits Times* reporter as his contribution to our cause. Before Conrad could burn the flag, we were told by the police that they would not tolerate littering. They further emphasised that we could do anything to the flag except litter. So we decided to stamp on the flag and spit at it. We finally tore it and threw the tattered flag into the dustbin. The police were glad that we did not litter the premises. Eventually, I was told by the commander to get everyone to disperse. He said he had given us enough leeway and that we must leave or he would have to use force to clear us. He asked the leaders to have a quick meeting with the students. It was agreed that we all leave. We could see the relief in the faces of the policemen as we did so. The ambassador ultimately did not take up the challenge to a debate. I don't blame him as his case was indefensible. The Americans had no right to be in Vietnam, and more and more Americans were beginning to realise it.

Not long after that, we organised a demonstration outside the Soviet Union embassy against the Soviet-led invasion of Czechoslovakia on August 21, 1968. The Czechoslovakian government had declared that the troops had not been invited into the country and that the invasion was a violation of socialist principles, international law and the UN Charter. Again, the student protestors were joined by outsiders who swelled the crowd. The Russians did not want to see any of us. They locked their doors and did not respond to the abuse thrown at them. Some of us decided that we should burn the embassy cars to teach them a lesson. Sunny Chew, who was one of the Students' Union leaders, told us not to do it. He did not want any violence. I was tired of singing and shouting, so I decided to go to the back of the embassy. I knocked on a window. A man opened it slightly and I asked him whether he could speak English. When he said he could, I asked if he could spare a few bottles of vodka. Our conversation was heard by some students who had followed me to the back of the embassy and they promptly reported my request to Sunny. He came immediately with some others and hauled me away. They were cursing me all the way, saying that I had cheapened the demonstration with my request for vodka. Other students thought it was funny and a little vodka would be welcome. Again, the police told us to leave or they would have to use force. I remember we marched off singing songs defaming the Soviet Union. For a few days, my request for vodka was a big talking point at Union House.

On another occasion during my university days, four of us went to a movie at the old Lido cinema, a classic standalone building with an airy 1960s feel to it. The cinema had front stalls, back stalls and circle seats. We bought half-priced tickets and proceeded to enter the hall. We were stopped and told we had to pay the full price. Our response was that we were students and that they had advertised that students pay only half the price. A commotion ensued and the manager of the cinema came and led us to his office. I explained to the manager that we were students and his advertisements had said that students pay half the price. He said the price was meant for schoolchildren. I told him we could not accept this explanation because if it was meant only for schoolchildren, this had to be stated categorically in their advertisements. The manager continued to argue with us. I got fed up. I told him that by the next day all Shaw Brothers cinemas, including Lido, would be picketed and we would make sure that no one went to his cinema. He looked worried and went to the next room to make a phone call. After the call, he told us we could see the movie with the tickets we had. I said that it was too late for us to view the movie and that he had to give us a refund and complimentary tickets for the next day. He agreed, but I told him that we needed more than four tickets as it was only fair to be compensated for all the trouble. I asked for about 30 tickets which he gave in to reluctantly. We went back to Union House and gave the extra tickets to our friends.

There were other times in university when I had to deal with situations on my own. As president of the Non-Hostelites Organisation (NHO), I had to attend inter-hostel meetings. Everyone else in those meetings was part of the academic staff. As a student, I was immediately disadvantaged. In one such meeting chaired by Peter Lim to ensure that the university sports meet was well attended, Professor Jansen of Dunearn Road Hostel called the NHO a dead-loss organisation. I responded by saying that it was a case of the pot calling the kettle black. The professor told me not to be funny, to which I replied I couldn't care less. Hearing my response, Dr Nalla Tan, the mistress of Eusoff College, an all-girl residential hostel, who was sitting beside me, shouted that I was showing a lack of respect to all the academic staff present. I lit up a cigarette and blew smoke into her face. This infuriated her even more and she looked at the chairman for help. He promptly called off the meeting.

Professor Jansen and Dr Tan reported me to Reginald Quahe, the deputy vice-chancellor. I was also banned from Eusoff College.

The resident students were told that they would face disciplinary action and possible expulsion from the hostel if they invited me there. I contacted the student leaders to tell them about the incident and that I would most probably be reported for disciplinary action. After a few days when there was no follow-up, I decided to see Mr Quahe myself. He offered me a cup of coffee and asked what I wanted to see him about. I told him I believed a report had been made against me and if that was so, what was he going to do about it.

He laughed and said, "Yes, a report has been made but I'm not going to act on it."

I was very surprised. "Why?" I asked.

This time he laughed even louder. It was almost a guffaw. "I have decided not to make you a martyr," he said.

Mr Quahe was a wise old man. He told me that to avoid such situations in future, he was instead going to appoint a master for the NHO who would be of equal status to the others at the meetings. He knew that if action was taken against me, there could be huge problems. It would have been a situation where no one would win but everyone could lose.

After graduation, I was advised by Norman Knight, a business administration lecturer who was also a chartered accountant, to pursue a second degree in chartered accountancy. He said to me, "Your law degree isn't very good. Why don't you consider going to London to do chartered accountancy to support your degree?" He was kind enough to offer to connect me with Coopers Brothers to do articleship. With that in mind, I toyed with the idea of going to London.

My elder sister was always very supportive of further education. She advised me to go. My mother, however, was not so keen on it as she knew that I would not be able to live on my own without her cooking.

I believe that deep inside she was also concerned that I would return with an English girl. Anyway, as I still had friends at university, I continued to frequent the campus. One day I met Professor S Jayakumar, dean of the Law faculty then and the present Deputy Prime Minister of Singapore. He called out to me, "Hey, Subhas, what are you doing here? You should be doing your pupilage."

"Yes, but I don't have a place to go."

"What do you mean? Did you speak to Mr Yang?" he asked. Mr Yang was a law faculty officer who was supposed to arrange for pupilage for everyone.

"Well, I didn't want to bother him." I didn't want to tell the professor that I had been thinking of going abroad for further studies.

He seemed a little agitated. "What are you talking about? Come with me." He led me to his office and made me sit in his room. I must say that he was very kind. He ordered a cup of coffee for me. He even told me that I could smoke if I wanted to. Then he coaxed me. "Look, Subhas, you must do your pupilage, you know. You must get called to the Bar. After that you can decide what you want to do. First things first, you know."

"Okay, but I have not got a place," I replied.

Without any hesitation, he picked up the phone and called Chan Sek Kiong (now Chief Justice of Singapore) who was then a partner with Shook Lin & Bok. He said: "Sek Kiong, I've got this guy here who has just finished his law and says that he's got nowhere to do his chambers. Can you take him in? He's very intelligent but prone to getting into trouble. I hope you can help him." After a few minutes, he put the phone down and said to me: "Okay, I've got you a place with Mr Chan Sek Kiong, a senior partner with Shook Lin & Bok. He's prepared to meet with you tomorrow. Most probably, he'll take you in. So please go down there tomorrow for an interview and hopefully, pupilage under him." A little reluctantly, I agreed.

As I walked away, he called out to me. "Subhas, for goodness sake, wear a tie for the interview, OK?" I smiled at him and assured him that I would wear a tie. I think if he did not say that to me, I would probably have gone in a T-shirt.

The next day I met Mr Chan at Shook Lin & Bok. He seemed a very unassuming man and even appeared shy at times. "So you're the man Jaya talked to me about yesterday," he said.

"Yes, sir, Mr Chan. I was there when he was talking to you."

"Don't call me Mr Chan. Just call me Sek Kiong. What is your area of interest?" I told him that I liked criminal law. He said: "Well we don't have criminal law here but law is not all criminal law. You'd better learn something else also. When the time comes, you can go and follow a criminal lawyer and get some criminal law experience. I'll arrange for it. In the meantime, I'll be your master."

Thinking I would have to report to work in a week or two, I asked him, "When do I start?"

"What do you mean? You start right now. Go and sit over there." I must have looked disappointed because he asked me, "Why, do you have another appointment? Do you have other plans?" Of course I said no and went to my table. That was how I started my chambers with Chief Justice Chan Sek Kiong.

At that time, the most senior partner in the firm was L P Thean. He went on to become the Justice of Appeal. After retirement, he joined KhattarWong as senior consultant. Today, I too am a senior consultant with KhattarWong along with him and Amarjit Singh, a former Judicial Commissioner. Even now, I may be talking with some junior lawyers in the firm and L P Thean will call out, "Hey, you rascal, come here. Are we having lunch tomorrow?" After he chats with me and leaves the room, everyone will look at me. I'll say to them: "You know, he can call me anything he likes because he was one of those people who shaped me in Shook Lin & Bok."

One day during my pupilage, L P Thean asked me, "Hey, aren't you interested in civil work? Don't you want some jam on your bread and butter? Don't you think you should do some civil litigation?"

"No, lah, L P, with my criminal law I think I can have enough jam," I said proudly. "I hate to do all these civil matters. Very boring."

He promptly replied, "Okay, I will not bother you anymore with this work but just think about it."

Pupilage under Chan Sek Kiong was very interesting. He was not a demanding pupil master. He was prepared to teach you everything that you wanted to learn provided you wanted to learn. He was not the type of person who would whip you into shape because if you didn't want to learn, that would be your problem. He made it very clear that if you showed interest in something and wished to discuss it with him, he wouldn't hesitate to sit you down and explain it to you. I tell you, this man really knows his law very well. He is such a learned person in law. You can ask him anything under the sun—from equity to trust to criminal law—and he would have an answer for you. If he didn't have an answer, he would give you the source where you can find your answer. He is a very brilliant man.

When he became a High Court judge, I appeared before him twice for two Magistrate's Court appeals. Knowing that he was sitting as an Appellate Judge, knowing that he was my master, and also knowing that I had always given him the impression that I was a lazy pupil, I made sure that he was aware that I was, by then, a changed person. Each time when I appeared before him, I was thoroughly prepared with my arguments and I won the appeals on both occasions.

Years later, when L P Thean also became a judge, I had to appear before him on a civil matter. I got a judgment before the registrar in the High Court and the other side was appealing against the registrar's decision. I argued against the other side. Justice L P Thean looked at me and listened to me. I did not know what was running through his mind, but I was very conscious of the fact that I had told him once a long time ago that I was not interested in doing civil law and that I could make enough 'jam' doing criminal work. I did not know if he remembered our conversation. Finally, he dismissed the appeal with costs. As we were leaving the High Court, he looked at me and smiled. Knowing L P Thean, he would have remembered everything because he has a very good memory.

I am one of the fortunate few to have had the likes of Chan Sek Kiong and L P Thean help me in my formative years as a lawyer. In many ways, both of them left a good impression on me. Contrary to some people's thoughts that he was ashamed to have me as a pupil, Chief Justice Chan has, on many occasions, introduced me to others as his pupil. I like to believe that he's done that with some pride.

Subhas and his father (1956)

The Anandan family. Seated from left: Surash, father, Subhashini, mother and Sugadha. Standing from left: Sudheesan and Subhas (1962)

Subhas, left, with his father and siblings, Sugadha, Surash and Sudheesan (1958)

Subhas, at 15 years old, with his mother
(1962)

Subhas with his elder sister, Subhashini (1975)

Graduation Day (1970)

Subhas with his red Sunbeam, outside the family home
in Kampung Wak Hassan (1975)

Subhas and his mother
in their Kampung Wak
Hassan home (1982)

Class of 1962, Naval Base School. Subhas is standing at the back row, third from left.

Subhas at a farewell party organised by his classmates of Naval Base School before he left for Loyola College, India, in 1963.

Before Subhas' departure for India. Standing from left: Chong Thee Kow, Cheng Lai Beng, Ramli, Chye, Mohd Noor, Ah Sai and Philip Pang. Seated from left: Chee Kok Meng, Ismail, Choy Sai Chee, Subhas, Wong Ah Soo and Narainasamy (Sam)

Another studio photo taken before Subhas left for India in 1963. Standing from left: Choo Poh Leong, Chong Thee Kow, Sandanasamy and Lee Chee San. Seated with Subhas is Michael Then.

Hanging out in the fields of Naval Base with friends. From left: Chong Thee Kow, Bernard Pereira, Michael Then, Choo Poh Leong and Lee Chee San (1963)

From left: Bernard Pereira, Choo Poh Leong, Lee Chee San, Michael Then, Subhas and Chong Thee Kow (1963)

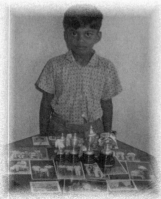

Surash, 8 years old, with his
first collection of medals
and trophies, and already
showing potential of much
more sporting achievements
to come.

Subhas with his trophies
for overall junior champion
won in Secondary 4 at
Naval Base School (1962)

University of Singapore Football Team (1968). Standing from left: Sudheesan, Mansor Marican, Ng, Chan Keng Fook, Rajayah and Lai. Front row from left: James, 'Tiger', Pak, Subhas and Gan.

FIVE

FIRST MURDER TRIAL

My family left the Base in 1971, about a few months after I was called to the Bar. As my father had retired, he was no longer entitled to living quarters there. We moved to Kampung Wak Hassan, not far from the Base, where my father bought a house with a small garden. The walls of the house were half brick and half wood and the roof was made of zinc. It took a long time to get used to the sound of raindrops hitting the roof but it eventually became therapeutic. We missed Block 9 but were intent on adapting to *kampung* life. We embraced the spirit of *gotong royong*, the Malay concept of doing things together and helping each other in the spirit of goodwill.

The Malays are generally very simple and humble people. They treated us very well, but they sometimes held us in awe because of the careers we had fashioned for ourselves. My elder sister was a doctor in Singapore General Hospital, I was an advocate and solicitor, my younger brother Sudheesan was then a senior officer at the Ministry of Defence, my younger sister then a schoolteacher and my youngest brother Surash later became an air steward with Singapore Airlines (he died in the SQ006 crash in Taipei on October 31, 2000). The *kampung* folk came to us with all sorts of problems including legal, medical and financial issues, and we helped them as much as we could. They often showed their gratitude by giving us food and drinks. During Hari Raya, our house would be filled with festive *kuih* and cookies, *ketupat* and satay. We used to invite our friends from the Base to celebrate with us.

One day while I was in the shower, Sudheesan yelled to me that there were people in the house who wanted to see me. He told me that he thought they were there to discuss a murder case. I was excited and quickly finished my shower. For me, to be briefed for a murder case was the ultimate. I went to the living room trying hard to look nonchalant even though I was trembling with excitement inside. I saw that my mother had already given them tea and made them comfortable. There were three of them—the elderly father of the accused and two others who were relatives. I was told that the accused had been charged with murder and was held in Queenstown Remand Prison. They wanted me to defend him. I told them I was new at the Bar and may not have the necessary experience to do a good job.

The father smiled. "I can't afford a senior lawyer, Mr Anandan," he said.

"The state can provide one free of charge," I replied.

"I'd rather have you," he said. "The state's lawyers are probably not so experienced either."

We discussed fees and he agreed to pay a sum that was equivalent to what it would take some of my classmates working in established law firms nine to 12 months to earn. It was also agreed that they would go to my office in Winchester House to sign the Warrant to Act and to pay a deposit for my services. Winchester House and the Singapore Rubber House flanked the famous Change Alley, which was like a labyrinth in those days, swarming with sailors, tourists and locals looking for bargain goods. Change Alley opened to Raffles Place on one side and Collyer Quay on the other. The site where Raffles Place MRT station is today was then an underground carpark below a public park with fountains and a huge floral clock. I had my office in Winchester House around the time of the infamous Robinsons fire when the department store was razed to the ground. On the Collyer Quay side you could see sampans and bumboats plying the open seas, gleaming in the sunshine.

So I had my first murder brief and capital case—defending a man called Tampines Raja who was charged with the murder of someone known as Beatle Raja. Because I was from Sembawang, I came to be known as Sembawang Raja. It was a tremendous feeling to be taking on the case though, after a few days, I realised the enormous responsibility that came with it. The only penalty for the crime was the death sentence and I had been entrusted to save Tampines Raja from this fate.

I went to Queenstown Remand Prison to see Tampines Raja for the first time. I sat in the visitors' room with my clerk. Tampines Raja was a young, cheerful man who had turned deadly for a moment at Beatle Raja's expense. I didn't know much about Beatle Raja, but as his nickname suggested, he must have been a Beatles fan. When I introduced myself to Tampines Raja, he smiled and said that he had heard about me. In fact, he may have been the person who started calling me Sembawang Raja. I took his instructions and asked several questions, some of which he could answer and some which he couldn't. I went back to Queenstown Remand Prison many times to discuss his defence with him.

His case was heard in the High Court before two judges, Justice A V Winslow, the presiding judge, and Justice T Kulasekaram. By then, jury systems had been abolished in Singapore. The deputy public prosecutor was Lawrence Ang, who had been my classmate in law school. It was also his first murder case. We were friends and I knew he would be fair and reasonable. The proceedings went on for a few days and one incident stood out for me. While cross-examining one of the prosecution witnesses after a weekend break, I put a question to him alleging something he had said in his examination-in-chief the previous week. The judges couldn't remember whether he had said it or not as their notes did not mention the facts I had alleged. Nothing in the DPP's notes reflected what I was alleging either. Justice Winslow asked me what my notes said and I replied that I don't take notes. Justice Winslow smiled and said he had noticed that. "Well, Mr Anandan, it looks as though it's a battle between your memory and all our notes," he said.

I remained silent. Justice Winslow was a great judge. He called for the notes of the court recorder whose job was to record everything in verbatim in shorthand. I told the recorder roughly when the witness was supposed to have said what I was alleging. The verbatim notes showed that I was right. Justice Winslow decided that their notes were useless and that they would rely on my memory from then on.

Unfortunately, Tampines Raja made a mess of his evidence. He departed from what we had discussed he was supposed to say. After his testimony, we made the final submission but I knew I had lost the case even before the verdict. While waiting for it, I went to see Tampines Raja in the lock-up cell of the High Court and asked him why he had changed his story. He looked at me sheepishly and told me that he had discussed his defence with his fellow prison inmates and they thought that the original version was not good enough. So, he amended and embellished it. I was very angry as our defence was based on the truth and the facts supported it. "You're a fool," I said angrily as I knew what the consequence would be.

Not long after that, Tampines Raja realised the seriousness of his error when the judgment was delivered. He was found guilty and sentenced to death. It was the first time I heard a death sentence being passed. It was extremely disconcerting to hear the judge pronounce it in such an emotionless way, as if he was proclaiming that the next day would be a holiday. We had to stand up when the death sentence was passed and my knees were trembling. It was sad to hear one human being being told by another that he had to die. As soon as court was adjourned and the accused taken away, the family and relatives sitting in the gallery came running out screaming and wailing. The women fell at my feet and started to cry, repeatedly asking me what had happened and what had gone wrong. Some were blaming me. I was angry and confused, but most of all, I was dejected. It was a terrible experience. That night I got completely drunk and didn't go home. I had lost my first murder case.

SIX

BECOMING A CRIMINAL LAWYER

I believe the changes in local criminal law have made things advantageous to the prosecution. Though there is a "presumption of innocence", according to our Constitution, the man in the street cannot be blamed if he thinks that he has to prove his innocence in court. The law is lopsided. So many aspects of the criminal law are loaded against the accused. The Constitution says one thing but in practice, it's different. The courts must also be blamed for this sad state of affairs. They rarely interpret the law in favour of the accused, though I feel things are slowly changing. One day, we may still have justice in the true sense of the word. Justice must be compassionate and it must be fair. It must endeavour to seek out the truth. It must balance the rights of the accused and the protection of society.

I argued the appeal of Tampines Raja in the Court of Criminal Appeal. The panel of judges comprised Chief Justice Wee Chong Jin, Justice Tan Ah Tah and Justice Freddy Chua. They were the most senior judges at the time. I was told I was the youngest lawyer to have ever appeared before the Court of Appeal. I was also told that Chief Justice Wee grilled the younger lawyers especially hard and I was prepared for the worst. That day in court, I was on my feet for nearly an hour; those 60 minutes were among the longest I've ever been through in court. Surprisingly though, the Chief Justice did not go after me. Instead

Justice Tan, who was reputed for protecting young lawyers from the Chief Justice, gave me a hard time. Chief Justice Wee actually took pity on me and started to protect me from Justice Tan. It didn't make a difference though. To crown my humiliation, the deputy public prosecutor was not even asked to answer my submission. The appeal was dismissed and the conviction was allowed to stand. Tampines Raja was one step closer to the gallows.

A few days later, the registrar of the Supreme Court phoned to tell me that I had been assigned to assist the solicitors in London to undertake my client's appeal in the Privy Council. For a brief moment, I thought I would be sent to London. I was told later that the extent of my assistance was to send the Record of Appeal to London. I was merely a courier with a parcel to deliver to the post office. I got the Record of Appeal together and sent it to a large solicitor's firm in London. I can't recall the firm's name, but it took on all the criminal appeals that went to the Privy Council for those who could not afford the fees. The accused has to swear that he has nothing "but the clothes he's wearing"—*In Forma Pauperis*—this is the term used for it. When the firm received the Record of Appeal, they sent me a letter of acknowledgement and I heard nothing further.

A few weeks later, I had a collect call from London. The operator told me a solicitor from London wanted to speak to me and asked if I was prepared to pay for the call. I said yes, more out of curiosity than anything else. A man speaking the Queen's English with a very condescending tone told me that a petition had been prepared by his firm for the Lordships of the Privy Council. He also said that their senior solicitor had decided to ignore my arguments as they were not well thought out and most probably doomed to failure. Instead, the senior solicitor had formulated his own arguments in the Petition of

Appeal. I was shattered as I put down the phone. The solicitor at the other end seemed to want to continue the conversation but since I was paying for the call, I wanted to end it. What I heard was a disaster and I was not able to sleep that night. If my arguments were so lowly thought of, I could be responsible for the death of my client.

The next day, I confided these feelings to my elder sister. Being a doctor, she was more concerned about my health. She told me to forget the case. After some deliberation, I decided to call London and speak to the same solicitor. I asked him if his senior solicitor was a Queen's Counsel. He told me that he was not. I then instructed him to get an opinion from a Queen's Counsel. In a tone laced with sarcasm, he asked me who would pay the Queen's Counsel's fee. I said I would and asked him how much that would be. He said it would cost around £150 which was about S$1,200 in those days. It was a lot of money but I had to do it. He intimated that they would only instruct a Queen's Counsel after receiving my money. So much for trust among fellow lawyers.

I remitted the fee the next day and heard nothing from London for two weeks. Then the same solicitor called me and, this time, it was not a collect call. When I spoke to him, I sensed that he was not so condescending any more. He told me that the Queen's Counsel's opinion was that my arguments were correct and he had amended the petition based on my arguments. I was overjoyed and relieved, but being the confrontational man that I was, I couldn't resist asking him whether his senior solicitor was still in his chambers. His silence spoke volumes.

I was glad I had decided to spend the money. If I had not done it, I would have continued to blame myself for losing the case. Who knows, I might never have taken up another murder case. Still, the appeal was dismissed by the Privy Council. When I was informed of the verdict, I was not surprised. Some messes created in the lower courts cannot be undone.

I was then told by the registrar of the Supreme Court to file a petition for clemency on behalf of the accused. I managed to get a specimen copy from David Marshall's clerk. I prepared the petition on behalf of my client and delivered it to the Istana. Benjamin Sheares was President at the time. My lawyer colleagues informed me that filing a clemency petition was a waste of time as the President, with the advice of the Cabinet and the Attorney-General, very rarely commuted a death sentence to life imprisonment. In subsequent years, I came to learn that this is true. Out of the multiple appeals I have done, only once was a sentence of death commuted to life.

For a country so small, Singapore has among the highest per-capita execution rates in the world, and the authorities have always been very cagey about executions. Under Section 216 of Singapore's Criminal Procedure Code, it is noted that "when any person is sentenced to death, the sentence shall direct that he shall be hanged by the neck till he is dead but shall not state the place where nor the time when the sentence is to be carried out." So, this uncertainty over executions is written into the law itself. A few months later, I received a letter from the President's office stating that clemency was denied. Tampines Raja had exhausted his last chance. An execution is typically carried out within a week of rejection by the President.

I made one last trip to Changi Prison, the 'condemned prison', to see my client and to inform him of the President's decision. I didn't know he had already been told the news. When I met him, he was smiling and before I could say anything, he told me he knew and that it was alright. He had become a Christian and accepted his fate.

"I'm not afraid of death any more, Mr Subhas." He spoke strongly about his faith and asked me if I would be angry if he told me he now believed in Jesus.

"Why should I be angry?" I replied.

"I thought you would be angry because you're the president of the Hindu temple," he explained.

"I could never be angry at someone changing his faith as long as he believes that what he's doing is right." I reminded him that Hinduism is a very liberal religion and Hindus are supposed to be tolerant.

He thanked me for all that I had done for him and assured me that his family would never blame me and that I should continue defending people with the same zeal I had shown in his case. He also told me that I was hot tempered and that I should try to control my temper. He laughed loudly as he said this, startling the prison guards who were present. "See what a hot temper has done to me," Tampines Raja said. As I stood up to say my last farewell, he hugged me and said, "May Jesus Christ bless you and your family."

I walked out of the prison with a heavy heart. Tampines Raja was a young man who had wasted his life over a silly argument. In fact, two young lives had been destroyed. *The Straits Times* announced shortly after my last meeting with Tampines Raja that he had been hanged. It was a tragic end to my first case, but I took consolation in the fact that I knew that it would be the start of an exciting career in criminal law for me. Tampines Raja's faith in me gave me the confidence I needed.

SEVEN

TEMPLE

This look at my early years would not be complete without including the time I spent in prison. It was a dark period for me. Throughout my life, I had been among the prime movers in many escapades and incidents, but my incarceration in Queenstown Remand Prison brought me back to earth. More importantly, it gave me a chance to rediscover who I really was as I gradually adjusted to life in prison.

My troubles began innocently enough at a temple called the Holy Sri Balasubramaniar Temple, which was then located at Canberra Road within the Naval Base. The temple was founded by a man called P Karupiah who worked at the British Royal Navy Dockyard. He dreamt one night of a very powerful golden cobra living in a tree in the Base. On the basis of this dream, some Hindus got together and built a small shed for the deity Murugan in the vicinity of the tree. Murugan is the God of War and the patron deity of Tamil Land. According to Tamil devotional literature, Murugan never hesitates to come to the aid of a devotee when called upon in piety or distress. A bigger building was constructed on the site when more and more devotees visited the temple. Naturally, a committee was elected to run it.

At that time, in 1972, the president of the committee was S Saravanan, an elder in our community. He had been president for almost 10 years. He was not popular with the younger generation of devotees because of the heavy-handed way he ran the temple. It was not unusual for the older generation to pursue matters relating to the temple without involving the younger devotees. But there were more immediate problems.

After I was called to the Bar, my childhood friend Sam, who was a committee member of the temple, approached me to discuss issues related to the rules and regulations of the temple. He needed my help to amend some parts of the temple's constitution. At the time, the committee was also having a problem with the Hindu Endowment Board. A member of parliament, N Govindasamy, had insisted that the temple join the Hindu Endowment Board but the committee was not keen to do so. I helped Sam draft some amendments to the constitution and to the rules. I also drafted a letter on behalf of the temple stating that we declined to come under the umbrella of the Hindu Endowment Board. The letter was practically a challenge to MP Govindasamy to show which part of the law required our temple to come under the board. That ended the matter.

Later that year, when my family had already moved to Kampung Wak Hassan, Sam visited us. He wanted me to attend the temple's annual general meeting. It was fixed for a Sunday and my appointment as the temple's legal advisor had to be formalised at the AGM. I told him: "There's no need for me to be present. Why don't you just ask the members to endorse it." Sunday was the only day in the week I could sleep in and the meeting was at 9.00 o'clock in the morning.

My mother overhead our conversation and said: "Can't you sacrifice just one Sunday for your temple? For God? Why don't you go to the AGM and get formally appointed?"

I turned to Sam. "Ok, then, I'll go to the meeting."

On that particular Sunday, there was a huge crowd at the temple, both young and old. Many were old friends and some were my father's friends. My father was also there.

Sam said to me: "Hey, the person who's supposed to stand for president against Mr Saravanan is unable to make it as something more urgent required his attention. Could you please contest the election? We don't want Mr Saravanan to be president of the temple committee again, and we just need you to contest and hold the position for a short period until we find someone to take over from you."

Many of our friends were there, and they were hoping that I would show my support and accept their proposal. After much coaxing from them, I agreed to contest the election. There were only two candidates: myself and the incumbent. The candidates were told to leave the hall and by a show of hands, I was elected president. The other candidate got only one vote—my father's.

My father was angry at the way his good friend Mr Saravanan had been humiliated. They had worked together for about 30 years in the Base and he was of the opinion that no one should be humiliated in that way. Even my father's friends had voted for me because I was his son. I had the support of both the older and younger generations. I accepted my victory with mixed feelings as I could understand my father's point of view.

My father proposed the defeated candidate as vice-president. Not wanting to hurt my father's feelings, no one objected and S Saravanan was elected unopposed. I realised, to my horror, that I could not resign. If I did, the former president would, under the temple's constitution, succeed me. I had no choice but to continue. When I got back home, my mother had a broad smile on her face. She had heard about my win and, to her, being president of a temple was a great honour.

After growing up among mostly Chinese boys, I found that the temple exposed me to the Indian community. I received great support. Youngsters came in numbers to help us change the face of the temple. We expanded its premises and it was common to see us digging the soil even after midnight. New friends like Dasa, Soman, Bhasi, Velayuthan, Puru, Vincent and many others were pillars of support and strength. Temple work brought me tremendous joy. I had to pull people from different factions of the community into the temple and unite them. I also became religious in the process.

Unfortunately, there was also a lot of politics to deal with at the temple. You can please people most of the time but sometimes what you do is never enough. There was at least one group of devotees who were not happy with what was happening. They became even unhappier when they saw that the temple was prospering under my leadership. However, they couldn't do anything about it and I was re-elected in 1973. In 1975, I decided that Sam, who had by then been vice-president for two years, should be the president. The election was contested and he won.

Although Sam had won, many people from the opposition camp had also been voted into the temple committee. I was reappointed legal advisor. There were numerous problems within the committee and some issues could not be resolved because of personality clashes. This created a lot of bitterness amongst the members. Even though I wasn't the president, many petitions and complaints were lodged against me. I felt these were mostly unjustified. Complaints were forwarded to then Prime Minister Lee Kuan Yew and to several government departments, stating that I was a gangster and that I was controlling the temple with the help of the Black Eagle Gang. Many allegations were made against me and some of my friends. To be honest, I didn't know that such a gang even existed. It was all ludicrous as I simply didn't have the time to be a gangster. I was too heavily involved in my law work and was also helping out at the temple in my free time. In 1976, I was arrested and detained under the Criminal Law (Temporary Provisions) Act and taken to Queenstown Remand Prison off Margaret Drive. Enacted in 1958, this Act is the longest temporary provisions in the history of Singapore.

Soon after my arrest, some of my good friends at the temple, including Sam and Soman, were also arrested. They were not put into the Queenstown prison like I was. Instead they were held in a CID lock-up and interrogated for about two weeks. I suppose the police was hoping they would say something that could be used against me. They never did, but the longer they were in custody the more worried I became. In the end, as there was already such a public outcry over my arrest, Sam, Soman and the others were released. I heard the news in prison and was quite relieved even though I still didn't have my freedom. If they had not been released, the case against me could have been very bad.

At the time of my arrest, my brother Sudheesh was working in the Ministry of Defence under Dr Goh Keng Swee. He wanted to speak to Dr Goh about my case but was told by his personal assistant that the minister was not free to see him. My brother was quite disappointed that his boss was not prepared to help him. Dr Goh was Singapore's first Minister of Finance after independence in 1965. He was also the chief architect of Singapore's early economic growth, including the creation of the Economic Development Board, the Port of Singapore Authority, the Jurong Town Corporation, the Housing and Development Board, the Ministry of Education and the Central Provident Fund. My brother held him in high regard as did many who worked under him.

After a few days, Dr Goh's personal assistant called Sudheesh to say that he would see him. Dr Goh explained to Sudheesh why he could not see him earlier. Because of the high profile nature of my case, he had guessed why Sudheesh wanted to see him but he said that he was not able to help at the time. He told my brother: "I knew at the time that you wanted me to help. I know your brother better than you. I've got his university record. I don't believe the charges against him are fair. Today, I have been appointed Acting Prime Minister as Mr Lee has gone overseas. I have asked the CPIB, which comes under the jurisdiction of the Prime Minister, to start an investigation into your brother's case. I can assure you that the investigation will be thorough and if your brother is innocent, he will be released." Sudheesh went away very happy that Dr Goh was able to intervene. Meanwhile, my friends went around collecting signatures from people who were living in Sembawang for my release, stating that I could not possibly be guilty of the fabrications levelled against me. I had support on many fronts.

Why was I was arrested in the first place? The story is one that relates to love scorned. The man who fabricated my involvement with the Black Eagle Gang was an Inspector Gopal and his two detectives, Vanampadi and Maniam. To understand the whole situation behind my arrest, I have to mention an episode concerning three brothers who lived at the Base. The brothers stayed in the same block as a married woman named Saroja. The eldest brother was having an affair with her. All the neighbours knew about it but everyone chose to mind their own business. One day there was a proposal for one of Saroja's sisters to marry one of the brothers. The eldest brother objected on the basis that if Saroja could be such an unfaithful wife, one could expect no better from her sister. The proposal was rejected and the two families became bitter enemies.

A few months after that, Saroja became involved with Inspector Gopal. She started poisoning his mind against the brothers. Without revealing her affair with the eldest brother, she alleged that they were gangsters and extortionists and were bullying her family. Subsequently, the brothers were arrested and detained under the Criminal Law (Temporary Provisions) Act.

The mother of the brothers appointed me as her sons' lawyer. I discovered there were many irregularities in the arrest procedure as well as in Inspector Gopal's pre-fabricated information. Inspector Gopal was the one who had made the arrest. As I delved deeper into the case, I found that he and his wife were bullying the people in his district. He was abusing his powers as an inspector with the support of a few police officers. Inspector Gopal realised that I was gathering evidence against him and his people, and decided that the only way to save himself was to fix me, which he did. He got people who had opposed me during my service at the temple to fabricate evidence against me. Finally, he managed to convince then Minister for Home Affairs Chua Sian Chin to sign a detention order against me. I felt then that Mr Chua was really not a capable minister. However, today his son is a good friend of mine and a capable banker.

Inspector Gopal and the other police officers thought that throwing me into jail would convey the message that any investigation on him would be over. But he didn't bargain on my family and friends fighting to clear my name.

EIGHT

PRISON

I was held in a solitary confinement cell as soon as I was put into Queenstown Remand Prison. I was stripped to my underwear and left to sleep on the cold hard cement floor. I could not tell whether it was day or night. There were no windows and light came through only when the wardens pushed the food through an opening in the heavy metal door. My mind began to wander to the many places and periods of my life. To keep my sanity and uplift my spirits, I played a game of 'mental' chess, holding both sides of the game. I focused on the strategies of chess. I didn't understand why I had to be kept in solitary confinement. I was told that it was for my own safety but I didn't believe that. It was a tough ordeal. Police officers would come occasionally to question me and ask me to sign statements. I never did sign them as doing so would not only have implicated me but also the friends with whom I grew up.

David Marshall visited me in Queenstown Prison. He was defending me along with Leo Fernando, a leading criminal lawyer, and Mak Kok Wing, a classmate of mine. One of the first things David Marshall told me was that he was very surprised that so many people had asked him to defend me. They were prepared to pay his fee because they felt that I should be defended by the best. He told me that he would not take a fee for defending me because he didn't believe in charging a fellow lawyer. But at the end of it all, we paid his disbursements as we felt it was the right thing to do. He was quite pleased to receive that.

David Marshall told me: "I've spoken to the people up there, my lad. Are you prepared? They may keep you here for a long time without a trial and this detention order by the minister can be renewed every year. So, nobody knows how long you'll be here, but they said if you are prepared to cooperate and sign those statements, you could make a deal and be out of here in the next couple of weeks."

"I know the statements that they have prepared for me," I replied. "Mr Marshall, those statements would get a lot of innocent people into trouble. They will all be remanded in prison and there will be no one there to fight for them except me when I get out. But if I've implicated them, I won't even be on their side. These are people whom I grew up with and they are my friends. I am not going to get them into trouble."

"But you know, lad, you can be here for a long time if you don't cooperate," he reiterated.

"I would rather be here for a long time than gain my freedom by betraying my friends."

David Marshall smiled and held my hand. He was a very kind man. "I'm glad you have made that decision, lad. If you had told me otherwise, I would have carried on with your instructions but I would not have liked what I was doing."

Once we had decided to fight my detention, my mind was at peace. The prison authorities treated me less harshly because I think David Marshall's name carried a lot of weight. Also, from that time on, David Marshall and I developed a very good working relationship. Many of the documents, affidavits and evidence that he required were obtained by my brother, Sudheesh, who visited him to prepare the case. Mr Marshall told me that my brother would have made an excellent lawyer.

I lost track of time, so I'm not exactly sure when they took me out of solitary confinement and put me into the main part of the prison with the other inmates. I do remember a medical officer called Dr Singh who saw me early in my incarceration. I felt he was a disgrace to his profession. His ill-treatment of the prisoners knew no bounds. His attitude was worse than that of the wardens, with no sympathy at all for the inmates. Every ailment was treated with aspirin. More often than not, he would just bark at you and accuse you of being a malingerer.

The day I came out of solitary confinement, I was taken to see him. There were two men dressed in normal office clothes with him. I didn't know who they were then and I still don't know who they are today. They were shadowy figures, the type you see in spy movies lurking in dimly lit underground carparks.

One of them asked me, "How do you feel?"

I told him I was feeling alright even though I was not. I didn't want them to know that I was physically on the verge of a breakdown. They continued to quiz me, trying to make conversation.

"You do a lot of criminal cases, right?" one of them said.

I realised they were trying to find out if they had broken me during my solitary confinement.

He continued, "If a person is charged for theft, under what section of the Penal Code would you charge him?"

"It depends on what sort of theft you are talking about," I replied.

"What do you mean?" the other man asked.

"Simple theft is Section 379, theft from dwelling, it may be 380, and if it is theft from employer, it's Section 381, and so on. These are the sections." They asked me a series of questions which I answered to the best of my ability. I hoped I wasn't making any mistakes because I really didn't want them to think that they were breaking me.

Finally, one of them looked at the other and said, "Wah, this guy is tough, huh?" They smiled and told me I could go to the clinic, which was like a small hospital, to sleep. The thought that I would get to sleep on a bed was such a relief. I had been unable to get any regular sleep on the cold cement floor of the solitary confinement cell. I slept very soundly but not for long.

About an hour later, I was rudely woken up and instructed to dress. Feeling disoriented, I asked where I was being taken. "Don't ask any questions," said one of the wardens who had aroused me from my sleep. They handcuffed me behind my back. As soon as I got into the van, an Indian officer who had looked uncomfortable when he saw me unlocked the handcuffs and cuffed me in front so that I could sit more comfortably. He even lit a cigarette and gave it to me to smoke. I was very grateful to him for his kindness. I didn't know where they were taking me but it seemed an endless journey. I couldn't see out of the van. Many things ran through my mind as I sat there. I even wondered if I was being taken somewhere to be shot. I thought about my clients who had been locked up in Queenstown Remand Prison and whether something like this had happened to them. It finally struck me that I was being taken to Changi Prison when I detected a faint smell of the sea in the air. In those days, you could still get the scent of the sea quite a way inland because there were no tall buildings to block the sea breeze as there are now.

I figured that I was being transferred to the psychiatric ward and sure enough I was dropped off there. I asked the officer why I had been brought there. He said that I had shown signs of claustrophobia when I was in solitary confinement, and the authorities wanted to investigate and observe me further. My new wardens had been told that I had been behaving strangely. Maybe they thought there was something remiss in my Bobby Fischer and Boris Spassky impersonations when I was playing mental chess in the cell. I thought that perhaps they were trying to make me mad or make me look mad.

I was given a bed in an open ward on the ground floor. It's funny because the movie *One Flew Over the Cuckoo's Nest*, starring Jack Nicholson, had just been screened the year before. I hadn't seen it but my friends had described it to me. I guess my status in the ward wasn't all that different. My sleeping companions were murderers who, because of their insanity, were kept there at the President's pleasure—we were all guests of Benjamin Sheares. I later learnt that some of the inmates had been there since the 1950s and were absolutely stark raving mad. Some of them were so mad that they had to be handcuffed to their beds and shackled. You could see the raw, mottled skin on their wrists and ankles where they tried to wrest themselves free of their shackles.

I was confused as I looked across the ward. Some of the inmates were smiling, others singing. It seemed like I was the only sane person around, apart from the officers. It was my worst nightmare and I thought I would become mad if I stayed there too long. An officer told me that there was a certain Denis Pinder upstairs in the medical ward. The former chairman of Sime Darby was put in jail for criminal breach of trust and cheating. Pinder was in the ward because he had a problem with his leg and he was not able to walk properly.

In the midst of my ordeal, I must say I got lucky. One of the officers knew me because I had defended a few of his brothers in court for various offences. I thanked God that I had got them all acquitted.

The officer walked me out of the ward and offered me a cigarette. He said: "I'm giving you some pieces of paper and this pen. Write your story down because a psychiatrist will be coming to evaluate your case. Tell him whatever you have to tell him because if he certifies you a nutcase, you're going to spend a lot of time here. So, please do what is necessary to show that you're not a nutcase. And if you're caught with this pen and paper, don't say who gave it to you because I'll get the sack if you do."

I assured him I wouldn't. I was so thankful to be treated as a normal person. When I got back to the ward, I hid the stationery under my pillow. I would sit up at night, almost in darkness, and slowly pen my thoughts about what had happened to me so far. I wrote about how I had been framed and my early experiences in Queenstown Remand Prison. I questioned why I was in jail in the first place.

I can't be sure, but on the ninth or tenth day at Changi Prison, I was told by one of the wardens that the psychiatrist would like to see me. I stuffed the paper down my shorts and walked with the warden to the psychiatrist's room.

"Good morning, Subhas," the psychiatrist said pleasantly.

"Good morning, doctor."

He tried to reassure me. "You don't know me but I know you. I've read about you. Your sister was a casual acquaintance a long time ago. We worked together but we have lost contact with each other. Do you smoke?"

"Yes," I replied. He got me a cigarette and offered me a cup of coffee which I was happy to accept as it was a luxury in prison.

"Let's talk," he said, as soon as I had taken a few sips of the coffee.

"Before we talk, doctor, I had the privilege of getting a pen and some paper to write about my ordeal. So, why don't you read what I've written and then you can start your evaluation of my mental condition."

"Good," he replied. I pulled out the paper from my shorts and gave it to him. He left a packet of cigarettes and matches on the table for me. As I puffed on another cigarette, the doctor read what I had written.

After reading my note, the doctor looked at me and said: "There's no reason for me to question someone who can write so lucidly. You can't be suffering from a mental disorder. Claustrophobia is not a mental disease. It's just a frame of mind that some people have. I don't see any reason why you should spend time here. What I'll recommend is that you be transferred back to Queenstown Remand Prison and that you be kept in a grille." He explained that in a grille, I would share a space that is enclosed with bars, not walls, with 14 other prisoners. I would be able to see beyond the cell. "I'll ensure that they do so and if they don't, there could be dire consequences. You can let your family know and they can tell the press," he added.

I heaved an audible sigh of relief and thanked the doctor. I asked when I could get out and he replied as soon as possible. With that expectation, I returned to the ward much happier than when I left it to see the doctor. But I was still not sure when arrangements would be made to send me back to Queenstown. I was very keen to get out of Changi because I was terrified that someone would strangle me in my sleep. It wasn't paranoia. On one of the nights, I had been jolted out of my sleep at about 3 o'clock in the morning by an inmate called Yusoff, who slept in the bed next to mine.

Yusoff had killed a security guard, the guard's wife and their two children for throwing sand into his rice while he was at work. He had flown into a rage when he discovered what they had done and then gone off to Sungei Road where he bought a secondhand *parang* but not before having a good meal first. He paid five cents for the knife to be sharpened and, at midnight, went to the security officer's home and decimated the whole family. He left an infant untouched because he said the infant hadn't done anything. He was charged and convicted for murder, but because of insanity, he had been kept in the psychiatric ward under the President's pleasure order. A very strong and violent person, Yusoff had required six to seven wardens to hold him down when he went mad. Everyone called him Raja Yusoff because he was king of the ward. He could even get away with hitting the superintendent because he was certified insane.

So, when he stood ominously over me in the dark at 3.00 am, I was terrified. But I couldn't show him that.

"What is it, Yusoff? What are you looking at?" I asked him calmly.

"I'm hungry," he replied in Malay.

A chill went through my body and I thought to myself: "Oh, my God! He's hungry and he's staring at me." I fought to stay calm and asked him again, "What do you want?"

"I want your biscuits."

My family had just visited that day and given me 2 katis (1.2 kg) of crackers. The biscuits that were allowed in prison were hard, tasteless, soda crackers, nothing like the Jacob's brand of cream crackers that you would have at afternoon garden tea parties. You had to soften the biscuits by dunking them in the concoction the prison passed off as a beverage every morning.

"You want my biscuits? Take and eat them," I told him.

You wouldn't believe what Yusoff did. He sat down and ate up all the tasteless crackers in one sitting. Some of the other inmates got up at the noise of crunched crackers from Yusoff's bed and stared sleepily at him but no one asked him for any. He was, after all, the raja of the ward. When Yusoff was done, he thanked me and went back to sleep. He was soon snoring.

Another inmate in the psychiatric ward was an Indian man charged with murdering his wife after finding her in bed with her lover. The lover managed to escape through a window but the wife was not so lucky. The man quietly took out a chopper from the kitchen drawer and chopped her head off. He then took a shower to wash off the blood on his body, put his wife's head in a bag and cycled to Bukit Panjang police station. He deposited the bag on a table without saying a word. It was the middle of the night and a sergeant asked him, "Hey, *mama*, what are you doing here at this time of the night?"

"I want to report a case," he replied.

The sergeant looked at him and said, "Okay, what case have you got? Report your case."

Apparently, the man calmly took his wife's head out of the bag. Holding it by the hair, he placed it on the sergeant's table. Clotted globs of blood and severed tendons and arteries were said to be dangling from the neck. It seems that the sergeant fainted and was later demoted for fainting, which sounds a bit unfair. How often do you see a decapitated head in Singapore? The man was ultimately charged but also put into the psychiatric ward because he was deemed insane. So you can understand my constant state of apprehension while I remained in Changi Prison.

Every evening, at around 4 to 5 o'clock, we were taken out to the yard for some sunlight and exercise. Another Indian man, who was in prison for committing a murder, would come up to me every day.

"You're a lawyer, is it?" he would say.

"Ya," I would reply.

"Lend me $10."

I would ask him why he wanted $10 as we were not allowed to have money. He always replied that he was being released that day and needed money to take a taxi home. Every day, I would give him the same answer: "There's no problem even if you don't have money. You see, when you reach home, your family will be there to receive you. They can pay the taxi driver."

"Ya, I never thought of that! No wonder you're a lawyer. You're a very smart man." He would walk away and the very next day, he would ask me for $10 again. This went on until I was transferred back to Queenstown Remand Prison.

A day or two after meeting the psychiatrist, the superintendent of Changi Prison informed me that the psychiatrist had reported that there was nothing wrong with me. The psychiatrist had said that I should not be kept in solitary confinement and had recommended that I be put in a grille. The superintendent was quite a good chap. He said that I would be sent back to Queenstown Remand Prison immediately.

I collected my belongings and said my goodbyes to the prisoners in the ward. Some of them understood what was going on but others just looked at me blankly. Now that I knew that I was leaving Changi, I was suddenly filled with compassion for them. I felt very sad as I didn't know whether they would be released at all because nobody seemed to bother about them. I thought: "These are the forgotten ones. Their families have forgotten them. The authorities have forgotten them. I think they themselves have forgotten who they are or what they are."

I walked outside and got into a waiting van. This time I was not handcuffed. The journey to Queenstown Prison seemed shorter than when I was being taken to Changi Prison. Perhaps it's because I knew the destination this time around. On arrival at Queenstown, I was received by the officer of my block, a very short and kind officer called Osman. He looked at me and said, "Welcome back to Queenstown, Subhas."

"Thank you, sir."

"You're not going to be in solitary confinement. You're not going to stay in a small cell with others. You're going to the grille upstairs."

I asked if I could be taken to the grille where my friend Anthony Heng was. Anthony was my school football captain and we had played for Naval Base School together. He was being detained for a second time. Officer Osman agreed. I was glad it was him and not some other officer who could have been mean to me and refuse my request.

Osman escorted me to the grille upstairs. I shared it with 14 Chinese prisoners. Normally, being the last one in meant that I had to sleep on the floor, but the inmates had agreed to let me have the corner bed. It struck me all of a sudden that they had taken it upon themselves to make sure that my stay at Queenstown was as comfortable as possible. I think Anthony had a hand in it. They gave me a spare blanket, but I told them that I didn't need one because I was used to sleeping on the balcony of my family's flat in Naval Base. From that day onwards, someone in the grille would take my *sai thong* (sewage pot) to empty it in the main sewage tank and wash my clothes. Everyone appeared to want to do favours for me. It was like having many personal butlers, though I regarded them all as friends.

On my second day back at Queenstown, I was taken to the yard for the first time. Prisoners were allowed to bathe there every day. They were also allowed to play games or exercise or engage in their own activity freely. Some of the prisoners would wash their clothes which was one of the things you couldn't do in the cells. The daily 'freedom' break was about two hours.

The officers were kind to me. They allowed me to shower early in the morning when everyone else had to get ready for work. They did not want to leave me alone in the grille as they were afraid I might lapse into the mental condition that saw me taken to Changi Prison. I think you could describe that condition as a depressed state.

Anyway, when yard-time came, Anthony Heng came along and sat with me, and we lit up our cigarettes. It was the first time I had felt relaxed since I was remanded. One by one, the other prisoners joined us, including one particular guy who was accompanied by two other men. He said: "Hey, lawyer. I'm the head of the Ang Soon Tong gang here and this is my deputy." He didn't bother to introduce the third person as obviously he must have been his 'bodyguard'.

"I'm glad to meet you," I replied.

"Do you have cigarettes?" he asked. Now, cigarettes are a precious commodity in prison. They are like cash. You could buy things with cigarettes. I thought that he wanted to extort cigarettes from me. I told him that I had enough for myself. Then he asked if I had biscuits. Again, I told him that I had enough for myself.

"Okay then," he replied. He smiled and walked away. Before I could ask Anthony what that was all about, others came to introduce themselves and ask me the same questions.

I was puzzled. After all the gang leaders had introduced themselves, I asked Anthony, "Hey, what's happening? What are these guys up to? Why are they interested in my cigarettes?"

"No, they're just showing you respect. Whether you like it or not, Subhas, to these people and to many others outside, you're one of the most high-ranking secret society triad members who have been detained. You're like their boss, you know."

I found the situation rather strange. All that they thought of me was untrue and I felt that Anthony had to tell them so. I was more concerned about clearing my name and reputation with the police, but here were people who believed that I was their triad boss. If they gave the jail wardens and police a wrong impression of me, I would be in trouble and would probably have to stay behind bars for a long time.

"You must tell them that this is all nonsense," I told Anthony.

He looked at me and said, "This is a different world, Subhas. It's a jungle here. Don't worry, just ignore it."

The next day, while I was sitting in the yard at the same time, all the leaders came up to me with biscuits and cigarettes. I had so much biscuits and cigarettes that I wondered what to do with them.

Anthony advised me: "Just ask them to keep the things for you."

So I told the leaders: "I'm very grateful to you but if I take all these cigarettes and biscuits back to my grille, we will all get into trouble. Could you do something for me? Why don't you keep these for me and you can give them to me when I want them." They agreed and took them all back.

I used to smoke nearly four packets of cigarettes, 70 sticks or more, daily before my arrest. When I was in prison, my family was allowed to give me only 60 sticks of cigarettes for two weeks which meant I could only smoke four sticks each day.

Anthony said: "Subhas, it looks as though you're going to be here for some time. You're a lawyer and the people in your case, like the three brothers, have been here for some time already, you know. So why don't you just resign yourself to the situation and don't make a big fuss about it. If you're going to be here for some time, you might as well enjoy all these benefits."

I kept quiet. What he said made sense. If I was going to be there for a few years, I might as well be No. 1 and enjoy the biscuits, cigarettes, extra storybooks or whatever it was that they were prepared to share with me. Although, at the back of my mind, I felt that something was not right. There are certain things you can't control when you're in prison. I realised that I was not only a special prisoner to the authorities, I was also a special prisoner to the prisoners.

NINE

PRISON INTERMEDIARY

In prison, I was perpetually hungry. Breakfast was at around 6 o'clock in the morning when we received a cup of something to drink. I still don't know what it is. It was not coffee nor tea nor Milo but more a concoction of substances that tasted a bit sweet. We were also given a bread roll which was so hard, we joked that if you were to hit a dog with it, you'd probably cause the dog to have a concussion. The bread tasted like rubber when you dunked it into the drink. It was so inedible that we would normally throw it away. I once asked the officer in charge why the bread was always so hard and he replied: "We have no choice on the matter. The bread that is served to you this morning was delivered to us one or two days ago. The bread doesn't come in fresh every morning." That was all we got for breakfast. For variety, we would dunk soda crackers that our families were allowed to give to us into our drink.

Lunch was at around 10.30 am. Every day of the week, we would get a block of *tauhu* (soya bean cake) with some gravy on it, together with some vegetables. The vegetables obviously weren't washed very well or perhaps not washed at all, as you could often find sand and grit in them. Sometimes we felt like cats and dogs feeding on discarded bits of vegetables from a restaurant rubbish bin.

If you thought lunch was served early, dinner at 3.00 pm was even earlier. This meant that from 3.00 pm to 6.00 am the next day when breakfast was served, we were not given anything to eat. There was no night snack. So, you can well imagine our hunger pangs between dinner and breakfast. Just thinking about my mother's cooking during that time made me dizzy. In prison, we didn't have the luxury of raiding the fridge in the middle of the night. It was one of the things I missed the most.

For dinner on Mondays, Wednesdays and Fridays, we would get a piece of fish with some gravy, vegetables and rice. On Tuesdays, Thursdays and Saturdays, we were given meat. The Chinese inmates got pork, which was actually pork fat, as the prisoners who were detailed as cooks would save the lean meat for themselves. The Indians got three or four pieces of mutton, served with a potato if we were lucky, while the Malays were given either mutton or beef. This dietary difference based on race was similar to that in army mess halls. I found out later that the meals we received in prison only just met the United Nations calorie count requirements for meat, vegetables and carbohydrates. The authorities ensured that they kept to the basic requirements. I suppose it was one way of punishing the prisoners. We did not expect to be given T-bone steaks or lamb chops but the authorities did not have to be so miserly with their food. We weren't convicted prisoners or Oliver Twists asking for more. Most of us were in remand, waiting expectantly for decisions about our fates. Anyway, when you're in there, you get used to the regime because you had to have some sustenance.

Still, all 14 of my grillemates including Anthony noticed that I found it difficult to eat. One day, they decided that they would do something for me.

"We will cook for you," one of them suggested.

"What?!" I exclaimed.

"Shhh. Cooking is illegal."

I stared at my grillemates incredulously. They just grinned at me. I was curious to find out how they could possibly cook inside the grille but they advised me to be patient. When the dinner trays arrived that day, they kept some food aside. In the evening, after everyone had returned from their work duties, they started a small fire with parts of our sleeping mats. They used the pots for drinking to heat up the food they had kept aside and added extras like chillis or pickles that the cooks among our group had squirrelled away from the kitchen. We all squatted or sat around the pots, eating the hot food as quickly as we could. We had to eat quickly as prison officers were always lurking and could unexpectedly check on our grille. Prisoners from another grille kept a lookout for us so that we could clear the area before an officer appeared on his inspection round.

That first dinner my grillemates cooked for me was the best dinner I had had for a long, long time. The dinners I have had as a free man were not comparable simply because I had not been so hungry.

From then on, my grillemates would cook for me once or twice a week. An interesting combination of food would be boiling in a soup over two fires. On some occasions, plastic would be used to start the fire. If it gave a burning smell, my grillemates would use a hair cream like Tancho which we were allowed to have, to rub on the plastic—this gave off the smell of Tancho instead of burnt plastic. I learnt how to eat piping hot food, straight out of the fire. I still drink hot soup very quickly, much to the dismay of my wife. She always asks me how I do that. I will just look at her with a smile, and she knows I'm thinking of my prison days.

Cooking in prison was a source of great excitement for me. My friends from the other grilles would sometimes engage the help of a 'friendly' warden, who was well aware that cooking in the grille was illegal, to pass a pot of hot soup to me to taste when they cook. After every cooking session, we would all light up a cigarette for a smoke that we did not have to share with anyone. It was a treat because most of the time when someone lights up, the cigarette had to be shared among a few grillemates. So, Anthony, someone else and I would normally share one cigarette. It was a sort of tradition in prison that you do not smoke a cigarette all by yourself. The only time we did was after a dinner we had cooked in the grille. I looked forward to those clandestine cooking sessions. I suspected that the wardens knew what was going on but chose to do nothing. Some of them had a lot of compassion while the others were like animals.

I still remember a warden who came to the grille as we were all seated and chatting. He remarked: "You know what you all remind me of? The animals in the zoo, caged behind iron bars." He laughed and went away.

I thought his remarks unnecessary and very cruel. The next day I met the superintendent and told him what that officer had said. I insisted that if the officer did not apologise, I would definitely ask my family to instruct a lawyer to write a letter to the Director of Prisons about it. Prison authorities were supposed to rehabilitate prisoners, not humiliate them. The superintendent agreed with me. That night he sent the officer to the grille. The officer looked at us through the bars of the grille and said: "I'm sorry for what I said last night. I'm sorry. I did not mean it and I will not do it again."

It was a positive response and word quickly spread within the prison that even officers had to behave. Otherwise they would be answerable to the prisoners. Slowly, I was building up a reputation among the prisoners. I was becoming their voice and leader.

During my time in prison, inmates would ask me to help write letters to their ministers, their girlfriends and families. I think many couldn't read or write. I was also asked to mediate in problems between gangs. Because of my perceived seniority in the hierarchy of gangs, the decisions I made were final and accepted without question. There was no appeal. In a way, I was enjoying the power that was bestowed upon me by the prison, but I don't think I abused my power or ever did anyone in by making a wrong decision.

It may come as a surprise to people who have never spent time in prison that prisoners share a certain code of ethics. These ethics have evolved over the years and help inmates survive. When we went to the yard in the mornings, we would put our wet clothes out to dry and hope that they would dry by the time we had to return to our grille. The sunniest spot would be reserved for the strongest gang. The rest of the spots for drying were reserved according to the strength and power of a gang. Thus the weakest gangs had to place their clothes to dry in spots that hardly received any sunlight.

I recall an incident that involved inmates who didn't belong to a gang but decided to form one of their own. The name of the gang was something like 'One Heart'. In true gang tradition, they even picked their leader and had council members. They asked the other gangs to recognise them but were rejected; they were told that the formation of their gang was simply for convenience and that they had not gone through the traditional rituals. The members of the One Heart gang decided to meet with me to discuss their rejection.

"This is difficult. They're not recognising us as a gang," the leader told me.

"What is your purpose? Do you want a better place to dry your clothes?" I asked.

Another gang member replied: "No, we just want an identity. We don't mind where we dry our clothes. We're not going to fight with them on where we can or can't dry our clothes. We just think it's time that we organise ourselves into a gang so that we will have some power for future purposes."

Basically, they just wanted to be recognised and if they weren't given that recognition, they were going to cause some problems. Some of the members were quite hot-headed and they were all generally unhappy. They felt that they were being unfairly treated by the other gangs. Because I sensed that the situation would only get worse if it was not resolved, I called for a meeting of all the heads of the other gangs.

Holding court, I told them: "Do you want trouble? These people are not fighting for any space to dry their clothes. They just want to be recognised and have the feeling that they, too, belong to some gang. They don't want to join any of your gangs. What is your problem?" The gang leaders said that these people simply formed the gang as a matter of convenience.

I reasoned with them. "This is a prison. They can't follow any rituals. They are unable to do anything. They can only do what they are doing right now. I suggest that to avoid a problem, you recognise them and give them whatever privileges they are supposed to get as a gang. They are not going to fight with you and I seriously suggest that you recognise them."

Very reluctantly, the gang leaders heeded my advice and accepted the new gang. The new gang was given a new spot to dry their clothes, a spot that was slightly better than when they were not united. As the drama unfolded over the next few days, I was constantly thinking: "This reminds me of the United Nations when a country wants to be recognised and the others choose not to do so because it has not met the required criteria." To a degree, these gangs were like countries in a small United Nations. The only difference was that my advice as the de facto 'Secretary-General' was always heeded. Mr Kurt Waldheim, who was Secretary-General of the United Nations during the time I was in prison, probably did not have as smooth a ride in his job.

In a similar vein, when other problems between gangs arose, I was asked to mediate and settle them. One of the biggest problems I encountered was a situation that involved the head of Gang 18 and his deputy. One day, while the two were showering themselves, two other men stabbed them with blades fashioned from handles that had been broken off from pots and sharpened. They didn't see the men coming as they had soap on their faces. Blood flowed freely on the floor, mixed with the bath water, as they lay crouched on the floor, groaning and pressing their hands against their wounds to stop the bleeding. Their gang members frantically called for help, creating a commotion that had other inmates craning over their cubicles to see what was happening.

Prison officers were on the scene immediately. The men were taken to the prison hospital and treated for their injuries which, while serious, were not life-threatening. The assailants were moved to a block for prisoners serving their sentences because the authorities anticipated a problem developing from the stabbing incident.

When the superintendent wanted to question the victims, he asked a prisoner named Danny, who was the chief clerk, to be the interpreter. But the victims objected to Danny as they claimed he had arranged for the assailants to be in the yard at the time they were having their showers. One of them said: "If you look at the roster, they were not supposed to be in the yard then. Danny had arranged for them to be there because he belonged to their gang." On investigation, the superintendent found their claims to be true. Danny was immediately sent away to a punishment cell. Almost all the inmates celebrated the move as Danny was not popular. They felt that he was growing too big for his boots since his appointment as chief clerk. Even though he was a prisoner like all of us, he behaved as though he was an officer in charge. I too felt that Danny was getting increasingly annoyed with me for encroaching into his areas of activity within the prison walls with my mediation efforts. I sensed he didn't appreciate them at all.

As the incident was a gang matter, the prison officers were wary of allowing the prisoners out into the yard. They were afraid of repercussions. In their experience, there were always repercussions. There would be more stabbings and it would be a never-ending cycle. It was likely that the prison officers were also concerned about their own safety when they had to break up fights. So, after the incident, prison officers escorted the prisoners in twos, threes or fours to the yard to have their shower and escorted them back to their grilles before the next group of inmates was allowed to shower. It was a tedious process but it had to be done to ensure there would be no violence. Because of this adjustment to our routine, prisoners were spending more than 23 hours in their grilles.

This continued for a few days. However, I was allowed to go to the yard and the prison officers would release me when it was yard time. I would sit there all alone, smoking a cigarette and reading the newspapers. One day, the superintendent came up to me as I was reading a recent copy of the *New Nation* and asked if he could have a word with me. I agreed and followed him to his office. There were two prison officers there, a Mr Wong and Darshan Singh. Darshan is now better known as the 'hangman of Singapore'. His identity was publicly revealed by an Australian newspaper in 2005, before drug trafficker Vietnamese Australian Van Tuong Nguyen was executed. As a result of the report, Darshan said he wasn't Nguyen's executioner but that someone from Malaysia was. The report could have come about because of Darshan telling the Australian newspaper that "with me (the prisoners) don't struggle. If (the executioner is) a raw guy, they will struggle like chickens, like fish out of water". As was to be expected from a country that doesn't have capital punishment, this comment wasn't well-received in Australia and then Foreign Minister Alexander Downer retorted: "I don't think an executioner is qualified to give useful advice. I think he seems to have found great appeal in making a spectacle of himself in the media. And I tell you that's completely inappropriate and I don't want to hear from him again."

I knew Darshan from before my time in prison. He had married a Muslim woman and converted to Islam. I recall him telling me that when we were alone I should address him only as Darshan. When I saw him in the superintendent's office, I knew there were problems.

The superintendent asked me, "How are things now that the inmates are not going to the yard?"

"It's very bad," I replied gravely. "Do you know that friends are fighting amongst themselves in the same grille? If you don't do something about it, the situation is going to explode. Prisoners are going to get violent. It's terrible for them to be confined for more than 23 hours of the day. All you need is for someone to instigate another and things will turn violent. And before you can act to control any outbreak of violence, it may spread all around."

The superintendent nodded in agreement. "Yes, we are aware of what is happening and we are very worried," he said. "That's why we want you to talk to the two gangs involved in the stabbing incident. We want you to try to solve this matter. They will listen to you."

"I can't," I said, shaking my head slowly. "Look, I've been trying to tell the police and the authorities that I have no connections with gangs and I am neither a triad member nor a gangster. Now you're asking me to mediate a settlement and say that I can solve the matter. I would be sending the wrong message to the police and the CID. They're bound to turn around and say that they were right all along about me—that I was connected and was placed high in the underworld. No, I can't take that risk. I don't want to do it."

The superintendent studied my face for a few moments before he spoke. "Subhas, you've been here for the past few months. They have been talking about your release and that the CPIB (Corrupt Practices Investigation Bureau) is investigating. They even said that the minister is going to release you but nothing is happening. We feel that you're going to be here for many years. So, you might as well help us and help the prisoners and be their boss here. This way, everyone will be quite happy with your role and you can help us solve a lot of problems. The police are not going to know about it and if they do, we will tell them that we asked you to do it as the prisoners respect you as a lawyer and wanted your help to solve their problems. We will make sure that there is no connection made to you."

I thought for a while about what the superintendent had said. I was inclined to trust him as he was an upstanding person. Many of my friends in the prison were suffering because of the recent clamp-down. It was also true that there had been rumours about my imminent release but I was still in prison. If I was going to be in prison for a few years as the superintendent said, I might as well make myself as comfortable as possible. You could say it was a survival instinct. I agreed to help.

After leaving the superintendent's office, I was taken back to the grille. I asked Anthony who the chiefs of the two gangs—Gang 18 and

Gang 24—involved in the stabbing incident were, and I was allowed to go to their grilles. I told the prison officers to let out the heads and deputies. I spoke to the gang leaders separately. I told them: "This matter must be settled. It is not going to do anybody any good." Their response was that they had to meet their 'important' people before they could make such a decision. I asked for their names and six prisoners from each gang were released on my request.

All eight members from each gang were sent to two separate locations in the yard to deliberate the matter at hand. I asked the superintendent if he could provide them with coffee as I knew they liked to drink coffee when they had such discussions. Coffee was a treat in prison and given to prisoners only on festive occasions. The superintendent smiled. "Coffee is your personal request, isn't it?"

I laughed. "So, are we getting our coffee?"

He arranged for coffee to be brought for all of us. We had cigarettes as well. There were plenty of contraband cigarettes in the prison, enough to pass around. The discussions which I helped to mediate took two days. At the end of the second day, the gang leaders came to an agreement and said there would be peace. Gang 18, whose leaders had been stabbed, gave their word that they would not retaliate, at least not in Queenstown Remand Prison. But they added that all bets would be off when they were transferred to Changi Prison.

I agreed and went to look for the superintendent and told him: "Sir, this is the position. They have given me their word that there will not be any fights here. There will be no more stabbings. There will be peace, but this will only apply in Queenstown and they are not going to give such an undertaking if they get transferred to Changi Prison. There could be a fight there."

He looked pleased. "As long as they don't fight in Queenstown, who the hell cares what they do in Changi Prison? That's not my problem, Subhas. So, can you trust them to keep their word?"

"Yes, I can."

The next day, the prisoners were allowed back into the yard. Extra guards were put on duty and I was told that some of the guards were armed and prepared to shoot if necessary. As the days passed without incident, the guard alert was slowly relaxed and, with that, the matter was settled. I learnt one thing: when gangsters give their word, they keep it. There was a lot of honour among them. I can't say the same about present-day gangsters. I've met some of them. They would sell you for a few dollars.

Life was a routine in prison. Many of the remand prisoners would seek my legal opinion. It was then that I realised that if any prisoner was not pleased with his lawyer's work, all he needed to do was to condemn the lawyer. Word would get around and nobody would engage his services. During my time in prison, many lawyers were mentioned. I won't tell you their names, but I did feel that their bad reputations were justified as I knew for a fact that they did not work hard for their clients and were more interested in the money they could make from them.

On many occasions, I would sit with the inmates to discuss their cases. It kept me in practice and alert. One day, as I was sitting in the yard having my customary cigarette and reading the newspapers, a prisoner came up to me. I asked him what he was in jail for.

"Well, they claim that I've committed seven murders, over 90 robberies, also extortion and many other offences," he replied as if he was listing out his lifetime achievements.

I was curious. "So, did you do all that?"

He laughed out loud. "Yes, lah, I did all that but sir, I'm very lucky they don't have enough evidence to charge me. None of the witnesses will come out."

Through conversations with prisoners like him, I found that many of them were actually guilty of the offences they were alleged to have committed. That's why when I was asked, after my release from prison, whether I would lobby for the abolition of the law that allowed people to be detained without trial, I said no. But I believe the authorities must have enough safeguards to ensure that this legislation is not abused. Many people were surprised at my response as I had been detained under the same law. I am being very practical about it as I've had first-hand encounters with prisoners remanded for wrongdoings. These prisoners are very happy to be there and not to be hanged.

I must cite one particular case from the 1970s (there were a few versions that I heard from some of the protagonists who were in Queenstown Prison at around the same time as I was). The case involved two women teachers who had kidnapped an intellectually disabled Indonesian boy. Because the boy was regularly picked up from school in a Rolls Royce, they decided he was worth kidnapping. However, they were not sure how to do the deed and engaged the help of a person called Ricky who agreed to kidnap the boy for a ransom of about $1 million. Ricky, who was just a salesman at the time, enlisted the help of Ah Lek, a man with underground connections.

After the boy was kidnapped, Ah Lek guarded the boy while Ricky demanded the ransom of $1 million which was eventually settled at $500,000. When the money was collected, the kidnappers kept their word and dropped the boy off unharmed on Old Upper Thomson Road. The money was shared between the teachers and the men. The three main protagonists, however, told Ah Lek that they received only $100,000 and gave him $10,000 as his share. They then shared the rest of the money amongst themselves. This was a very large sum in those days, when nice houses with gardens could still be bought in many parts of Singapore for less than $100,000.

The women resigned from teaching and started a company that financed hire-purchase loans for cars. Ricky, on the other hand, bought a flashy car, wined and dined, and gambled. He soon lost his money. With no remorse, he approached the two ex-teachers for more money. They gave him some money and he squandered that too. He went back to them again but this time they refused him. He threatened to confess to the kidnapping and expose them. Not knowing what to do and wanting to continue their legitimate business, the women approached Danny for help—the same Danny who had set up the stabbing incident in Queenstown Prison. Danny sent his men to threaten Ricky into silence but Ricky didn't comply. Instead, he did a very stupid thing. Realising he couldn't take on Danny and his gang, Ricky immediately thought of Ah Lek. He told Ah Lek that the ransom money had actually been $500,000 and the teachers had taken most of it.

"They are doing so well and when I asked them for some money, they refused to give it to me. I think you should ask them for your full equal share," Ricky said.

Ah Lek was hopping mad. "How dare they cheat me!" he shouted.

He immediately sought them out. The women again approached Danny for help, claiming that Ah Lek was extorting money from them. Danny went to Ah Lek who said to him: "Look, I am not Ricky. You can't just push me around. What gang do you belong to?" Danny and his gang identified themselves and they decided to have a 'settlement talk'.

All this time, Danny and his gang did not know that it was a kidnap case and ransom money that was being discussed. Danny thought that it was a case of extortion and protection money. When they sat down to talk in a coffee shop, Ah Lek asked Danny why he was interfering. He related the kidnapping incident. He felt he had been taken for a ride and wanted more money from the women. Word soon got around in the underworld that there had been a kidnap and the kidnappers and others were sitting down to talk. Someone leaked the information to the police who arrested the whole lot, including the ex-teachers. After interrogating them, the police found that the women, Ah Lek and Ricky had committed the act of kidnapping and that Danny and his gang were trying to extort protection money from them. All of them were detained. The women were put into Changi Prison. Ricky, Ah Lek, Danny and all the others spent more than 12 years in remand.

It was Ricky who narrated this story to me in prison. Ah Lek shared a different version with me and of course, Danny also had another story. But after putting all the various pieces of the story together, I decided that it all started because of Ricky's gambling habit. No one would have been caught if he had not gambled away his share and demanded money from the women that second time.

A few years after my release from prison, an attractive woman came to see me for my services. Her friend had been charged with kidnapping a very wealthy man for ransom. I went to see her friend, the accused, in prison and she said to me, "This is the second time, you know. I think the police will not give me any chance." She then told me what had happened.

"I know," I replied. "Ricky, Ah Lek, Danny and all the others were in prison with me." On hearing that, she treated me like an old friend and pleaded with me. "Can you do me a favour? Please ask the judge to give me the death sentence."

I explained that as her lawyer, it was not possible for me to plead with the judge to grant her a death sentence. However, she insisted and I told her, "In that case, I am going to discharge myself. You can ask the judge for the death sentence yourself."

I stood up as Justice Kan Ting Chiu, the presiding judge, walked into court. I said that I had to discharge myself as I could not comply with my client's instructions. He looked at me as though he knew what the problem was. He said, "Alright, you're discharged." I left the court and I believe she did ask for the death sentence. Justice Kan sentenced her to life imprisonment. She is presently in Changi Women's Prison. For all her misdeeds, I thought she was a brave woman to ask for the death sentence.

The Straits Times

M.C.(P) 426/76

TUESDAY, NOVEMBER 16, 1976

25 CENTS

Estd. 1845

Crafted Exquisitely Designed
nd & Gem Set Rings
or 18ct White Gold a treasure
ear with Pride and Cherish forever

C. DE SILVA (PTE) LTD.
JEWELLERS

14, THE GALLERY, STRAITS TRADING BUILDING
8, BATTERY ROAD, SINGAPORE • TEL: 915695

Sequel to pleas alleging frame-up

SUBHAS FREED AFTER PROBE

By N.G. KUTTY and GERALD PEREIRA

LAWYER Subhas Anandan who
had been in detention under
the Criminal Law (Temporary
Provisions) Act for alleged secret
activities, since Jan 27 this
was freed yesterday.

Home Affairs state-
that Subhas, 28,
the Supervision

release
into

om-
for

r. Chua
the peti-
nt Com-
vestigations
has, the
the Attorney-
requested the

'Release Subhas' plea to Govt by legal firm

A SOLICITOR'S firm
has appealed to the
Home Affairs Minister
for the release of law-
er Subhas Anandan,
detained under the
riminal Law Act last
uesday, the New Na-
reported yesterday.

ing to the report,
appeal was sent by
M.P.D. Nair, in
firm an associat-
e years.

letter to
Chin,
d, was cop
Attorney
the p
lawyer, S

'Kept in dark' claim: Law Society hits out

THE Law Society of
Singapore yesterday
hit out at some lawyers
here who reportedly ac-
cused it of keeping as
bers in the dark
ters relating
arrest and d
lawyer, S

Detained lawyer: Inspector charged

Former police Inspector G.
Gopala Krishna was this
morning charged with using a
false statement to mislead his
superior officer about the alleged secret society and criminal activities of lawyer Subhas Anandan s/o R Anandan.

Krishna, who is charged
under the Prevention of Corruption Act, was alleged to
have submitted an undated
joint diary on Subhas' activities
purportedly prepared by two
detective constables, P.S. Parmaiyah and P. Kupusamy.

The report was submitted to
Asst. Supt. Chang Pei Hwa, the
Officer-in-Charge (Crime) of
Paya Lebar police station be-
tween Sept. 1 and 15 last year.

The charge stated that
Krishna "did knowingly use
with intent to mislead" ASP
Chang Pei Hwa, the Officer-in-
Charge (Crime) of Paya Lebar
police station, a certified true
copy of an undated joint diary
purporting to have been prepared by the two detectives.

It alleged that the document
contained a statement which
was false in a material parti-
culars, to wit, that Parmaiyah
and Kupusamy did
make inquiries into
and reported on

Krishna

12

Some of his clients

▶ Tan Chun Seng (2003)
He was sentenced to death for murdering deaf-mute Krishnan Sengal Rajah, 44, in Little India in 2001.
He won the appeal and was, instead, jailed for 10 years for culpable homicide.

▶ Quek Loo Ming (20...)
The retired forensic sc...
(above) was jailed for ... years for culpable ho... and another three ye... causing grievous hur... the sentences to run currently.
He had spiked a ... water with pestici... poisoned three pe... drank from it. On... the other two bec... seriously ill.
On appeal, h... was increased t...

▶ Ng L...
The for...
was se...
jail an...
for m...

Murderers.
Maid abusers.
Rapists.

And he defends them all

PHOTO: DESMOND WEE

Top criminal lawyer Subhas Anandan believes every accused person deserves a proper trial

▶ Elena Chong

IF SOMEONE'S in big trouble and needs a lawyer, chances are he'll call Subhas Anandan.

And when he meets the 55-year-old lawyer to talk, he may find him dressed in a T-shirt or kurta (loose collarless shirt), un-

two sentences run concurrently instead of consecutively.

Mr Anandan said he turned him down because he felt that the jail terms — 18 years for robbery with hurt, and life for kidnapping — were fair.

Even the most heinous offender, he said, deserves a proper trial.

He said: "We cannot say: 'This is a rapist. This is a terrorist. We do not want to defend him.'

"Let's put it this way: Who is the lawyer to decide if the person is guilty or not? The moment you decide about the guilt or innocence of people, then there is no

"His cross-examination is all in the head because he's got a remarkable memory, almost photographic.

"He doesn't waste time on hopeless points. He goes for the nitty-gritty and he knows what the kernel of a case is."

Mr Anandan isn't just a local legend.

In late 2001, for example, he made international headlines when he defended Julia Suzane Bohl, a 24-year-old German who faced the death penalty for drug trafficking. She was eventually jailed on the lesser charge of pos-

dles but that his face is so recognisable and that he delivers such good soundbites.

"The media always likes to quote me. In my submissions, I became like a quotable quote sort of thing," he said.

For instance, he said of the disgruntled retiree who missed his target and poisoned three other people by accident at a grassroots party: "The man is 57 years old, do we need to use a sledgehammer to finish him off?"

He joined Harry Elias Partnership as a consultant in July 2000, when the firm was looking to beef

ing courtroom tactics.

He's also called "Gangster" and "Mafia" — usually affectionately.

He covers cases, he said, in a precise way and doesn't beat around the bush.

In the recent trial of the hotel rapist, he was sharp and focused, cross-examining the victims based on his instructions and keeping details to a minimum to avoid distressing them.

When he has a case on, he relaxes by playing snooker at the Singapore Cricket Club, just across the street from the Supreme Court.

They offer him arm and le...

Lawyer's death-row clients impressed by his commitment

By Khushwant Singh

HIGH-PROFILE criminal lawyer Subhas Anandan so impressed some clients who were found guilty and sentenced to hang that they offered to donate their organs to him.

"They know of my three heart attacks and kidney problems, thus the offer. But it's impossible for me to accept. Yet, I'm deeply touched," he said.

Lately, Mr Subhas, 55, has taken on practically every high-profile case, the most recent being the trial of former TV presenter Vidya Shankar Aiyar, 37, who was convicted on Jan 6 of molesting a 30-year-old woman.

In 2002, he acted for graphic designer Anthony Ler, 32, who engineered the killing of his wife by a 15-year-old youth. Ler was sentenced to hang.

But Mr Subhas, of Harry Elias Partnership, has achieved several notable successes.

In 1997, he convinced the Court of Appeal to overturn a conviction and free Mr Nadasan Chandra Secharan, then 42, who had been sentenced to death for the murder of his wife.

Last year, he saved Tan Chun Seng, 28, from the gallows for killing deaf-mute Krishnan Sengal Rajah,

44, in Little India in 2001. Upon appeal, Tan was jailed for 10 years for culpable homicide.

Many people consider Mr Subhas to be in the same league as the late David Marshall, undoubtedly Singapore's greatest criminal lawyer from the 50s to the 70s.

Few will remember that he once acted for Mr Subhas who, as a young lawyer in 1976, was detained without trial under the Criminal Law (Temporary Provisions) Act.

Mr Subhas was accused of heading a secret society and spent nine months in detention until he was cleared in an inquiry in which Mr Marshall and Mr Leo Fernando defended him, for free.

Asked for his view of detention without trial, he said: "I'm not against it, but it must be carefully monitored to prevent mistakes. In my case, it was a frame-up by my enemies."

He is offended by criticisms that he seemed to act only for those who are guilty.

"The State must prove its case before anyone can be judged guilty and for me to deny my services to a client because I think he's guilty is tantamount to me acting as the judge," he said.

He could easily have ended up being a doctor, he said, as he attended a medical college in India, but gave up after three months because of homesickness.

So medicine's loss is law's gain.

His next high-profile case will be in April when he defends Mr Ng Kwang Lim, 46, who is accused of murdering a professor at the National Un...

...ge juice fights back

LAKELAND, Florida — Tired of losing orange-juice drinkers to low-carb diets, US citrus growers are fighting back.

The Florida state Department of Citrus last week changed its marketing strategy to convince consumers that orange juice can go with the Atkins diet as well as the popular weight-loss plan pushed by TV talk show host Phil McGraw.

It will spend US$1.8 million (S$3 million) on the new campaign.

The department's lawyer is also reviewing legal options against some books, such as The South Beach Diet, that discourage orange juice in diets because of its high sugar levels.

Florida's US$9 billion citrus industry has reason to be concerned.

Citrus officials said that a noticeable drop occurred last March when low-carb diets began to reach a critical mass.

Already, some in the industry are making changes. PepsiCo Inc's Tropicana earlier this month introduced Light 'n Healthy, which has a third less sugar and calories than regular orange juice. — AP

THE CASES

Magnet

Drugs, Stupidity and Abuse

Constance Chee

Took Leng How

Ramu Annadavascan

Nadasan Chandra Secharan

Leong Siew Chor

Abdul Nasir

Muhammad Nasir

Anthony Ler

Tan Chor Jin

Chua Tiong Tiong

Pal (Milk), the Bookie

Johnny Tan

University Martin

Public Prosecutor vs Heng Boon Chai

TEN

MAGNET

Unlike civil cases, criminal cases can have severe penalties for those who are convicted. When your clients face the death penalty or life imprisonment, it makes you focus your mind and efforts. I had my first taste of this with Tampines Raja. The primary job of criminal lawyers like me is to ensure that the accused receives fair and just treatment. To do that, I need to have a full grasp of all aspects of criminal law.

I think you need to be a different breed to be a criminal lawyer, especially in Singapore, where many lawyers seek to specialise in areas that are more lucrative. There are only a few lawyers in Singapore who specialise in criminal law. I think there may be about 200 lawyers altogether in Singapore who take on criminal cases even though it is not their area of specialisation. These lawyers may be helping a family friend or doing some pro bono work or perhaps have been assigned to a criminal case by the State.

It is often said that people who want to engage a lawyer to handle a criminal case should not get one whose primary practice is something other than criminal defence. This explains why I get a large number of cases and I am featured in the press very often. I can't help it if editors like to devote column space to cases involving murders, sex crimes and crimes of passion. The exposure is not something I seek consciously, but some of the cases I am involved in understandably generate a lot of interest in the media. I have no control over that.

For example, in June 2007, I was assigned by the State to act for Tan Chor Jin in his appeal against his death sentence for killing nightclub boss Lim Hock Soon. Tan had requested that I conduct his appeal after he unsuccessfully defended himself in the capital trial. The State assigns lawyers to those charged with capital offences if they cannot afford a lawyer's fees. Tan's wife had also asked me, separately, to defend him, but as the State had assigned the case to me, Tan's family would not have to pay my fees. Instead, the State would cover my fees.

Tan, also known as the One-eyed Dragon because he is blind in the right eye, was sentenced to death for discharging a Beretta pistol with intent to injure Lim Hock Soon. If Tan had asked for me to defend him in his original capital case, I wouldn't have accepted. I knew Lim casually and I would have felt uncomfortable having to cross-examine his wife during the trial. Such a situation would not arise in an appeal as no cross-examination of witnesses is required. I only have to look for loopholes in the judgement and the applications of law to argue the case in Tan's defence. The One-eyed Dragon's appeal is described later in this book.

I am known to take on complicated cases, with a degree of success. I do get sentences reduced on appeal because my experience allows me to spot errors in judgement. I also know enough of the law to get charges amended. This is not the easiest thing to do in Singapore courts, but the numbers are increasing especially with the new Chief Justice Chan Sek Keong on board. Perhaps it's my track record that makes me a sort of magnet for accused people from all walks of life. I also have a reputation as a fighter. I fight for my clients till I've exhausted all possible legal avenues and usually myself in the process.

Over the last three decades, I have defended many, many different kinds of people, some of whom were accused of the most heinous crimes. Some may have been guilty of what they were charged with, some probably weren't, but I never take the high moral ground when it comes to defending an accused person. I always accept or reject cases on a case-by-case basis. To me, there can be no other way if you respect the law and believe that everyone deserves a fair trial regardless of how serious a crime has been committed. If I pick and choose my clients, I believe my practice will fail because people will start to lose faith in me. For instance, they wouldn't call me out for drinks to discuss their problems, as some do, and eventually retain me as their lawyer if they didn't have this faith in me. I've become friends with many of my clients even after I've lost their cases. Like Tampines Raja, they see that I do my best for them and their appreciation is heartfelt even when the prosecution's case is stronger and they are found guilty. It's quite well-known in legal circles that my health is not the best and I'm beset by a variety of ailments. I have a team of four specialist doctors at Gleneagles Hospital who keep me going. I take about 30 pills a day, including vitamins and supplements. In my trouser pocket, I also carry a little bottle containing a white pill that when taken will prevent my heart from seizing up. Knowing about my ill-health, some of my clients who have been sentenced to death have offered me their organs. Anthony Ler, with his signature smile, offered me his kidneys before he was hanged.

In fact, my clients show their gratitude to me in many ways after their cases are concluded. The chief executive officer of a listed company whom I defended with some degree of success takes me out for drives in his fancy cars. Others just hug me and thank me at the end of the case. Once, when I got a client's death sentence squashed, his family came to me and said that I was a god to them. They knelt in front of me and touched my feet. The victim's family, on the other hand, cursed and swore at me, but that is to be expected. By the same token, I've received letters containing death threats. I don't take much notice of them though I do report the threats to the police, just in case. I've even been told that someone has carried a *kavadi* during the Thaipusam festival to take revenge on me so that I will die. Of course, this sort of thing worries my family, but I see it as part of my job. You have to take the good with the bad.

I think I turn down about 10 per cent of the cases that I'm offered. For me to consider taking on a case, I will always insist that the accused has to be honest with me. How can I defend him in court if he lies to me? It makes me look bad if the prosecution picks up on something he didn't tell me or lied to me about. This can have nasty repercussions on my defence of the accused. My client must also trust that I will be honest with him and keep our communications confidential at all times. This has to apply to all discussions made during the relationship, and even after the case has been concluded and the relationship has ceased. If a client doesn't have this trust in me and shows this distrust by questioning my every move, I will reject the case.

I also need to find some chemistry with the client. I feel chemistry is often an overlooked factor in lawyer-client relationships. I need to know all aspects of my client to be of best use to him or her. If the right chemistry is not there, the client may not be as forthright with me and that can lead to problems further down the road. So, if I don't feel especially comfortable after talking to someone, I will not take on the case.

Sometimes, the family and friends of the accused interfere too much and that puts me off too. I've had cases where family members would call me practically every hour which is irritating. In some cases, the accused people are very arrogant, especially when they come to see me in my office. That turns me off too. If they show remorse, they definitely have a better chance of hiring me. One interesting thing I've noticed in my career is that when I go to see someone in prison, he or she is invariably remorseful. I suppose the prison experience is a humbling one, as the accused soon realises that arrogance will not take him or her far. I saw that first-hand too when I was in prison.

What are some of the cases I've rejected? It's not easy to recall. I'm not a busybody in the sense that after I've rejected a case, I don't really follow up on it. I just don't have the time to do that. I remember a case involving acid thrown at a trade union leader. The victim was the father-in-law of Justice M P H Rubin, who was a Supreme Court judge and is now Singapore's High Commissioner to South Africa. Justice Rubin wanted me to hold a watching brief for the family of his father-in-law. A watching brief is an instruction to a lawyer to follow a case on behalf of a client who is not directly involved in a case as a defendant. Justice Rubin told me that the family of the accused would most probably come to see me and ask me to take on their case, adding that they were rich enough to pay my fees. Sure enough, that same day, the family visited me. I declined saying that I was already holding a watching brief for the family of the deceased.

On another occasion, I was in the Subordinate Courts when someone grabbed my hand. It was a middle-aged woman. She was dabbing a handkerchief on her puffy eyes. Before I could say or do anything, she pleaded with me to take on her son's case. She said he was a good boy and it was his first offence and so on—the usual things doting mothers say about their recalcitrant sons. I discovered that the boy had been caught red-handed in the act of stealing. It was pointless for me to take up the case because he was going to be found guilty as charged and sentenced to time in prison. Her son also had a previous conviction for theft. I told her it would be futile to hire a lawyer. Obviously she disagreed with me and engaged one. As expected, they lost the case and he received a higher sentence. Not long after that, I chanced upon her at the corridors of the Subordinate Courts. She was weeping and when she saw me, she wept even more. I suppose she was thinking of my advice to her.

ELEVEN

DRUGS, STUPIDITY AND ABUSE

Though I'm probably best known in Singapore for representing clients in murder cases, my case load has been diverse. I've handled every kind of crime you can possibly think of and probably worse. If you ask me how many cases I have handled during my career, I couldn't tell you for sure. They have to be in the thousands. I couldn't even work out an accurate number for this book.

Among the many requests for representation that I receive, the more common ones are for drug-related offences. As in murder cases, the penalties can be very serious. I must say I dislike drug traffickers. I support the death penalty for those who sell hardcore drugs because they exploit people's weaknesses. They obviously don't care about the dangers of drug addiction and the harm it can cause addicts and their families. Still, I can't turn down a request to represent them in court just for those reasons. No matter how bad they are, drug traffickers still have the right to a proper defence. There is some frustration with defending drug offence cases in Singapore because the prosecution seems to have an advantage in many of them even before hearings start. I've also seen first-hand how judges' hands are tied by the laws that govern drug offences in Singapore. In the Misuse of Drugs Act, death by hanging is mandatory for anyone aged 18 years or over who is convicted of carrying 15 grams of heroin, 30 grams of cocaine, more than 500 grams of cannabis or more than 250 grams of methamphetamines. It is a well-known fact that Singapore's stand on drug trafficking is controversial around the world. Darshan Singh, for example, is reputed to have hanged more than 850 condemned prisoners in his career and is also believed to have hanged 18 prisoners in one day.

Critics of Singapore's liberal application of the death penalty for offences which are treated with less severity in many other countries say that Singapore has reversed the burden of proof, requiring the accused to prove they are innocent. In many other countries, it is a fundamental human right to be presumed innocent until proven guilty. There are still many inconsistencies in the way the courts treat drug offenders. I brought this up in 2005 in the inaugural issue of *Pro Bono*, the newsletter of the Association of Criminal Lawyers of Singapore. I cited the big cocaine bust in Seletar Camp involving a former internet entrepreneur. The accused pleaded guilty to a single charge of cocaine consumption and had his 12-month sentence reduced to eight months on appeal. I was approached to handle his appeal but there was a conflict of interest because I represented Guiga Laroussi, the man who had supplied him with the cocaine. In the appeal by the former internet entrepreneur, Justice V K Rajah ruled that all first offenders should be jailed for six to 18 months. Fines, he said, should be imposed only "sparingly" and in "purely exceptional" cases involving Class A drugs or hardcore drugs like heroin and cocaine. But I wrote that the court's ruling did little to clarify the position on sentencing. Justice Rajah did not clarify what he meant by "sparingly" or what constituted a "purely exceptional" case.

I pointed out that there was a "clear conflict" between the views expressed in the former internet entrepreneur's case and in four other cases heard by then Chief Justice Yong Pung How, who has since retired from the bench. In an earlier case involving Ecstasy abuser Ooi Joo

Keong, the Chief Justice upheld a decision by Senior District Judge Richard Magnus to jail him for 12 months, ruling that first offenders should be jailed for 12 to 18 months. I pointed out that three other cases sent out different signals. In a case involving insurance manager Ng Kheng Tiak, who had a couple of puffs of cannabis, the Chief Justice fined him $20,000 and set aside the 12-month prison term imposed by the Lower Court. In another case, footballer Muhammad Razali Ishak's one-year jail term for smoking cannabis at a birthday party was set aside and replaced with two years' probation, a $5,000 bond by his parents and 100 hours of community service. Polytechnic student Pililis Nikiforos escaped an eight-month jail term in 2001 for morphine use and the Chief Justice instead imposed a $5,000 fine. Our take on this is that when sentencing an offender, which of these decisions should district judges follow?

Another problem in my view is the use of entrapment to snare drug offenders. I believe it should be allowed to a certain degree, otherwise you'll never catch the crooks. But the Central Narcotics Bureau (CNB) should not overdo it. I've said on record before that I think the CNB crossed the line in the case of insurance agent Teo Ya Lin in 2003. She was pressured by an undercover CNB officer to procure an Ecstasy pill for him, promising that he would buy an insurance policy from her in return. Teo got him a pill and the result for her troubles was a prison term of more than six years. This girl had no intention of selling drugs until she was persuaded by the officer. Under normal circumstances, she would not have been categorised as a trafficker. There is also the issue of whether the CNB officer should be guilty of abettment for the offence. He instigated the offence by putting the idea into her head through misrepresentation. Indeed, there is a lot of grey area in Singapore's Misuse of Drugs Act. I believe this has partly to do with the fact that the law is so out of sync with other First World countries which Singapore aspires to be.

The differences between Singapore's drug laws and those of other countries were clearly illustrated in the case of German national, Julia Susanne Bohl. She faced the gallows following a drug bust at her downtown apartment in Singapore on March 13, 2002. The 22-year-old student at the German school in Singapore was arrested, together with her 21-year-old Singaporean boyfriend and nine others, on suspicion of running a drug ring. Authorities seized 687 grams of cannabis, 60 pills of Ecstasy and a number of designer drugs at the apartment. Under the "presumption clause" in the Misuse of Drugs Act, anyone caught in possession of a certain amount of a specified drug is presumed to be trafficking in the substance. Friends and teachers of Bohl at the German school said she was a very inconspicuous and polite woman. Some ventured to say that it was her boyfriend who had introduced her to the party scene and was more at fault for her problems. Bohl had been living in Singapore with her parents for about five years, but at the time she was apprehended, her parents had divorced and separately returned to live in Germany. Her father had been an engineer with Lufthansa in Singapore while her mother taught at the German school. Her mother had objected to her boyfriend, whom I only knew as Ben. Bohl subsequently moved out of her parents' home not long before they returned to Germany, and stayed with Ben and his friends. The apartment was leased under Bohl's name because she was the only one who was gainfully employed. She was working under a job training scheme with Daimler-Chrysler. I felt that she was an attractive young woman mixing around with some ugly people.

Bohl's parents flew back to Singapore to be by her side during the case. On March 15, Bohl was charged in court with two others for being in possession of 687 grams of cannabis for the purpose of trafficking. If found guilty, she would be hanged. Bohl was the first female Caucasian foreigner to face execution in Singapore since Johannes van Damme, a Dutch man caught with 4.6 kg of heroin in his suitcase as he was leaving Singapore in 1991. Van Damme was hanged in August 1994 despite pleas for clemency from the Dutch government and Queen Beatrix. Singapore firmly rejected pressure from the Netherlands to stop the execution and dismissed suggestions of a "cultural gap" between the two countries.

As soon as Bohl was caught, the German government and its ambassador in Singapore mounted a diplomatic offensive on her behalf, meeting several senior Singapore government ministers in the process. Coincidentally, it was a technicality that saved Bohl from the gallows in the wake of this campaign. Tests revealed that the amount of pure cannabis seized in Bohl's apartment weighed in at only 281 grams, below the 500 grams threshold. This meant that Bohl faced a jail sentence of five to 20 years instead of execution. After negotiations with the Attorney-General's Chambers, Bohl still faced several charges but none was on trafficking in drugs. Her lawyer then was Michael Eu. Bohl's parents later came to see me through my pupil Ravi Isaac, who was responsible for me getting the brief. After I took up the case, many people erroneously thought that I had been responsible for getting her charges reduced, but that actually happened when Eu was still her lawyer. I also recall being asked by some European journalists why I didn't advise Bohl to jump bail. This is not the type of question that a lawyer can answer and, in any case, it didn't deserve an answer as it showed a lack of respect for me and lawyers in general.

Bohl was eventually sentenced to five years in prison. She's now in Germany having served her time. Anti-death penalty activists would cite her case in their efforts to save Vietnamese-Australian Van Tuong Nguyen who I mentioned earlier in the book. I didn't represent Nguyen. He was caught with heroin while on transit through Changi Airport on December 12, 2002. He had been on his way back to Melbourne from Cambodia. The amount of heroin Nguyen carried was 25 times the amount which meant an automatic death sentence. He was convicted and, despite serious diplomatic efforts by Australian authorities, was hanged on December 2, 2005. I remember telling the Australian media just before his hanging that the only chance of saving Nguyen would have been before he went to trial, when prosecutors were finalising the charges and still had the prerogative to make changes. I told them: "What is the point in coming in now? The President has already refused clemency and the presiding judge in capital drug cases has no discretion. Death is mandatory. It is like visiting a patient in hospital when he is already dead."

While the Australians were slow off the blocks in their diplomatic efforts on Nguyen, the German ambassador impressed me with his handling of the Bohl case. Volker Schlegel stood by Bohl all the way. He was a fantastic man, who gave me all the support and encouragement I needed. He would come to my office and we would spend hours discussing Bohl's case. I have acted for other nationalities and observed that the dedication shown by their ambassadors is not the same. Some can't be bothered if their nationals get into trouble in Singapore. Others only show an interest when the accused person is someone famous or important or well-connected. These ambassadors could have learnt a thing or two from Schlegel. Another embassy that I thought really cared for its nationals was the Belgian embassy. I saw this in a high profile cocaine case in which a Belgian lady's only crime was being married to a Sri Lankan national charged with drug consumption. She was charged with abetting her husband to escape the jurisidiction of Singapore. A person at the Belgian embassy, whom I only remember as Claire, stood by the lady through to the end of the case.

I visited Bohl quite often in jail as her parents were overseas and couldn't come to Singapore on a regular basis. I persuaded her to study and got permission for her to read economics through the prestigious London School of Economics. She did well in her first year. When she called me from Amsterdam after her release, she told me that she was going to work and would continue her studies later. To her credit, she turned down all offers from publishers and TV stations for interviews. I think she just wanted to forget the whole affair. In 2006, she offered to be my guide if I were to go to the World Cup tournament in Germany. I didn't attend it and haven't spoken to her for a long time now. Wherever she is, I hope she won't be tempted by drugs again.

Another case that comes to my mind, and which is different from my usual murder cases, is the Residents' Committee (RC) poisoning case which was classified as culpable homicide. The reason I want to mention this case is that it highlights the stupid things people can do when they are offended or 'lose face'. In this case, the culprit didn't even realise that his actions could hurt people he didn't intend to hurt. The worst thing about it is that he wasn't a hot-headed youngster. He was a retiree from a responsible job who should have known better.

The year 2002 started and ended badly for former government laboratory officer Quek Loo Ming. He is in jail today because he had a petty beef with the chairperson of the Bukit Timah Zone 5 RC, Madam Doreen Lum. He felt she took advantage of him and did not give him enough credit for his volunteer work at the RC. Most people would settle such problems face to face, and murder can virtually be ruled out. It couldn't be ruled out in Quek's case, however, because his frustration with Madam Lum eventually led to a death.

The setting for the 56-year-old retiree's crime was a New Year's Eve party in 2001 which the RC was organising. Madam Lum had asked Quek to buy 20 packets of chicken rice for the people who were helping to organise the party. Quek was aggrieved at being given the task at short notice and hatched a plan to get back at her. He had some powdered pesticide called methomyl, commonly used by orchid growers, in his possession. It was a controlled poison under the Environmental Pollution Control Act. Methomyl is a cholinesterase-inhibitor; it acts on the nervous system, causing muscular paralysis and death in large doses. Quek had obtained it at the Toxicology Laboratory of the Department of Scientific Services when he was working on a case in which a Filipino maid committed suicide by drinking methomyl mixed with coffee. Quek put about one teaspoon of methomyl into an empty mineral water bottle, filled it up with water and placed the bottle on the cabinet opposite Madam Lum's office. This was where the centre's supply of mineral water was usually placed. He hoped that the chairperson would drink the contaminated water.

His plan failed because she never drank it. Madam Fong Oi Lin, Richard Ho Sin Shong and Wong Ah Kim did instead, and they all became gravely ill, foaming at the mouth right from the outset. Before she lost consciousness, Madam Fong had the presence of mind to pour away the remaining water in the bottle as she had found it smelly. All three were taken to National University Hospital. Madam Fong never recovered and died on January 3, 2002. Ho and Wong survived, though they endured a lot of suffering as they battled with the poison.

The police linked the methomyl in the water to Quek and he was arrested. It was a clear-cut case. He maintained he had no intention of killing anyone and had only wanted Madam Lum to have diarrhoea. He pleaded guilty to the charges of culpable homicide and voluntarily causing grievous hurt. Because he was not a layman but a former lab technician who knew the dangers of methomyl, the punishment meted out to Quek was severe. He was viewed as acting with complete disregard for the lives and safety of others. On November 8, 2002, Quek was sentenced to 10 years on the first charge and five years on the second charge. He is currently serving his time in prison.

With Quek, it was certainly a case of hell having no greater fury than a retiree scorned. I found Quek a very foolish man who took offence over petty things and his reaction which led to Madam Fong's untimely death was totally uncalled for. I believed him when he told me he just wanted to "get" the chairperson Madam Lum. He wanted her to suffer diarrhoea. In his determination to get her, he forgot about the amount of poison he put in the water. He should have known that the poison could kill because of what had happened to the Filipino maid. There had also been many cases of methomyl-related murders in other countries which Quek should have become aware of at the time of the Filipino maid's suicide case. In contrast to Quek, I thought his wife a remarkable lady. She was calm and emotionless throughout the proceedings. She even paid my fees without bargaining. She told me she had moved out of her neighbourhood and was living elsewhere in Singapore. I believe she was thinking of emigrating. She was concerned about whether her husband could eventually join her when he was released from prison.

One of the issues that angers me about Singapore is the treatment of domestic maids. We have seen a constant stream of maid abuse cases over the years, even by professionals who should know better. Is it the Singapore mentality to get what they perceive as value for money that leads to these abuse cases? In the process, Singaporeans forget that maids are human beings too and deserve respect. Maids take a big risk to come to Singapore to earn money for their families back home.

I defended the accused in Singapore's "worst case of maid abuse so far"—those were the prosecution's words. I can tell you right now that what happened to the maid made me sick to my stomach. Muawanatul Chasanah was a healthy, optimistic 17-year-old when she first arrived in Singapore from Indonesia to work as a maid in 2000. She was probably already thinking of how she would send money back to her family in Indonesia, like many others had done before her and many would do after her. But her luck ran out the moment she entered Ng Hua Chye's home. Only nine months later, she was dead.

Muawanatul had weighed 50 kg when she came but only 36 kg when she died. Her body bore the scars of more than 200 separate injuries, all probably inflicted on her by Ng. Now, maids in Singapore are required to go for six-monthly medical check-ups. During her nine months of torture, Muawanatul had two check-ups. Though her physical condition and injuries must have shown that she was in deep distress, no alarm was raised by the doctors and nurses. Neighbours had seen the woman always appearing tired and unhappy. They didn't know that Ng, a 47-year-old tour guide, had repeatedly abused the Indonesian with his fists, a cane and a hammer, burnt her with cigarettes and scalded her with boiling water. It is understood that Ng's wife was present at some of the beatings but didn't appear to do anything about it. He later told the police: "There were so many times I beat her, I lost count of them."

Muawanatul had been starved, occasionally given only packets of instant noodles for her lunch and dinner, and it was hunger that provoked the assault that finally ended her life on December 2, 2001. On that day, Ng accused her of stealing leftover porridge from his infant daughter and kicked her so severely that her stomach ruptured. She died several days later of peritonitis, lying in agony in a vomit-stained T-shirt before police arrived too late to save her. Fearing she might die, Ng had gone to the neighbourhood police post to report that he had assaulted her.

Ng was initially charged with murder, but the charge was reduced to one of culpable homicide as the prosecution was not in a position to prove murder. In the plea bargain, the parties agreed that the prosecution would not ask for life imprisonment and would leave the sentencing to the judge. Ng's history of violence against Muawanatul suggested that such a concession should not have been made. On July 19, 2002, Ng was sentenced to a total of 18 years and six months imprisonment and 12 strokes of the cane for what the prosecution described as the worst case of abuse of a domestic worker in Singapore. Deputy Public Prosecutor Lee Sing Lit described Ng as "inhuman".

Ng's treatment of Muawanatul struck a nerve with most Singaporeans. Like most other maids in Singapore, she was not guaranteed a minimum wage, could be required to work all her waking hours and was not automatically entitled to even one day off each week. She could also be dismissed without notice or right of appeal and sent home immediately on the whim of her employer. Her extreme bad luck was to be assigned to a despicable man who thought nothing of dehumanising her. In the end, he took her life.

Ng's wife approached me to defend him. She was later charged for assaulting the maid and sentenced to a few months in jail. I represented her too. Ng's charge was reduced to one of culpable homicide under Section 304(a) of the Penal Code because the prosecution agreed with us that it would be difficult to prove murder. I agreed that my client would plead guilty to the reduced charge. It was the most horrendous assault I have come across where a maid is concerned. It must have been a living hell for her. When I looked at the autopsy report, I felt sick. How could one human being be so evil to another? I suppressed my emotions and decided as usual that I would do the best for him as it was my job to do so.

Negotiations were difficult because of the nature of the injuries and the way they were inflicted. Finally, we reached an agreement and I persuaded Ng to accept the offer of the prosecution. Justice Choo Han Teck heard our mitigation and the prosecution address on sentence. He agreed with us that in this case, life imprisonment would be excessive and since he was in a position to give more than 10 years because of the multiple charges, he agreed with me that he could give more than 10 years but less than life—a total of 18 years.

If I'm not mistaken, Ng came to court to testify for his wife. He said that he was to be blamed for everything that had happened to the maid and that he was a monster. He found religion in prison and hopefully his new-found faith will make it easier for him to live with what he has done. He had an infant daughter whom he loved very much, so I cannot understand how a person who can love so deeply can behave so barbarically.

One final case that I want to highlight in this chapter involves another man who behaved very badly. Vidya Shankar Aiyar was labelled a "wolf in sheep's clothing" and it appeared an apt description. He was a well-known, amiable face in Singapore media circles, fronting the blue-ribbon business news programme 'In Conversation' on Channel NewsAsia. It was a job everyone agreed he did very well.

But Aiyar, an Indian national, got randy on November 2, 2002, at a colleague's housewarming party at Holland Village. He took a girl home from the party to his Lorong Chuan apartment and outraged her modesty. According to his 30-year-old victim, who was never named in public, she woke up the next morning feeling flesh pressing against the back of her body. She was naked in his bed and being spooned by Aiyar's naked body. She repeatedly asked him, "Why am I naked?" and "Where are my clothes?" Aiyar claimed at the trial that the woman was tipsy and had welcomed his advances. He said he had taken her clothes off because she said she was hot and also because she had vomited. Fighting her anger, the woman dressed up and stormed out of Aiyar's apartment at around 6.20 am. Aiyar followed her to the main road where she hailed a taxi and went home.

It was a classic case of one person's word against another's. But the case against Aiyar was strongly supported by a statement from the taxi driver who had taken the two of them to Lorong Chuan the night before. Eric Tey was initially dismissed by police as being immaterial to the case against the 37-year-old Indian. But the victim's father tracked him down and Tey became a key witness in the trial. The taxi driver noted that the victim had asked him to take her home first when they got into the taxi near Holland Village, but Aiyar had insisted on going to Lorong Chuan first. He had heard Aiyar telling the woman: "Let's go to Lorong Chuan. When you are sober, I will send you back." She apparently threw up once during the ride, putting her head outside the window, and passed out after that. Tey also heard Aiyar say: "I'm not going to bed a drunk."

Aiyar's trial started in September 2003 and lasted three months. It captured the imagination of the public mainly because Aiyar was a media personality and had interviewed industry leaders and prime ministers. Scandals involving media personalities are rare in Singapore. When one erupts, it's bound to be closely covered by the media and followed by the public. It perhaps also helped that Aiyar was a foreign national and didn't have a particularly deep network of friends, family and contacts in Singapore. Even other prominent criminal lawyers like Choo Si Sen, Peter Fernando and Kertar Singh were curious onlookers at this case. The victim turned up in court everyday even though she did not have to and had already given evidence. But she was not present when the judge's verdict was read out on December 30, 2005.

It was quite clear that District Judge Victor Yeo took great satisfaction in chastising Aiyar and sending him to jail. He did not mince his words as he handed down the guilty verdict. He described Aiyar as deceitful, crafty, unreliable, pretentious, cunning, evasive and absurd. Aiyar bowed his head a few times as the judgement was read. On January 6, 2006, Aiyar was sentenced to 15 months in jail and four strokes of the cane. He managed to escape the caning because of health reasons. He served his time without further incident and is now back in India working for the media.

Shankar Aiyar's family gave him full moral support. But in the process of doing so, they acted like royalty. His elder sister from the Middle East told me that the courts should be very careful before they convict her brother because Singapore needs India more than India needs Singapore. I then asked her whether the whole of India was supporting her brother and whether there could be a political disaster. She didn't reply, perhaps realising the farcical nature of her words.

I was not Aiyar's original lawyer. He was first represented by Shashi Nathan, a partner from the firm I was with at the time. Even before Aiyar was charged, the whole office knew he was in trouble. As a famous personality, anything about him was news. After the initial court appearances, Shashi Nathan was removed. Aiyar and his family wanted me to represent him and I was told specifically to get any assistant except Shashi. Of course I chose my usual assistant then, my wife's nephew Anand Nalachandran.

The family decided not to appeal the long-winded and sometimes unnecessarily harsh judgment of District Judge Yeo. But we made an appeal to the President to take away the caning on medical grounds and it was accepted. Shankar served 10 months in prison (with remission for good behaviour). On the day of his release, he was taken to an immigration department holding centre from where he was sent to the airport and back to India.

Neither he nor his family called me after his departure. I think they were upset that I insisted on my full fees. I didn't consider it an honour or a privilege to defend Aiyar that I had to reduce my fees, especially as the family had been quick to let everyone know how wealthy they were.

I believe the case jolted many men who have been in similar situations as Aiyar. Unfortunately, it's not an unusual situation. The Aiyar case was a good reminder that men should think twice before taking advantage of a woman who is intoxicated. I should also say that, during the course of the trial, Aiyar applied for permission to leave the jurisdiction of the country to go to India. Leave was granted and people were taking bets as to whether he would return. When he returned, both the deputy public prosecutor and I were surprised as we thought that he would not come back. Extradition would have been difficult with his political connections as his uncle was a minister in India's central government. Sometimes, I wonder whether he would have returned if he knew he would be convicted and sentenced to 15 months imprisonment with caning.

TWELVE

CONSTANCE CHEE
The Air Stewardess Who Fell From Grace

Whenever a child dies, emotions run high, and so it was that the death of four-year-old Sindee Neo generated a lot of anger, despair and frustration. The public could not comprehend how former SIA stewardess, Constance Chee Cheong Hin, could cause a child to fall from a block of flats on October 7, 2004.

It all started with an unlikely love affair between Chee, a university drop-out and Sindee's father, Neo Eng Tong, who was running a *karang guni* (rag-and-bone) business at the time. He said he first met her when he approached her at her doorstep asking if she had any unwanted household items for sale. From then they chatted and became acquainted.

Being a married man with a child, Neo was cagey about these facts at the hearing. He said Chee would stay with him overnight in his Telok Blangah Crescent flat when his Thai wife, Kittiduangrat Ketkanok, who worked as a hawker's assistant, and their daughter Sindee were away in Bangkok. He also said that during the affair, Chee lent him about $40,000 to start a business but he gambled it away. Chee said in court that she had actually lent him $50,000. He never paid back what he borrowed and broke off their affair in July that year. But Chee continued to demand for her money after that. She would call him often on his mobile phone and turn up at his doorstep unexpectedly.

Neo said she would create a scene outside his flat when he refused to let her in. "She would knock on the window, knock on the door and shout that she knew I was at home," he said.

Things came to a head on October 3, 2004. Between 8.00 pm and 9.00 pm that day, Chee called him on his mobile phone while hiding behind a wall outside his bedroom window. Spotting Chee outside, Neo hid Sindee behind the bedroom door as Chee tried to barge into the flat. Neo's tenant, Joseph Wong Tai Fatt, failed to keep her out. She had a quarrel with Wong in the living room but fled when she saw Madam Kittiduangrat returning home. Over the next few days, Chee must have thought about what she could do to get back at Neo and also how she could get her money back.

On October 7, she entered Neo's unlocked flat at 4.30 am and kidnapped the sleeping Sindee. Less than 15 minutes later, Sindee plummeted down the block. Just before the girl fell, her parents, who had discovered almost immediately that she was missing and had been frantically looking for her at the foot of the block, heard her screams pierce through the night from the upper floors. Sindee's fall was broken by an awning, but she still suffered a fractured jaw and serious head injuries. She died five days later in the Singapore General Hospital.

Chee was accused of kidnapping Sindee and causing her death. Neo said he had seen Chee walking away from the scene and told his wife to apprehend her. He had recognised Chee even though she was wearing a wig. Caught by Madam Kittiduangrat and Wong, Chee was handed over to the police. In her statement, Chee said: "Who in the right sense of mind would want to throw somebody down, what's more a child?" This was the question that reverberated around Singapore.

The court was packed on October 10, 2005, for Chee's trial which began more than a year after Sindee's abduction. On the advice of

High Court judge, V K Rajah, the prosecution rephrased the culpable homicide charge against Chee. Instead of accusing her of causing Sindee's death by throwing her down a block of flats, it alleged that Chee had intentionally caused the child to fall from a floor at the block of flats. Which floor it was could not be accurately determined despite tests by forensic teams. When the case was adjourned for the day, an emotional Madam Kittiduangrat hurled insults at Chee in Hokkien and Thai. There continued to be an undercurrent of strong emotions during the proceedings.

The defence team was angry at one of the expert witnesses for the prosecution, Dr Tay Ming Kiong, who was Head of the Criminalistics Laboratory of the Health Sciences Authority. We nicknamed him "The Pig" because he used pork in his experiments to decide whether Chee had thrown the child. Three bags of pork—weighing 25 kg in total and packed in three jointed sections to represent the head and neck, torso and arms, and lower limbs—were used to simulate the child's weight and body. A policewoman about the size and height of Chee was then deployed to first tip and then throw the bags down the block. The experiments were conducted from the fourth, sixth and tenth floors of the block to find out if the bags would land in the vicinity where Sindee had landed. Dr Tay concluded from his experiments that Sindee was not tipped but thrown. But I felt otherwise and so did our expert whose evidence was rejected by the judge.

On January 24, 2006, Justice Rajah found Chee guilty of two charges: culpable homicide and kidnapping. But he reserved judgment after the prosecution's forensic psychiatrist, Dr Stephen Phang, raised several issues about Chee's mental health. Dr Phang told the court that Chee, who was diagnosed with schizophrenia, had in the previous two months rejected suggestions she was mentally ill and refused treatment.

Dr Phang said: "For all cases of schizophrenia, it is said that one-third will be cured, one-third will have relapses and be in and out of hospital, and another one-third will have a downward slide. Chee falls in the last category." He was convinced that Chee should be locked away for a long time, like life imprisonment. But Chee told me that Dr Phang did not like her because she asked him too many questions that he could not answer. I found Dr Phang a very officious psychiatrist and was worried that his opinion might sway Justice Rajah to impose life imprisonment. Thankfully, the judge went against established mode of sentencing and, on April 7, 2006, imposed a 10-year sentence on Chee for culpable homicide as well as another three years for the kidnapping of Sindee. Justice V K Rajah showed that he was a courageous judge who knew the meaning of compassion. In the relatively short time he sat as a trial judge, he earned the respect of the whole Bar, especially the Criminal Bar.

Chee claimed that she knew my late brother, Surash, well. According to her, Surash was the only person who remembered her birthday and once, when they were overseas, he went to her room with a cake and conveyed his best wishes. I thought that was typical of Surash. Hers was a case of a woman who literally flew very high and came crashing down to earth fast. When I first saw her in prison, I could see that she must have been attractive once. She was teasing me when we first met, asking me whether I was as good as people said I was. I just smiled. She gave funny answers to questions I asked and it took some time to get information from her. She got along very well with my nephew, Sunil Sudheesan, who was assisting me. I didn't find it unusual when she told me that I made her nervous.

After the trial had been going on for a few days, she called me to the dock to tell me that I was a better lawyer than people said.

She was teasing again. I felt Chee was not a good witness. She was nervous and temperamental on the witness stand, but she came across as very intelligent and could hold her own against the deputy public prosecutor, Wong Kok Weng. Wong was a thorough gentleman but he was assisted by two other DPPs who I felt were not as good. In fact, the lady DPP gave me the impression that she was disappointed that Chee would not be hanged.

At the end of the trial, Chee's sisters, though reluctant to pay our full fees, stood by her through the case. They swore affidavits to show that they were prepared to take care of her when she was released from prison and said that they would be responsible for her welfare. The affidavits made a difference when sentence was passed. After Chee was convicted and sentenced, I went to see her in prison. She was all smiles when she saw me and thanked me for a job well done. I asked her whether she wanted to appeal and she said no. I told her that her decision was right and that she should take her medication faithfully. She said she would and that when she is released from prison, she would look me up to take me out for dinner. I said that would be okay and left. That was the last time I saw her.

THIRTEEN

TOOK LENG HOW
The Man Who Should Not Have Been Hanged

By all accounts, Huang Na was a normal eight-year-old who was a familiar sight at the Pasir Panjang Wholesale Centre where her parents, both Chinese nationals, worked. She was known to be friendly and respectful of anyone she met. On October 10, 2004, the lovable girl went missing.

Her mother was believed to be away in China at the time and the girl was being looked after by a friend. The initial reaction of her parents was possibly not to be too worried. After all, Huang Na was rumoured to have once returned to her parents' village in China on her own. But as the days passed, her mother became more frantic and her worry spread like wildfire to members of the public. A massive search that stretched to Malaysia was conducted. Hundreds of volunteers started looking for her in isolated places. In Johor, taxi drivers joined in the search. The media ran stories of the missing girl almost daily. But people didn't have to look too far from the wholesale centre to find her. Three weeks after Huang Na first went missing, police found a brown cardboard box sealed with adhesive tape in undergrowth at the nearby Telok Blangah Hill Park. It contained her decomposed body, wrapped in several layers of plastic. The police couldn't immediately confirm if it was Huang Na's body but did so later.

Twenty-two-year old Malaysian Took Leng How was initially classified as helping the police with their investigations. He had been the last person seen talking to Huang Na before she disappeared. Took, a vegetable packer at the wholesale centre, was a former colleague of Huang Na's mother, Huang Shuying. He lived in the same flat with both mother and daughter and was said to be very close to them. Indeed, people had some reservations about Madam Huang in the weeks after the body was found and when details of the case were starting to surface. She had an earlier conviction for overstaying in Singapore but managed to return to Singapore with a false passport and as Huang Na's guardian. Because she had burnt all her fingers and thumbs, her fingerprints could not be matched when she arrived in Singapore the second time with a different passport. Some people suspected that the girl was "adopted". In any case, Took was charged with sexually assaulting Huang Na, then kicking and stomping on her until she died.

Took's case began on July 11, 2005. The court was told by public prosecutors that he had initially lied to the police during the search for Huang Na and given them the slip. He had agreed to take a lie-detector test which was to be held on the morning of October 21, 2004. The night before the test, he told police officers that he had the contact number of someone who he claimed would lead them to Huang Na. He asked to return to his flat where this person's mobile phone number was kept. At around 1.15 am on the day he was supposed to take the lie-detector test, police officers accompanied Took to his flat in Telok Blangah. Took, however, was unable to find the number and they left for the police station. Along the way, Took said he was hungry and they stopped at a food stall on Pasir Panjang Road. He ordered a plate of *roti prata* with chicken curry. Halfway through his meal, he excused himself to go to the toilet. This was when he was believed to have slipped away. It was later learnt that Took went to Woodlands in a taxi and sneaked across the causeway around 3.40 that morning. He then travelled to Penang where he went into hiding until he surrendered to the Royal Malaysian Police and was brought back to Singapore.

The details about what Huang Na went through were gruesome. She had been lured into a storeroom at the wholesale centre on the pretext of a game of hide-and-seek. According to Took, the game went horribly wrong. Took claimed he had tied Huang Na's hands and feet as part of the game and that she had accidentally hurt herself falling on some boxes. When he saw her bleeding from the mouth, he panicked and started to strangle her. He undressed her to give the impression of a rape. There may have been some truth to this last claim because semen was never found on Huang Na or in the storeroom. The medical examiner found bruises on her right temple, scalp, chin, jaw and lips. It was also concluded that the nature of death was asphyxia.

During the case, Took appeared gaunt and pale but was calm. He occasionally looked at reporters and smiled. On August 26, 2005, Took was found guilty of murder and sentenced to death. I would describe this case as the case of the man who shouldn't have been hanged. From my first meeting with Took, I realised there was something wrong with him. The sickly smile, which was different from Anthony Ler's arrogant one, and the confused and often irrelevant ranting convinced me that Took was mentally retarded. His IQ was 76 which suggested that he wasn't playing with a full deck of cards. The defence expert, Dr R Nagulendran, agreed with me and testified on Took's behalf. I felt his testimony was much better than that of Dr G S Devan from the Institute of Mental Health, whose evidence didn't stand up to cross-examination. I am still mystified at Justice Lai Kew Chai's decision to accept Dr Devan's evidence. However, I was not surprised at the conviction. Neither was I surprised at his judgment which had lots of unexplained portions.

Took appealed the conviction. There had been some worrying gaps in his case which prosecutors and the police couldn't address. A major technicality was that the cause of death could not be established. Huang Na could have choked on her own vomit due to fits or she could have been strangled by Took. More than 30,000 people signed a clemency petition for Took which was doing its rounds at the time. His murder conviction was upheld on a two-to-one vote. The last time the Court of Appeal was split in a capital case was 10 years before that. Then, a Myanmar national was acquitted by the trial judge of drug trafficking. The prosecution appealed and the Court of Appeal set him free with a two-to-one majority.

The Court of Appeal's decision on Took was heartbreaking. At the hearing, it was quite clear that one of the three judges, Justice Kan Ting Chiu, was with me. Justice of Appeal Chao Hick Tin came alive during the arguments, especially when I started reading the evidence of the expert from the script. He asked some questions and seemed to be satisfied. He gave me the impression that he was at last following my arguments and I thought I had won him over. The third judge in the Court of Appeal was Chief Justice Yong Pung How. So, when we returned a few weeks later and were told that Justice Chao would read the majority decision, we thought for a moment that we had succeeded in the appeal. But as he read the judgement, we realised that Justice Chao was not with us. To me, Justice Kan's dissenting voice was a clear and logical judgment which explained why the appeal should have been upheld. Members of the Bar were full of praise for him and his courage to dissent. I expected nothing less from him as I knew him from my Raffles Institution days. An attempt to win clemency for Took also failed, though the President took five months longer than the usual three months to make the decision. I believe this was partly due to the number of people who signed the clemency petition. Took was hanged on November 3, 2006.

Although I do not attend my clients' funerals, I attended Took's wake. I went in the afternoon with my two legal assistants, Anand Nalachandran and Sunil Sudheesan, to avoid the crowd and the press. We had received some donations for him which we gave to his family along with our own contribution. Took's parents were glad to see me, and his mother and aunt hugged me and thanked me for what we had done for them. I felt sad when I saw Took lying in the coffin and, for a brief moment, I wished I was not a criminal lawyer. I wished our legal system had more room for compassion. It reminded me why I am so against the mandatory death sentence. In my opinion, when there is a split decision as was the case for Took, the death sentence should be commuted to life imprisonment either by the Court of Appeal itself or by the President.

I also think the local media didn't help. It started off by practically convicting Took before the case started. The hype was great because it involved the murder of a child. Hundreds thronged the corridors of the courts, queueing up to view the proceedings. People waited patiently for an empty seat. But as the case progressed, I got the feeling that the media and members of the public began to realise that their first impression of Took may have been wrong. From what started out as a hopeless case, the odds began to shift in favour of Took. I felt it became a 50:50 case. People who initially condemned him became sympathetic. The case was a talking point in many coffee shops. Because of the extensive media coverage, it became difficult for me to go anywhere without being recognised. My son was amused at the number of people who would approach me to shake my hand and say a few good words about what I was doing for Took. Apart from the massive public interest, I should note that even representatives of the Chinese government were curious onlookers during the case.

During the case, I took to calling him Ah Took. The police made Ah Took demonstrate what he did in the storeroom when he was with Huang Na. The scene was recorded and shown in court. Everyone saw how he had stamped on Huang Na and kicked her. It was a very violent demonstration which probably did a lot of damage to his case. I recall when we first took instructions from him, Ah Took told us that sometimes he remembers things and sometimes he doesn't. When we asked him why he agreed to re-enact the scene, he accused the police of persuading him to do it. Ah Took also said that he was asked to do specific things for the recording but couldn't remember if he really did them to Huang Na. He said the police told him that if he co-operated, it would help them solve the case. Ah Took himself felt that if he co-operated and did what the police told him to do, they would certainly help reduce his charge. That was why he did it.

Despite Ah Took's low IQ of 76, he did several clever things. One was to choose only those dustbins at the wholesale market that did not have any CCTV cameras pointing at them when he threw away Huang Na's things. The other was the way he escaped from Singapore. I asked the psychiatrist how such things could be explained. He replied that though the measurement of intelligence quotient can be low, that does not discount the possibility that a person can do intelligent things. In fact, some of these acts can be brilliant, but when you are examining people for their intelligence levels, you can't just take one or two specific acts to give a broader assessment.

When the police became suspicious and started interrogating Took, they had still not arrested him. He was considered a witness that they were interviewing. They asked Took if he was prepared to take a lie-detector test and he said he would. The police told him to go home and come back to the police station the next day. But Ah Took volunteered to be held in the station overnight, saying he would not be able to wake up on time the next day. He was truly a co-operative witness asking to be kept in custody. The police were sufficiently impressed and agreed.

While they were on the way back to the police station where he would be held in custody, Ah Took said he was hungry and needed something to eat. They went to a food stall and ordered some *pratas* for him. Ah Took said he needed to go to the toilet and from there he made his escape. As he was under police custody and was treated as a visitor during his interrogation earlier, he had been given a visitor's pass which he wore around his neck. The pass had the emblem of the CID on it and with the pass, he walked quite boldly through Singapore customs checkpoint at the causeway. I think the immigration officers must have thought he was a police officer because of the pass.

After he escaped into Malaysia via Johor, Ah Took met up with some loyal friends who helped him to get to Penang. In Penang, I think such relations came into play again. He gave press conferences through a friend of his, telling all sorts of stories and even citing political issues like the Malaysia-Singapore relationship. He said he would sacrifice his freedom and surrender to preserve the relationship between the two neighbouring countries. He appeared to want to paint himself as a hero. I think, by this point, some delusions of grandeur had set in. There was probably some evidence of this when he had the CID pass on him too. He was deluded in that he thought he could be a saviour of two countries. That's why he eventually surrendered.

Many people have asked me why Ah Took remained silent in court when he was given the opportunity to provide evidence. Once the prosecution has established a prima facie case, the accused is given two choices. He can remain silent and if he does, the court can draw an adverse inference if it wants to because he remained silent. Or he can go to the witness stand and give evidence, in which case he can be cross-examined by the public prosecutor and by the court. Ah Took had this choice.

From the instructions he gave us, we could not make head or tail of what he was saying. He was full of delusions by then. At one point, he was talking about hired killers from China who had come to murder Huang Na because of what her mother had done to some people in China. And since Ah Took knew what was happening, they made him strangle Huang Na and leave his fingerprints on her body so that he would not be able to squeal on them. They forced him to pack up the body and told him where to dump it. When we told him that the CCTV did not show any foreign killers at the scene, he replied that they were so good that they could remain invisible if they wanted to. Ah Took was giving us plenty of such obviously delusional stories, and all the time, he wore a smile on his face. When we asked him to clarify the statements he gave that he was the head of a gang and some other stories, we were unable to get proper explanations from him.

I knew my old friend Lawrence Ang was dying to cross-examine Ah Took because the prosecution had made him say so many incriminating things in his many statements. I don't know why they had to record that many statements. I suppose it was a strategy to show the inconsistencies in his statements. Together with the enactment, there would have been too many things to explain. I felt that it would not help to put Ah Took on the stand because by the time the prosecution was done with him, he would be literally finished.

My assistants agreed with my assessment. Our defence was one based on diminished responsibility. The first, that he was suffering from a mental illness. The second was on causation—how the girl died, for instance, it could have been how she got into a fit, vomited and choked on her own vomit. We were going on two defences for which Ah Took could not contribute at all. As such, the best thing for him to do was to remain silent. In fact, I even consulted our psychiatrist, Dr Nagulendran as to whether I should put Ah Took on the stand. The doctor said putting him on the stand would not help at all. It was very sound advice. Putting Ah Took on the stand, we felt, would have done irreversible damage to his case. If by remaining silent, the judge drew an adverse inference, then so be it. A talking Ah Took would have been worse than a silent one.

During the case, many members of the public came to our office, wanting to sign a clemency petition. Seeing the interest the case had generated, we made many copies of the clemency petition for people to sign. Hundreds and hundreds of people streamed into the office to sign the petition. It was quite a nuisance, but we thought we should entertain them in our office as they were there to support our client. I was personally surprised that more than 30,000 people actually signed the petition asking for his life to be saved, especially when one considers the fact that Ah Took had no sympathy when the case first started. He was condemned long before that.

That's why in cases such as this, I think the Singapore media must be cautious. They should not build up the hype, give sordid details and write reports that may create bias. All this can give the impression that the person under investigation has already been found guilty. This is exactly what happened to Ah Took. Even before the trial, people were saying that he was Huang Na's killer and he deserved to hang. This is because too many unnecessary things were reported before the trial which created an unfair bias against Ah Took. In some ways when the trial ended and people started to say that he wasn't so guilty after all, we felt that it was a sort of moral victory for our defence team. Finally, when the Court of Appeal gave its two-to-one verdict, with one judge saying Ah Took should only be sentenced to a maximum of one year, it was again a victory for us.

One last thing I want to mention about Ah Took's case is that there were at least three workers at the Pasir Panjang wholesale market who came to see me personally on the condition that their names would not be revealed. They did not want to be subpoenaed as witnesses. They told me about Madam Huang and how she carried on with some of the men in the market. They confirmed to me that Ah Took had an affair with Huang Na's mother and that she subsequently left him for his boss. They insisted that she went with many men, took their money and subsequently dumped them when she met somebody better. They added that Ah Took gave all his money to her and was practically her slave, running errands for her.

This news interested me because I wanted to explore whether Ah Took could have killed Huang Na out of hatred and anger towards her mother. After listening to the three witnesses on different occasions—two in my office and one outside as he did not want to come to the office—I went immediately to see Ah Took in prison. I told him what I had heard and asked him whether there was any truth to it and whether he was angry with her for leaving him for his boss, a richer man. He denied this, saying he did not have that sort of relationship with her and that they were just good friends. Ah Took, however, admitted that he knew that his boss was carrying on with Madam Huang and there were rumours that she was carrying on with other men at the same time.

Once my client denied having relations with Huang Na's mother, I had to believe him rather than the strangers who had talked to me. Still, it was interesting to hear what people were saying. Sometimes, I wonder if there is any truth in what these people told me. Why would they bother to go out of their way to meet me, only to tell me lies? We can never fully understand people and their intentions.

FOURTEEN

RAMU ANNADAVASCAN
A Rake And The Burning Man

Ramu Annadavascan had a history of bad blood with Kalingam s/o Mariappan. They often argued and fought over petty issues. At about noon on September 20, 1981, Ramu and a friend went to a coffee stall at a hawker centre to have a drink with Kalingam. Ramu and friend had beers while Kalingam had a stout. After their drinks, Ramu invited Kalingam to go with them to Changi Airport for more drinks. Terminal 1 was newly opened at the time and was a popular hangout for many Singaporeans. Kalingam initially declined but agreed after some persuasion. It would be the last decision he ever made.

The three men piled into a lorry which Ramu had borrowed from an uncle. On the way, Ramu had another argument with Kalingam and pulled over on a deserted track next to the East Coast Parkway. All three men got off the lorry. Ramu suddenly became violent, grabbed a rake from the lorry and hit Kalingam on the head with it. Kalingam stumbled, picked himself up and started to run. Ramu could not stop him but his 17-year-old friend managed to. Ramu caught hold of Kalingam and dragged him along the ground for a few metres. He then gave the rake to his friend who struck two blows on Kalingam's face. Kalingam collapsed. Ramu placed his foot on Kalingam's chest. Thinking that Kalingam was already dead, Ramu asked his friend to fetch some petrol from the lorry. He poured the petrol over Kalingam, lit a match and dropped it on him with the intention of disposing of the body by burning it. But Kalingam leapt up, howling in pain. He began to run around and set some bushes on fire. His time, however, was up and he died soon after.

Both men were eventually caught and convicted. Ramu was sentenced to death while his accomplice was ordered to be detained under the President's pleasure as he was below 18 years of age when the offence was committed. (The President's Pleasure Review Board is appointed by the Minister for Home Affairs to review the cases of underaged prisoners who have been detained during the President's pleasure. The role of the Review Board is to assess the prisoners' suitability for release and make recommendation to the minister.)

In the appeal against Ramu's conviction, it was argued that it was never the intention of the accused to kill by burning. Ramu and his friend didn't wait for Kalingam to die; they climbed onto the lorry and drove off. It was argued that there was an absence of common intention to cause injuries in the ordinary course of nature to cause death. It was also argued that by that time, the senior forensic pathologist, the late Professor Chao Tzee Cheng, had determined that it was the second blow from Ramu's friend which was the fatal one. Finally, it was argued that at the time the men poured the petrol on Kalingam and set him on fire, they thought the victim was already dead. None of these arguments held and the appeal failed. Ramu's death sentence was upheld.

That was the official version of this terrible murder. There are, however, a few things that I would like to add. I remember defending Ramu twice before. In the first case, he was charged with murder, but I managed to get the charge reduced to one of affray which is one of the lowest offences in the Penal Code. He pleaded guilty to the charge and was sentenced to a fine of $230 by district judge, Rahim Jalil. Shortly after that, he was charged again for assaulting a police officer during a Thaipusam festival event. I got the charge reduced for that too and he was fined $500. So, when he was charged and finally convicted of Kalingam's murder, it made me reflect on my previous efforts in getting his earlier charges reduced. Did he feel that he was invincible and could get away again? It is one of those cases where I still feel a tinge of regret about doing the best I could.

There is another detail about this murder case that not many people know about. At the time of Ramu's trial, the police suspected that there were more than two assailants. But since Ramu and his accomplice insisted that they were the only ones involved, the investigation stopped there. Many years later, I had a call from the registrar of the High Court informing me that a person in Queenstown Remand Prison who was charged for murder was asking for my services. The man had stabbed another person to death in a fight over drugs (ganja).

My first reaction was: "Look here, sir, you just cannot allow an accused person to decide who should be assigned to him. If you allow that to happen, you will find that the accused persons would generally want lawyers who are more reputed and well-known. Then what's going to happen to those with less experience and who wish to practise criminal law? Where would they get their opportunities? This request would set a bad precedent."

The registrar replied: "I am aware of that, Subhas, but he is turning down all the other assigned counsels and we do not want to prolong this matter. The case is long outstanding and before it blotches up our record, please do me a personal favour. Accept the assignment and go see him."

When it was put to me like that—the registrar requesting a favour of me—I could not say no. I requested the letter assigning me to the case. I received it the next day, ironically thanking me for accepting the assignment as though I was eager to take it on. Whatever it was, I took the letter and wrote to Queenstown Remand Prison seeking permission to interview the man.

After taking his instructions, I told him what I thought—that there was a very good possibility of reducing the charge to culpable homicide. In all probability, he would get eight to 10 years if I succeeded in getting the charge reduced. I asked him if he would accept the reduced charge and plead guilty. He agreed to it.

As I was about to leave, I asked him, "By the way, why did you keep on insisting that I should defend you?" I may have done a few murder cases but I was not fantastic, especially at a time when I was just making a name for myself.

"Do you have some time?" he replied. "I'd like to tell you." I said yes and sat down again. He asked me for a cigarette and we lit up a stick each. In those days, we could give prisoners cigarettes and we could smoke with them in the interview room. The situation is different now. No cigarettes are allowed.

He took a long puff on his cigarette and as he exhaled, he said, "You were the lawyer for Ramu Annadavascan?"

"Yes. All the more you should not have asked for me to defend you. I lost the case. He's hanged and gone."

"I'm aware of that. It was a very bad case for you. I'm not holding it against you. He was a friend of mine. Do you know the case where you defended him for murder? I was involved in that."

I was astonished to hear this. "You were involved? How so?"

He just nodded. "Yes, I was."

"Come to think of it, there was talk that there were four persons involved in that murder, but the prosecution just didn't have evidence about the other two and so investigations were closed. How were you involved?"

He explained. "I was in the lorry which took Kalingam to East Coast Parkway. I didn't know that Ramu and his friend were going to kill him. When they returned to the lorry, I realised that they had killed him but I kept silent as there was nothing more I could do."

"Well, I guess you played a very minor role," I said. "You did not take part in the murder."

"I was the third person involved out of the four of us."

I asked him where the fourth person was. His reply shocked me again. That person was the one that he was now charged with for murder. "What, you killed the fourth person?" I exclaimed.

There was some remorse in his voice. "Yes, we were good friends but we fought over some drugs."

In the end, justice had caught up with the Kalingam murderers because the third person involved was being charged for the murder of the fourth person. It took a while but it eventually got there. I appeared before Justice Chan Sek Kiong, who was a High Court judge at the time, on a reduced charge of culpable homicide and put up a mitigation plea for this client. He was sentenced to eight years in prison. That was the end of the whole episode.

In my many years of practising law, I've come across some strange coincidences such as this where justice ultimately catches up with the bad guys. Somehow, if you are not dealt with by the court, you will be dealt with outside the court. It's almost like a force of nature. In some way or other, punishment will be meted out.

There are people I've defended who have been acquitted and walked out of court free men and women. But in all honesty, they walked out free because the prosecution could not prove their case beyond a reasonable doubt. The court does not at any stage say: "I am discharging and acquitting you because you are an innocent man." The statement is always: "I find you not guilty. Therefore I discharge and acquit you."

It is a myth that everyone who is acquitted is innocent. I personally know of many who have walked out of court as free men and women even when they were guilty of the charge.

FIFTEEN

NADASAN CHANDRA SECHARAN
Escaping The Death Sentence

One landmark case which gave me great satisfaction was that of Nadasan Chandra Secharan vs the Public Prosecutor. Nadasan was a mechanic who used to worship in the same temple that I attend. Sometimes he would go to the temple with his wife. On the occasions that I saw him there, we would exchange greetings. He was one of Lord Ayappan's devotees who would go through a penance and fast every year for 40 days during the months of November and December. Devotees also go on a pilgrimage to Shabrimallai in South India, the historical abode of Lord Ayappan. Nadasan made the pilgrimage regularly.

Nadasan also used the grounds at the back of the temple to wash his Toyota Lite-Ace van or do repairs to it. I remember asking some of the temple employees why he was given the privilege of using the temple premises and facilities to clean his van. They assured me he was contributing to the temple and that the amount he put into the temple donation box covered all his expenses. I was also assured that he was a good man. So, it came as a shock when I learnt that he had been arrested for the murder of his ex-mistress, Ramipiram Kannickaisparry. Thirty-nine-year-old Ramipiram was separated from her husband at the time of her death and lived with her sister, a Madam Kasturi Bai. She was last seen alive by a colleague at 12.15 pm on the day of the murder at Apple Computer where she worked. Nadasan and she had parted ways some years back, but the parting was not amicable. I wondered why he was arrested.

Nadasan's family appointed me as his lawyer. I found out from his wife that Nadasan had a long affair, which she knew about, with Ramipiram and that it was all over well before he was arrested. When I rang the Special Investigation Section to find out more, I was told Nadasan was being held for suspicion of murder of his ex-mistress. A few days later he was charged with her murder and I realised they were building a case against him.

The body was found by a jogger in Jalan Ulu Sembawang at the edge of undergrowth. In front of the body were tyre marks. Ramipiram was lying on her back with her left leg flexed over her right leg. She was dressed in a light purple Punjabi suit which was torn in some parts. Part of her brassiere was exposed and she was still wearing her watch on her left wrist. A forensic report showed that a van had run over her and she had 13 stab wounds on her face. The body was in a bad shape and there were teeth missing because of the impact. It was quite a brutal murder.

When I first interviewed Nadasan, he cried and said he was innocent. I asked him about Ramipiram's background and what he was doing on that particular day because, based on the autopsy, the coroner and the pathologist had determined the time of the murder. I needed to know exactly where he was at that particular time. Unfortunately for him, he didn't have an alibi. He was working as a mechanic at Seletar Country Club but was not there at the time of the murder. While he could account for some of the activities during his absence, he couldn't do so for a crucial 30 to 40 minutes. According to Nadasan, he was on his way home to have lunch, which he often did as his flat was very near the golf club, but on that day his van broke down. It was an old van which often broke down. Nadasan said he spent some time at the side of the road cleaning the carburettor. He also said that it was drizzling which was why he took more time to fix it.

I was told by the forensics team that they had found a tooth belonging to the deceased stuck under a wooden panel at the bottom of Nadasan's van. They surmised that this could only have happened if his van had driven over the victim's head, knocking out her teeth. The prosecution also said they had evidence to show that the tyre marks found at the scene, especially those in front of the body, belonged to the tyres of Nadasan's van. Circumstantially they had a very good case—a tooth had been found underneath Nadasan's van, the tyre marks matched his van and Nadasan couldn't explain where he was at the time of the murder.

Unfortunately, by the time they found the tooth, the body was on its way to the crematorium. The police arrived too late and the body had been cremated. The only recourse was a DNA test to ascertain if the tooth belonged to the victim. Subsequently, the tooth was sent to Scotland Yard; at that time, Singapore's forensic team were not able to conduct DNA tests. Test results showed that the tooth was indeed Ramipiram's.

Next came a report about the tyre marks. Drawn up by an expert in New Zealand engaged by the prosecution, it stated that the tyre marks were caused by the tyres of Nadasan's van. The case was getting worse for my client. I decided to hold a meeting with Nadasan's family. Together with my capable assisting counsel, Amolat Singh, I told them that we needed to get our own experts in and asked whether they could afford the fees. They assured us they could. So I engaged the help of a DNA expert from Sydney, Dr Malcolm MacDonald. Through him, I got an expert to analyse the tyre marks. He was also prepared to give evidence contrary to that of the prosecution's New Zealand expert. So I had two experts from Sydney while the prosecution had one from Scotland Yard and one from New Zealand. The trial also saw a few local experts, like the forensic pathologist, and two others from the Department of Scientific Services.

The case started before Justice Lai Kew Chai. The deputy public prosecutor was Ong Hian Sun, who is currently director of the Commercial Affairs Department in Singapore. He was one of 10 scholar engineers who were offered scholarships in law because there was a shortage of good lawyers, according to the government. They were promised quick promotion, a promise that was kept. When Ong graduated, he was attached to the Attorney-General's Chambers. I didn't have any dealings with him before and we were polite to each other. In the course of my conversations with him, I found him to be a deadly serious person, devoid of any humour.

When I told him that lawyers at the Bar were referring to Nadasan's case as 'the toothless case', he got annoyed and retorted, "What do you mean by 'toothless case'? I'll make sure your client gets convicted."

"Hey, come on, don't be so serious. It's just a joke, you know," I told him.

He smiled in relief. "Oh, it's just a joke, is it?" I knew then that I had better not joke with this guy as he was far too serious.

The trial progressed. Our experts gave us tutorials to help us brush up on our knowledge of DNA. We also learnt how to cross-examine the prosecution's DNA expert from Scotland Yard. This expert was prim and proper and gave evidence as though she was talking to lesser human beings, presumably because she believed her knowledge in the area to be superior. I had a lot of fun questioning her and played up my Indian accent just to irritate her. I knew she was having difficulty understanding me. I cross-examined her at length and finally managed to get her admission that her own laboratory did not follow established protocol. I drew from her many admissions that were not very complimentary to her and her laboratory. I ended the cross-examination by telling her "… and you call yourself an expert". Obviously, she didn't like the way I put it. I must say Justice Lai gave me a lot of leeway.

The prosecution then called its tyre expert. The young New Zealander admitted that his final conclusions were done in Singapore after he had seen the tyre marks and other evidence related to it. When it was my turn to cross-examine him, I put it to him that his preliminary opinion that the same tyres caused the tyre marks was mere speculation. He did not respond and kept quiet. He also remained silent when I asked if he just wanted a free trip to Singapore. I remember Justice Lai asking me to go slow on that.

The prosecution finally finished presenting their witnesses and it was now the defence's turn. I asked the judge to make an exception and to allow me to call my experts first before calling in the accused because the longer the experts stayed in Singapore, the greater the expenses I had to incur. It is the usual procedure in criminal cases that the accused takes the stand before the witnesses. Justice Lai consented because the two witnesses whom I wanted to call were expert witnesses and I had cited cases where there was a precedent. The prosecution made no objection.

My first witness was Dr MacDonald, the expert on DNA. He gave his evidence and explained that the evidence of the prosecution experts could not be accepted because the method used was wrong and thus the finding could be wrong. He said that the experts had ignored important issues and gave his reasons. He was cross-examined extensively by the deputy public prosecutor, with the prodding and prompting of his own expert who was sitting beside him. Next, my other expert on tyres took the stand. He explained why the prosecution expert's findings were not reliable. He was also cross-examined extensively.

Subsequently, Nadasan gave evidence. He said he had nothing to do with the murder and didn't know how the tooth came to be impaled on his van. Apparently, according to Ramipiram's husband and son, she would open beer bottles with her teeth. Nadasan said that they used to rendezvous in the van and were sometimes intimate and would share a beer underneath the van. It was possible that she could have cracked her tooth on one of those occasions.

The prosecution also produced an expert witness to say that it would not take 30 to 40 minutes to repair the carburettor of the van, as Nadasan had claimed. Under cross-examination, that testimony was shredded to pieces because it was obvious the witness did not know much about Nadasan's old van. Nadasan explained why his van would start and stall over and over again.

When the trial ended, we handed in written submissions. Despite our efforts, Justice Lai convicted my client and sentenced him to death. There was much wailing and crying in court. The judge called the DPP, Amolat Singh and me into his chambers, and we remained there until the crowd was cleared by the police. Only then did he allow the DPP to leave through the back of the court. I was very disappointed with the judgment. I felt that Justice Lai always dealt more harshly with people who commit adultery. I also felt that as a church elder, and because of his personal convictions, he tended to take issues other than the law into consideration. Of course, I filed the Notice of Appeal.

I should also share that some gold items were found in the van too. The prosecution said they belonged to the murdered woman but did not provide any expert evidence to back up their claim. Nadasan explained that he hired out his van for transporting guests during weddings and the gold items could have been accidentally dropped by them. Since there was no proof to connect the gold items worn by the deceased with the items found in the van, the evidence was referred to as neutral evidence. I remember Justice Lai saying that his father was a goldsmith and he knew a little about gold and had his opinion about things.

Anyway after we had filed our Notice of Appeal, Justice Lai wrote his Grounds of Decision explaining why he convicted my client. When I read the Grounds of Decision, I found the judgment to be very weak and one that did not reflect what actually happened in the trial. It was a 'wishy-washy' sort of judgment with the usual 'mumbo-jumbo' when you want to convict somebody, stating nothing much other than that he accepted the evidence of the prosecution's forensic experts and did not believe my client.

When it was time for the appeal, the family had no more money. They had spent it all on the experts. I got myself assigned by the Supreme Court registrar and did the appeal as an assigned counsel.

Together with Amolat Singh, we argued before the Court of Appeal comprising Chief Justice Yong Pung How, and Justices of Appeal M Karthigesu and L P Thean. We put forward our case and argued why Justice Lai had erred in convicting and why he should not have accepted the forensic evidence submitted by the prosecution. Of course, the DPP fought back aggressively. In one instance, when arguing about the tooth in the van, Justice Thean retorted: "So what if the tooth was found? Does that mean that he killed her? There was an explanation given, wasn't there? Why don't you look at the explanation?" He cut the DPP short on that. I was a bit surprised. I think he found Justice

Lai's judgment weak and the arguments of the DPP even weaker. The judgment of the Court of Appeal was reserved.

A month or two later, judgment was delivered and the Court of Appeal unanimously allowed the appeal. They squashed the death sentence and ordered Nadasan to be freed. He cried loudly when he heard the result. When I went to see him in the underground cell at the Supreme Court, he was still wailing. I shouted at him to stop and the wardens told me that they were tears of joy. I said, "Even with tears of joy, there's a limit." I told him to shut up and listen to what I had to say.

They took him back to Changi Prison and returned his belongings to him. That evening he was released. He made headlines in all the newspapers and on TV. Winning the appeal gave both Amolat Singh and I great satisfaction. It's very seldom that you get a conviction on a capital case squashed in the Court of Appeal. The system very seldom allows such things to happen. So we had good reason to celebrate.

One of the things I must say that struck me as funny was the extent to which an accused would go to impress a judge. Nadasan, who was a staunch Hindu, somehow learnt that Justice Lai was a Christian and a church elder. After a couple of days of hearings in court, Nadasan started carrying a Bible. The interpreter who had earlier thought that Nadasan was a Hindu informed me that Nadasan now was carrying a Bible. I said, "Never mind, let him carry whatever he wants." I did not question Nadasan's decision to carry the Bible. However, when the time came for him to give evidence, he told the interpreter that he wanted to swear on his own copy of the Bible. I went towards him and told him: "You can be a Christian, you can be a Buddhist, I don't care what you are. But if you want to swear on the Bible, you take the oath on the court's Bible. Why the hell do you want to use your own Bible? What are you trying to prove?" He felt a little embarrassed. I demanded that he not make an issue out of this. He swore on the court's Bible. I knew that it was just a ploy to impress upon the judge that he was a good man. Still, Nadasan was promptly convicted and taken to the condemned cell. The first letter he wrote from the cell was to ask me to do the appeal because he was not guilty. At the top of that letter, he had written "*Om Shakti*". So, he had forgotten about the Bible. Since he was now convicted, he had chosen to revert back to Hinduism. These are some of the things that accused persons sometimes do when they are under pressure or in a depressed state or if they want to impress somebody in the hope that it will help their case

I still see Nadasan in the temple with his family. He always comes to me and says hello. His wife still complains that I have yet to go to their house for a meal, an invitation that has been long-standing. They are very grateful. Each time I meet with his family, his wife says to me: "We pray to the God that we cannot see but whenever we see you, we feel that we see our God in you because you saved my husband's life." I always reply that I didn't save her husband's life and that sometimes the system works.

SIXTEEN

LEONG SIEW CHOR
The Body Parts Murder

Factory supervisor Leong Siew Chor looked like any ordinary Singaporean. Slightly built, bespectacled and balding, the 51-year-old was described as a loving father and husband by his family. He was seemingly not a danger to anyone. So, it came as quite a shock to everyone who knew him when he was arrested in connection with one of the most brutal murders that Singapore had seen in recent times. The body of 22-year-old Liu Hong Mei was hacked into seven pieces, stuffed into five cardboard boxes and plastic bags, and dumped in various locations. Madam Liu had worked as a production operator in a semiconductor company, Agere Systems Singapore, at Serangoon North Avenue 5. She was under Leong's supervision. She was also his lover.

Their love affair apparently turned sour after Madam Liu lost her POSB ATM card. She reported the loss to the police on June 14, 2005, and told her sister and a colleague that she had lost her bank card. Police later learnt that Leong had withdrawn a total of almost $2,000 from her account at different teller machines within cycling distance from his home. The next day, Madam Liu failed to turn up for work. She worked the same night shift as Leong, starting at 7.00 pm. On June 16, a box containing the lower torso of a woman was found by a cleaner along the shores of the Kallang River. Shortly after that, police discovered another box in the vicinity containing the upper torso of a woman. Further investigations revealed that other parts of the body might be at the Tuas South Incineration Plant. On June 18, while sieving through rubbish collected from the Singapore River, police officers retrieved a plastic bag containing a decomposed head. A further search into the rubbish uncovered a pair of lower limbs. The severed feet and the personal belongings of the deceased could not be found. DNA tests conducted by the Health Sciences Authority confirmed that all the dismembered parts belonged to Madam Liu's body.

Leong was charged with the murder of Madam Liu on the same day. He had done the horrible deed in his own Lorong 3 flat in Geylang on the morning of June 15. His wife and one child were away on holiday in Thailand; his two other children were not at home, though his daughter was due home by 6.00 pm. The actual killing was relatively straightforward—strangulation with a towel. Leong claimed that Madam Liu's death was part of a mutual suicide pact which he backed out of after seeing her turn blue. Leong said Madam Liu had wanted him to leave his family and return with her to China, but he had told her he couldn't bear to leave his family.

After her death, he had to dispose of her body. Imagine killing your lover in your own home, knowing that one of your daughters was due back in a few hours. His mind must have been racing. He didn't have the cover of night to steal away the body nor did he have a vehicle other than his bicycle. So he dragged the body into a toilet and started hacking it into seven pieces. He then systematically dumped the body parts. He cycled to the Kallang River and made two taxi trips to Clarke Quay and Boat Quay respectively where he disposed of some parts and then threw the other parts into the Singapore River. He said that he recalled a Chinese belief that ashes of the dead should be thrown into the sea in order to set the spirit free. But Leong showed attributes of a cold-blooded killer because he went to work on the same day he murdered Madam Liu. When a colleague informed him that Madam Liu had not turned up for work, he asked her to give Madam Liu a call to find out what had happened to her.

The police only caught up with Leong during the evening shift on the following day. Leong was convicted of murder and sentenced to death in May 2006. In August 2007, he failed in his second appeal to escape the gallows. A plea for clemency from the President also failed and Leong was hanged in November 2007.

The Kallang body parts case, as the media called it, was truly an unforgettable case. First, the photographs of the dismembered body were gruesome. I've seen some horrifying photographs in my life but these were the worst: legs here, a head there, some parts already decomposed. Some of the girls in the office felt nauseous looking at the photographs while others, strangely enough, were studying them with great intensity and commenting on the size of the bloated legs and the clarity of the colour photographs. I've noticed over the years that there are very different reactions to gruesome murder pictures. Some people feel nauseous and sick, some are drawn in a kind of morbid fascination, while others are indifferent.

(When I showed these photographs to my current colleagues, I recall a nasty trick I played in the 1970s on the three girls in my office, one of them my wife-to-be. On that day, I had forgotten to ask them to get me lunch. I was hungry and when they came back with their lunch, I beckoned them to my desk and said, "I've got something interesting to show you." I showed them photographs of a murder case I was working on. Two of them immediately lost their appetite. My future wife was not affected and I had two lunches that day.)

The body parts murder case attracted many people to the court hearings. It is no surprise to me that the gruesome cases tend to draw people out of the woodwork. There appears to be a thirst to find out details. I don't think it has anything to do with wanting to learn from the case to prevent the same thing happening to you. It's just a deep curiosity that's innate in most people. It's really difficult to put your finger on what drives this but it's always evident. Perhaps it's the same driving force you see when people gather around fatal traffic accident or murder scenes.

Right at the start, I could not understand why Madam Liu became involved in a relationship with Leong in the first place. He was married with grown-up children, while she was attractive and young. To better understand her motivations, I had to analyse why the affair took place. It could have been because he was a supervisor in a different department, got her transferred to his department and quickly promoted her. I think, being from China, Liu was interested in getting promoted and earning a better income. One would expect such factors to typically drive people who are settling down in a new country. So, she must have been grateful to him. In fact, there were complaints from other employees that the couple was kissing in the factory but nothing came out of the complaints.

As mentioned earlier, Leong said that his reason for killing her was that they had made a suicide pact. The prosecution, however, contended that he had killed her because he had taken her money and she had reported the theft to the police. The police was going to produce some CCTV photographs for Liu to see which would idenitfy the culprit. The prosecution's stand was that Leong was afraid that Liu would identify him. I asked Leong, "Why did you go and take the two thousand over dollars? Surely you're not that hard up for that money."

If I remember rightly, the theft of the ATM card occurred when they were in a room in Geylang. While she was taking a shower, he had looked into her handbag for a comb, saw the ATM card and took it. He knew her Personal Identification Number and that night he withdrew money from different teller machines.

I asked him: "You were doing quite well. You were having enough money for yourself. Why did you need to steal her money? I find this very odd. Why did you do that?"

His reply was strange. "I suppose it's greed," he said.

While the investigations were going on and when the public knew that I was acting for Leong, I received two phone calls informing me that my client had killed Liu because she was unfaithful to him. I asked the person on the line, "Why do you say that?" On both occasions the response was: "She was seen with other men. Mr Leong knew about it and that's the reason." I had to ignore the information because the people who gave it never came forward. But there may have been some truth to what they said. While Liu was supposed to be having a steady relationship with Leong, she was also registered with a dating agency, apparently to be introduced to other men in the hope of marriage. Was she thinking of leaving Leong because she realised that there was no future with him? We do not know.

Was there any other reason why Leong killed her? Was it because he was afraid that she would find out that he was a thief and report him to the police? If they were intimate, he could have easily confessed to her and asked for her forgiveness. Did he need to kill her because of that? I don't think so. Was there a need for a suicide pact? Would the suicide pact solve anything? What was he going to do? She was having a good job and he ostensibly had a stable family life. Why the sudden need for a suicide pact? Or was there any other reason that prompted him to kill her? There were so many questions that could not be answered in the course of the trial because Leong stuck to his suicide pact story. We just have to wonder about what really happened.

I can say though that Leong's family suffered a lot. Their flat was ransacked. Some people burnt joss sticks outside it while others threw things into the flat. They were eventually forced to move out to get some peace. I felt really sorry for his wife and the three children. They were very good children too. No one wanted to buy the flat and they had to sell it back to the Housing & Development Board at a loss. We had to prepare a Power of Attorney for Leong to sign for the flat to be sold back to the HDB. No one wanted to buy it because, generally, Asians believe that it is bad luck to live in a flat where a murder had been committed.

I visited Leong before he was executed. He had put on a lot of weight in prison. He was very calm and relaxed, nothing like the mad man when he was first charged in court. He told Sunil and I that he was very grateful for all that we had done for him and that he had no complaints. He knew that we had done our best for him and we had fought hard to save his life. But he said it was fated that he must hang and there was nothing we could do about it. He said that certain things cannot be prevented and this was just one of those things. He was quite philosophical. On the day I met him, he also told me that he had just shared his lunch with Tan Chor Jin, the One-eyed Dragon. They had become friends and talked to each other quite often. He was ready to go and was not afraid.

DEATH BY HANGING

Took's lawyer says overturning murder conviction is rare in appeals, but possible

A LAWYER'S HOPE

Dawn Chia
dawnchia@sph.com.sg

THERE is always hope. Took Leng How may have been sentenced to death for Huang Na's murder, but there are still avenues available to appeal against the verdict, says his lawyer Subhas Anandan (below).

He told The New Paper on Sunday last night that the first thing to do is to file a petition to the Court of Appeal.

Said Mr Subhas: "Since there are three judges looking at the documents, they might see something that the defence or prosecution might have missed.

"They are experienced and have been sitting there for years, and they know what to look out for. There is always hope with the Court of Appeal."

He added that Took has indicated he would appeal.

Mr Subhas, who has been practising law for 35 years, has achieved several notable successes on appeal cases.

In 1997, he convinced the Court of Appeal to overturn a conviction and free Mr Nadasan Chandra Secharan, then 42, who had been sentenced to death for the murder of his wife.

In 2003, he saved Tan Chun Seng, 28, from the gallows for killing deaf-mute Krishnan Sengal Rajah, 44, in Little India in 2001.

Upon appeal, Tan was jailed for 10 years for culpable homicide.

While it's rare for the Court of Appeal to overturn a conviction, Mr Subhas said that it is worth a try, especially if a person has been sentenced to death.

He added: "In Took's case, we don't kn chances of success yet.

"It's an uphill task trying to overturn conviction, but it has been done."

Even if the Court of Appeal dismiss petition, lawyers can still submit a cl petition to the President.

STUDY THE COMMENTS

The President will, on the ad Cabinet, study the comments Court of Appeal before he de commute (a legal term mea punishment to one that is sentence to life imprison

Mr Subhas explained want to go to the Court straight to submit a cl

"Making the clem President is like a n months, and Too Chinese New Ye his avenues for

(See report)

FRI NEWS

ONE-EYED DRAGON'S APPEAL

First, he acts arrogant in court

He then tries to defend himself...

... but makes a mess of it

Now, he makes U-turn

THE NEW PAPER

I want top man to fight for me

HE refused to have a lawyer to defend him on his capital charge. He was almost be-chap (couldn't be bothered throughout the trial cocky even when his life was at stake.

But now that he has been sentenced to death, Tan Chor Jin, 41, also known as the one-eyed Dragon, seems to have had a change of heart.

From "no need for a lawyer", now wants the best.

He has asked the State to assign criminal lawyer Subhas Anandan defend him.

He was convicted of discharging firearm with the intent to kill Mr Lim Hock Soon ...day, Mr Subhas, who is the ...ttarWong's criminal ...firmed that he will be

said that one of Tan's ...approve of the ...of the trial. But he ... it was too late to

Entering the trial ...day the ... would have

Lawyer Subhas Anandan say he is used to handling tough cases.

Tied up and shot

TAN Chor Jin, 41, was found guilty of discharging a firearm with intent to nightclub owner Lim Hock Soon, 41 last year.

Mr Lim's wife, teenage daughter and maid were also in the flat that morning when they barged in. He tied them up to tap the others Mr l also tied up.

Alone with then with a...

上诉判决保留

阿豪或有
一线生机

二奶跪求苏峇士

第2至4版

SEVENTEEN

ABDUL NASIR
A Landmark Case

Chocolate and milk—these were what Abdul Nasir bin Amer Hamsah loved most. Whatever spare cash he had, he would buy himself huge bars of chocolate and eat them in the morning, afternoon and night. He loved to drink milk too. This was reflected in his physique. He was a big man and looking at him you could see that he was strong. Abdul Nasir was also quite a good-looking person, and it ran in the family. His two sisters who came to court when I was defending him were really beautiful women. They had no make-up on, yet looked simply exquisite.

Abdul Nasir had gone for a job interview at the Oriental Hotel with his friend, Abdul Rahman bin Arshad. It was for a position as a bellboy. After the interview, the two friends decided to rob somebody as they were short of money. At about the same time, a busload of Japanese tourists arrived at the hotel. One of them was Isae Fujii, who was visiting Singapore for the first time. In fact, it was the first time she had ever left Japan. She took a lift with her roommate Miyoko Takishita to the ninth floor where they had been allocated a room. By chance, Abdul Nasir and Abdul Rahman had, minutes before, taken a lift to the same floor and were hiding at the end of the corridor. When the women entered the room, Abdul Nasir and Abdul Rahman rushed in after them and each attacked one woman. The petite Japanese women, who were in Singapore on a company-sponsored holiday, were both overpowered and knocked down to the floor. The men took their valuables and fled the scene. Takishita survived the robbery but Fujii didn't. Abdul Nasir had stamped on her face and hit her so badly that her nose broke and her jaw bone cracked.

According to forensic pathologist Dr Paul Chui, Fujii suffocated to death because of her facial injuries. He testified that she had six fractures on her face which caused swelling in the tissues as well as bleeding into the tissues of the nasal passage. The jaw fracture also caused her tongue to block air from entering her lungs.

Police found a palm print, including a thumbprint, on the wall of the room. However, they were not able to trace whom the prints belonged to because, at that time, only fingerprints of known criminals were available in the police database. Abdul Nasir did not have a record. As there were no further leads, the case was put aside.

Some 18 months later in Woodlands, Abdul Nasir attempted to rob and strangle a taxi driver. While trying to escape, he was caught by police and arrested for attempted robbery and attempted murder. At the Criminal Investigation Department (CID), his fingerprints were taken and sent to be cross-checked against recorded fingerprints. It was then discovered that the fingerprints found at the Oriental Hotel murder scene belonged to Abdul Nasir.

Investigations into the attempted robbery and attempted murder of the taxi driver were shelved, and Abdul Nasir found himself facing a murder charge. He confessed to being one of the robbers at the hotel. On the back of his statement, his friend Abdul Rahman was also arrested and subsequently sentenced to 10 years jail for the charge of robbery with causing hurt. But since Abdul Nasir had inflicted the deadly blow on Fujii, he was charged with murder. I was assigned to defend him and I chose Amolat Singh as my assisting counsel. At that time, the press referred to us as "Batman and Robin".

We went to see Abdul Nasir and received his instructions. He admitted that he had punched Fujii and that she had fallen heavily. He explained that he had bent down to take her wallet and as he was getting up, he felt dizzy because of some pills he had taken earlier. To balance himself, he held on to the wall, but it did not help and he fell on her. It was accidental. In one of the statements he made to the police, Abdul Nasir stated that he had stamped on her face. According to him, however, he had told the interpreter that he had stepped on her face but she wrote "stamped". I cross-examined the interpreter very strenuously on this matter. She admitted that though the Malay word he used was "stepped", he had demonstrated to her a stamping action. The demonstration was a stamping action but his word was "stepped". She finally conceded that it was not her business to interpret the action but to translate exactly what he had said. We argued that the fingerprints on the wall were the result of Abdul Nasir having to steady himself and that the stepping on the victim's face was accidental. There was no intention to cause death or any injury.

Of course the deputy public prosecutor's interpretation was different. He said Abdul Nasir was holding on to the wall to steady himself so that he could use force to stamp on the victim's face. Our counter-argument was that if that was so, why wasn't he charged for murder under the particular limp where the intention was to cause death and nothing else. The charge said "an act which is likely to cause death". It was a technical argument, but if there was truth in what the DPP said, the charge had to reflect an intention to kill. The charge did not reflect this. There were arguments all around and judgment was reserved for Justice Choo Han Teck to give his verdict.

The DPP in this case was Francis Seng who was then the acting head of crime in the Attorney-General's Chambers. He had not come to court for a long time as he had been doing mostly administrative work, but he participated in this trial as it was a high profile case. The Japanese TV media was covering the proceedings, and with the Japanese government and population upset over the incident, the Singapore government was going to make sure that justice was done as they didn't want the incident to stop Japanese tourists from visiting Singapore.

We also cross-examined the forensic pathologist on the force used by Abdul Nasir and matters related to it. I believe the pathologist was quite new as his evidence was not convincing. He tended to side with the defence a little more than expected. The judge also made Abdul Nasir draw the tread pattern of the shoes that he was wearing at the time. According to Abdul Nasir, he was wearing heavy boots and the soles were essentially of metal. He showed the design and if you look at the drawing you would know that if the shoe had landed on somebody's face, it would definitely cause great damage.

All these points were argued and taken into consideration. The verdict was to be given at about 4.00 or 5.00 pm. The registrar, Mr Chiam Boon Keng, came up to court and said: "After the conviction, whatever application you wish to make for the disposal of the exhibits, please make it in chambers because it would be quite messy after the death sentence is passed because of the emotions in open court."

I remember telling Chiam, "What do you mean when the death sentence is passed? We do not know yet whether he would be convicted or not."

Chiam replied, "Okay, I'm sorry, but I just thought that he would be convicted."

At 5.00 pm, Justice Choo came back into court and acquitted my client of murder. He believed that there was no intention to kill and it was possible that what Abdul Nasir said could be true. He was giving him the benefit of the doubt. He sentenced my client to 18 years for the other charge of robbery with hurt. We were very happy that we got an acquittal. I remember Abdul Nasir thanking me and I told him he was not going to get any chocolates and milk in prison. He laughed as I left the court to meet his sisters who were very grateful. We thought that this would be the end of the matter. But the prosecution was not happy with the decision and appealed.

The Court of Appeal comprised Justice of Appeal M Karthigesu, who was the presiding judge, Justice of Appeal L P Thean and Justice Goh Joon Seng. There was a split decision. The appeal was dismissed with the sentence to stay. Justice Karthigesu and Justice Goh dismissed the appeal. Justice Thean, in a dissenting judgment, was in favour of allowing the appeal. It came as a surprise to me because as I was arguing the case before the Court of Appeal, I thought that Justice Thean was with me—he was nodding his head and asking questions while the other two were quiet. So, when I was told that there was a dissenting judgment and Justice Thean will read his dissenting judgment after the majority judgment had been read, I thought: "Oh my God, that means I've lost the appeal." I thought Justice Thean was going to dismiss the appeal and the other two would be allowing the appeal but it happened the other way around. I don't know why Justice Thean dissented. Today, although we are senior consultants at KhattarWong, I've never asked him why. I don't think it's fair to do that.

Abdul Nasir escaped by the skin of his teeth and he was taken to prison. We thought that that was the end of the matter but it wasn't. The prosecution brought on a charge of kidnapping a police officer while in custody in the CID. With another detainee, Abdul Nasir had held a female police officer and asked for ransom—they wanted a getaway car, a gun and some money. While negotiations were under way, an elite police squad burst into the detention area where Nasir and his accomplice were holding the policewoman captive. They were arrested and subsequently charged with kidnapping. Abdul Nasir's accomplice was later found guilty of drug trafficking and sentenced to death. I suppose the authorities were hoping that Abdul Nasir would also receive a death sentence for the murder of Fujii. When he didn't, they brought the kidnapping charge on him. Abdul Nasir again asked for me to be his defence counsel. I believe he had some faith in me. I got Amolat Singh to assist me once again.

We went to visit him in prison to take his instructions. I asked him, "Why the hell did you do this?" He said: "First I was arrested for robbing a taxi driver. When I was brought to the CID, the police said I would be charged for the murder of a Japanese lady. I was in shock, confused and worried."

That day itself he had bought some milk and six bars of chocolate which were kept by the police while he was in custody. It seemed he asked for them but his request was turned down. He claimed that he quarrelled with the police officer, demanding to know why he couldn't have his own things. He said that he would eat the chocolates in front of them to allay any fears they might have but they refused. He saw other inmates enjoying food that their families had brought for them or they had brought themselves. He was frustrated and said to this particular detainee: "Hey, look, since both of us are going to hang, why don't we kidnap the woman police officer?" They decided that they might not succeed on their own and asked two other detainees to assist. Those detainees were going to be charged for a possession of firearm offence which would also have given them a life sentence. (One of them eventually became my client. He pleaded guilty and received life imprisonment.) They initially agreed to join Abdul Nasir and his new accomplice but decided against it at the last moment as they felt it would not succeed. So, Nasir and the other detainee carried out their plan to kidnap the police officer. The plan was simple. They decided that one of them would pretend to be ill and the other would call for help. The plan worked in that they managed to get a hold of the officer. I thought that the incident would not have happened if the police had given Abdul Nasir his milk and chocolates.

The kidnap case went to trial. Amolat and I produced the accomplice who said it was all his idea and that Abdul Nasir had played a very passive role. We tried to argue this case by referring to the Hansard parliamentary reports that this was not the type of kidnapping legislators had in mind when they passed the law. It was to prevent rich people from being taken for ransom. But looking at the law strictly, you could fit in any sort of situation, even Abdul Nasir's.

Finally, Justice Sam Sinnathuray, who heard the case, found him guilty and asked for arguments in the afternoon for sentence. DPP Madhavan, who is now a lecturer in a polytechnic, argued for the death sentence. He put forward a very strong case. I counter-argued that the death sentence should not be imposed and gave the reasons. After listening to our arguments, Justice Sinnathuray reserved the sentence to the late afternoon. When he returned, he sentenced Abdul Nasir to life imprisonment but ruled that Abdul Nasir would serve the life imprisonment only after serving the sentence for armed robbery which Justice Choo had imposed. This meant that the life sentence and the sentence of 18 years would run consecutively. He said it did not make sense that the sentences be allowed to run concurrently because Abdul

Nasir had committed two very serious offences.

I was quite happy with the verdict because as far as I was concerned, I had saved Abdul Nasir from the gallows twice. I told him to be satisfied with the outcome. Life imprisonment, which is 20 years less the one-third remission for good behaviour, means only 13 years. So, he had 13 years plus 12 years—that is, plus the 18 years less the one-third remission—totalling 25 years which he had to serve. He would still be a young man after his sentence. Abdul Nasir was 25 years old at the time of the Oriental Hotel incident in 1994. I advised him to forget about appealing.

Abdul Nasir asked for me to visit him again in prison because he wanted me to argue the appeal that he had taken upon himself to lodge. I told the registrar that I was not interested and I didn't think that he should be assigned any counsel anymore as there was no death sentence involved. I was not going to argue it as I thought the sentence was fair. Justice Sinnathuray could have imposed the death sentence and justified it if he wanted to. He had shown Abdul Nasir some compassion.

Abdul Nasir was not happy. He filed and argued his appeal on his own. After listening to his appeal, the Court of Appeal decided that it would be dismissed. On studying the matter further, the Court of Appeal concluded that it was incorrect to interpret life imprisonment as a 20-year imprisonment. Life imprisonment should be till the end of natural life with entitlement to parole after 20 years. Abdul Nasir was not affected by this change because it was to apply to all future cases. So, because of this case, Abdul Nasir vs the Public Prosecutor, the interpretation of the law was changed from "life" to "natural life". I don't know if Abdul Nasir realised what he had done but if he did, I suppose he wouldn't care.

EIGHTEEN

MUHAMMAD NASIR
The 16-Year-Old Lover

They say that sometimes justice and law are distant cousins. In the case of some countries, you'll be lucky to say that justice and law have the same parents. In Singapore's case, it is sad to say that sometimes we feel that justice and law seem to be indifferent to each other. The law says something but when it is interpreted in the courts, it says something else. Most of the time, it is to the detriment of the accused person. This is sad. If it is not kept in check, one day we'll come to a stage when justice and law will not only be indifferent to each other, it can be hostile. That will be a sad day for Singapore.

The case in question is that of 16-year-old Muhammad Nasir Abdul Aziz who killed his lover's husband, Manap Sarlip, at Whampoa Drive in 2007. Singaporeans were shocked when they read that a disc jockey had been found dead outside his flat. He had been stabbed viciously in the chest and through the neck several times. Any of the stab wounds would have been fatal. Police called the victim's wife, Aniza Essa, who was sleeping inside the flat, for her statement and let her go after recording it.

In most cases, when one spouse is killed, the other is always high on the list of suspects. I believe even though she was released after questioning, Aniza was high on the police's suspect list. Investigations revealed that her marriage was an unhappy one. Manap had been known to assault his wife, taking money from her to settle his debts. For Manap, it was his second marriage—he had a child from the first marriage. He had also gone to prison for going AWOL while serving national service in the Civil Defence Force. Out of prison, he was apparently even nastier to Aniza who had been holding two jobs in his absence, trying to support their child and Manap's child from his previous marriage.

Aniza was working at Razcals Pub on Beach Road and young Nasir used to frequent the bar. The fact that he was below the legal drinking age seemed to be of no significance to anyone in the bar. If you look at Nasir, you'll know straight away that he must be below 18 years old. Still, he was served his favourite drinks. He struck a rapport with Aniza, who was eight years older than him, and she would tell him her problems. Nasir also shared his problems with Aniza but they weren't as serious as hers. Nasir left school early to take care of his father's shop when his father suffered a stroke and couldn't walk properly.

When a vacancy for a bartender came up at Razcals, Nasir applied for the job even though he had no experience in bartending. Since the owner knew him as a customer, he was prepared to take him in and teach him the ropes. The owner taught Nasir how to mix drinks and also asked Aniza to help him. Nasir became a bartender working alongside Aniza. Their friendship blossomed. They would go for supper after work and would take the same transport that the pub provided back to their respective homes. They soon became lovers. Nasir had his first sexual encounter with Aniza at the pub, when both of them were there early one day. From then on, they continued to have these early sex encounters at Razcals.

To the 16-year-old boy, Aniza was the most beautiful thing in his life. He didn't realise that she was manipulating him. She kept on emphasising the problems she was having with her husband and told Nasir that she could not tolerate looking at her husband's face anymore. Nasir told her many times to divorce him but her answer was always no. "He'll never give me a divorce. Even if we are divorced, he'll come back to pester me," she said. I was defending Nasir and it appeared to me that she was subtly telling Nasir that the only way to solve her problem was for her husband to disappear—in other words, she wanted him dead.

Aniza broached the subject with Nasir about having her husband dead, saying that it would prove his love for her if he killed Manap. When Nasir was hesitant, she said: "Look, if you don't want to and are afraid, my ex-boyfriend is prepared to do it. If he did it, I would have to leave you and return to him because he killed my husband for me. You would be out of my life." When Nasir heard this, he was afraid he would lose her and agreed to do it. He made one attempt to kill Manap but didn't have the heart to carry it out. He told Aniza that he was unable to kill him as a neighbour had come by. Aniza was furious with him. She told him: "This is an excuse I cannot accept. I think you can't do it. So why don't I ask my ex-boyfriend to do it." Nasir replied: "Don't worry, I've got somebody else to do it for you. He knows a hired assassin who will do it."

Nasir didn't realise that his friend was just boasting that he knew how to hire assassins. At first, the friend had asked for $500 for the assassin, who was supposedly a Thai. When Nasir agreed to the sum, the amount was raised to $4,000. Nasir wasn't daunted. He said he could still afford it and told his friend to instruct the assassin to do the job. His friend even asked him for a photo of Aniza's husband. Nasir duly got a photo from Aniza and told her that he had made all the arrangements. Days passed but nothing happened to Manap.

Nasir called his friend but he was avoiding him. The friend had by then realised that Nasir was serious about the matter and prepared to pay the $4,000. There was no assassin after all and, in his mind, Nasir had little choice as to what he had to do if he wanted to keep Aniza as his girlfriend. She had threatened to leave him and return to her ex-boyfriend who was apparently prepared to do the deed. (To this day, nobody knows whether she had lied about the ex-boyfriend.) Nasir was so in love with Aniza that he could not live without her. So he decided he might as well do what she wanted.

He told her not to worry and assured her that he would kill Manap. Aniza instructed him: "Don't contact me. I will contact you. I will contact you with my friend's phone. It's best that we don't have any communication during this period." Nasir agreed. That night they left the pub together. Nasir had a knife and his crash helmet with him which he would use to disguise himself. He went to Whampoa Drive and waited for Manap. He had been told by Aniza that if he was asked why he was there, he was to say that he was going to borrow a video tape from Aniza. Finally, Manap returned home and saw Nasir outside the flat. He knew Nasir because he had seen him before, but before he could react, Nasir stabbed him in the neck a few times. As Manap collapsed, he asked Nasir: "Why are you doing this? I've done you no harm." Nasir just shook his head because he knew what Manap said was true. He had done Nasir no wrong, but Nasir had stabbed and killed him because Aniza wanted him to do it. As Nasir was running down to the next floor to take the lift, he heard groans from upstairs. Realising that Manap had not died and that he could identify him, he ran up the steps and stabbed him again. This time, he stabbed him through the chest to make sure that he was dead. Then wearing his helmet, he ran back home.

Although the police had released Aniza after taking an initial statement from her, they arrested her a few days later. They had managed to trace earlier phone calls between her and Nasir which indicated that there was a plot to kill her husband. At the police station, she broke down during questioning and confessed to the whole scheme. But in her confession she put the entire blame on Nasir, saying he had initiated the move to kill her husband. She made it look as though her role in the murder was minor and Nasir had masterminded the whole plot. The police arrested Nasir and told him that they knew everything, that Aniza had confessed, that there was no point in lying, and that it was better that he told the truth.

Upon learning what Aniza had told the police, Nasir lost his cool and related everything that had happened. He said he did it for the love of Aniza and related how her repeated threats to leave him forced his hand. He managed to convince the police that he was telling the truth. The police questioned Aniza again and after looking at all the evidence, decided that it was Aniza who had made use of Nasir. She had everything to gain with her husband's death. Both of them were charged with murder.

I was briefed to act for Nasir. Aniza was represented by my close friend, Noor Marican. After a few appearances in court, the prosecution decided that Aniza would be charged on a lesser offence of culpable homicide not amounting to murder. The charge against Aniza was reduced because a psychiatrist from the Institute of Mental Health certified that she was going through depression and that it impaired her thinking. As such she was entitled to the defence of diminished responsibility which is an exception to the charge of murder. I was very surprised that the prosecution readily accepted the psychiatrist's report and reduced the charge against her based on that report. In many cases, the prosecution demands a second psychiatric opinion.

Noor Marican was, of course, very happy that the charge was reduced and had his client plead guilty to the reduced charge. The prosecution, in their statement of facts, focused the blame squarely on Aniza, stating that she was the main cause of the tragedy. She had instigated Nasir to commit the act and the statement of facts disclosed that she manipulated Nasir. The prosecution asked for the maximum sentence, that is, life imprisonment, on Aniza. But Justice Chan Seng Onn, who heard Aniza's case, did not impose it. Instead, he imposed a sentence of nine years and since she was a woman, she would not be caned. With good behaviour, she could be released in six years because of one-third remission for good behaviour. The sentence was also backdated to the time of arrest. In essence, it meant that she would serve about five years before being released from prison.

In the meantime, we wrote to the prosecution to reduce the charge for Nasir, saying that they had themselves admitted that Nasir was manipulated by Aniza. Although she did not do the actual stabbing, it was quite clear that she was responsible for my client holding the knife. In fact, in my mitigation for Nasir, I called Aniza a manipulative monster but it would have been fairer to call her a mad manipulative monster. The prosecution did not want to reduce the charge for Nasir. They said it had to be murder and since he was below 18 years at the time of offence, he would not be sentenced to death but would instead be held under the President's pleasure. In other words, Nasir could be held for a very long time until the President decides when he should be released. In my experience, people who are held under the President's pleasure stay at least 10 to 12 years in prison. I said it was not fair that Aniza would be released in less than six years and this boy, who was clearly manipulated by her, should pay such a heavy penalty.

We wrote many representations to the prosecution with all the factors in favour of Nasir. Every representation was turned down and the prosecution insisted that they had to go on a charge of murder. I believe they were afraid that if they reduced the charge, Nasir might get the same sentence as Aniza or even less. The prosecution did not want that to happen. I don't know why they wanted Nasir kept in prison for such a long time, especially when he had shown so much remorse and cooperated with the police. According to the psychiatrist's evaluation, he showed remorse. He realised that he had been made use of by Aniza. He was just a tool for her vengeance. His love for her turned to hatred because he now knew how she had used him. There was no love left in him for her. Everything we could throw into our mitigation, including remorse, was not accepted by the prosecution. They insisted on charging him for murder.

For the first time in the legal history of Singapore, a person was allowed to plead guilty in a capital case without the prosecution calling witnesses to prove its case. Justice Kan Ting Chiu, who heard Nasir's case, agreed that there was no need to waste everybody's time by calling witnesses, when I as defence counsel, assisted by my nephew Sunil, had agreed that there was no need for it. We had advised our client of his rights and there was an agreed statement of facts which clearly brought out the ingredients of the charge. Nasir was prepared to accept the statement of facts.

The DPP Tan Kiat Peng, who was assisted by DPP Samuel Chua, was not happy, stating that it might lead to criticism. The judge laughed and said: "The only person who should be worried about any criticism would be the defence counsel who is experienced enough to advise his client, and he told me that his client had no problem with the agreed statement of facts. So, you take instructions from your superiors in the afternoon and tell me whether we have to go through the fuss of calling all these witnesses for nothing because I can still rule against you." The DPP returned in the afternoon and said they were not very happy but would leave it to the court. The judge said: "Well, I'll just agree to the statement of facts and Mr Anandan has already explained to the accused of the consequences. That's good enough for me."

It was also the first time that we were allowed to state points in our client's favour as our mitigation. Normally, when a person is found guilty of murder, there is no mitigation as there is no other sentence but the death sentence. In this particular case, as there was no death sentence due to his youth, the case would be reviewed periodically by the President. The judge allowed me to point out those facts that were in Nasir's favour so that when the authorities review his case, they would know what sort of a person he is. I raised all the mitigating factors: how a 16-year-old boy had been manipulated, how he thought his lover was so great and how he was not prepared to lose her.

Nasir had written a letter to the judge acknowledging that he was foolish. (A section is reproduced on page 209.) He thought that his love would last forever but he now realised that it doesn't. In it, Nasir asked the judge for a chance to reform. It was a very touching letter in which he described his feelings and explained why he killed Manap. The judge said that he understood what my client and I were trying to tell him but under the law, his hands were tied and he had no choice but to send him to prison at the President's pleasure. He also pointed out to Nasir that no matter what he said, he was still responsible for causing the death of a man. Nasir just nodded and was taken away.

I had a chat with Nasir just before he was taken away. He thanked me for all that I had done for him and he said he would try to study in prison. I told him that if he had any problems with the authorities, he could let me know. I would arrange for him to do his 'O' and 'A' level exams. He was going to be there for a long time. The judge was kind enough to allow his family to have a word with him in court. There were a lot of tears. When I was walking out of the court with Sunil and my intern, Michelle Chua, Nasir's family who was outside stopped us. They held my hand and thanked me for my work on the case. I told them that I couldn't do very much. However, they were very grateful for the points of my mitigation. The press had asked to interview the family but they declined.

That was the end as far as the case was concerned, but when I went back to my office, I started thinking about how ridiculous Nasir's situation was. Here was a woman who had instigated and practically caused the death of her husband and who would serve less than six years in jail, while a boy, still in his youth and completely under the control of this woman, would spend a longer time in jail. He was madly in love with her and she would use sex to entice him to do anything for her. She even threatened to leave him. She did everything possible to ensure that this boy would heed her demands. Where is the justice in this case? Where is the fairness? I believe the judge wanted to show compassion but had no choice. He had no opportunity to show any compassion as the law decreed that Nasir had to be sent to prison under the President's pleasure. The judge's hands were tied.

Why didn't the prosecution reduce the charge? Wouldn't that be fair if the charge for the main culprit was to be reduced for whatever reason? Shouldn't the prosecution have given this 16-year-old boy the same chance? Many a time the prosecution has erred in exercising its prosecutory prerogative which is so rigid and strong that compassion is considered a weakness. Why they must take such a tough stand,

I cannot understand. Reducing Nasir's charge to culpable homicide would have been the fairest thing to do. In this case, justice and law were not distant cousins. They were total strangers.

Number ___RC5540/07___   Name ___Muh'd Nasir Bin Abd Aziz___

___Queenstown Remand___ Prison

Singapore (   )

Date _12.04.08_

Your Honour,

My name is Muh'd Nasir Bin Abd Aziz and im currently as remanded inmate at Queenstown Remand prison. I am writing this mitigation as to hope that the judge refering to your Honour judging on my case, at the most possible to have me sentence at a very light and a very least possible sentence. I'm very sorry for what i have done, I wish i had never met anisa in any way at all to have her in my life and i wish i had never listen for follow what ever she had asked me to do. I'm very remorsefull of being influence by her and because of her, a man who was not guilty had been murdered by me. I'm the second and last child in my family. I have a brother and a father who had brought me up well. My father and my mother had a divorce earlier on when i was only two month. At that time i was only a child and i didn't receive a love from a mother before. I don't know how it feels to have a mother by my side every time. I didn't receive it before but i received it from my father instead. My father by the name of Abdul Aziz is a handicap ever since he was in his early twenties. He had a tragic accident and lost one leg and now walking on a plastic leg. He owns a stall around Bedok and it was me and my brother who operates the stall but every since things happen this way, my father had to rent out the shop and my brother is now as a speedpost driver. He's the currently the sole bread winner. My brother by the name of Muh'd Khamil is the one supporting my father and himself now because i'm not around to help my father to operate the stall. Now my father is sick again as he just had recovered from a brain tumor past two years. When he came to visit me in prison he could not afford to even have a check on his health just because im not around to support him. I actually quited school just to take over my father stall because he was in coma. I was in secondary then when i quited school. Although my father wanted me to continue my studies but i was didn't want his business to fall apart that is why i didn't continue studying. I know now that i have let them down and i wish i had a chance to pay them back for all their support. All this incident happen because anisa suggested the killing though i convince her to have a divorce but she was the one who said her husband will never let her go but although but i just wish i didn't have met her in my life at all. She even told me that she had a friend to do it, and she reassure me if i never do it i have to leave here and her friend will do it. I was so threaten that i myself didn't know why i was afraid to lose her. After everything she even for everything, instructed me and told me not to do. She even asked me to delete everything im in my phone and act normal as if nothing had happened. I did everything because i was afraid to lose her. Even on that day, she told me if the police were to call me up and investigate me, she asked me to say that i had come to borrow a DVD by the title of "American Pie" which is mine. I'm very remorseful and very sorry i have committed an offence which is against the law. I'm so sorry for so stupid to listen to her and murder an innocent man. Now i pray and i hope dat your honour will at least have leaniency and give a second chance to have a bright future. It's all because of anisa, my future is gone but now my hope is in the hands of god and the

ANTHONY LER
That Certain Smile

The case of Anthony Ler was particularly heinous and tagged the crime story of 2001 because it set loose a range of emotions amongst Singaporeans. There were three things that struck members of the public as they looked on in morbid fascination during the trial: How could a man kill the mother of his own daughter? How could he coach a teenage boy to commit murder? How could he put his young daughter in a position in which she ended up with no parents?

Ler did all these things. He was accused and convicted of abetting in the murder of his estranged wife Annie Leong Wai Muen, an insurance agent. In May 2001, Ler had enticed a 15-year-old boy to murder the mother of his own four-year-old child by offering him $100,000 and the promise of beautiful women. Because of his youth, the 15-year-old could not be named in the newspapers. While Ler was hanged for his part in the crime, the youth escaped hanging because he was too young and was detained at the President's pleasure. It is believed that the boy, now in his early twenties, is still detained.

Some people have likened Ler's case to the O J Simpson trial, albeit a watered down version. The local media recklessly added to the sensationalism by showing a smiling Ler chatting with policemen. During his trial, Ler tried to defend himself by claiming that the idea to murder Madam Leong had been a joke. However, the motivation behind the murder was greed as Ler's web design business was apparently in dire financial straits and he was in need of cash. He wanted his wife out of the way so he could, as the sole owner, sell their flat. Ler offered the boy money to do the deed. Together, they plotted out the details.

Ler arranged for his wife to sign some documents with him. Meanwhile, the boy lay in wait for her to return to her flat on the fourth floor of Block 923 Hougang Avenue 9. Without suspecting that anything could be amiss, Madam Leong went down to the void deck of the block with her four-year-old daughter to meet Ler. Apparently, she went back to her flat without her daughter and was less than 50 metres away from the flat when she was attacked. She staggered towards the front door and collapsed in her mother's arms. She was bleeding profusely and died later in Tan Tock Seng Hospital. Madam Leong's mother later told police that Ler appeared only a few minutes later, saying he was at the void deck and had heard screams. He supposedly told his wife not to close her eyes and to try to stay awake. A neighbour noted that his daughter had come up with him.

Fingers were pointing at Ler as soon as the murder was reported in the media on May 17, 2001. Some members of the public even said he had hired someone to kill his wife though the motives were unclear until the case reached the courts. Ler was apprehended with evidence found in his computer by the CID's Technology Crime Forensic Branch, Technology Crime Division. After the murder, to avoid being overheard, Ler and the boy had communicated by typing messages to each other using Ler's computer. They did this sitting side by side in Ler's flat. Even though Ler had not saved the files in his computer, the police were able to retrieve the correspondence using advanced software. The communication between them led to Ler's downfall because it offered hard evidence of his involvement in the case.

I went to Queenstown Remand Prison to take instructions on the evidence given to me by the prosecution. I showed Anthony Ler the messages between him and the boy from the computer. He was shocked and asked me how they could recover the evidence when he had erased them. I told him it was possible and legal. He just looked at me and for once, he lost his silly smile.

There are similarities in the cases of Aniza Essa and Anthony Ler. Both had enticed young boys to commit a serious crime. Ler used a 15-year-old boy while Aniza goaded her 16-year-old lover. Both manipulated the egos of the teenagers. Initially, Ler had chosen and trained the boy's friend to do the act but the friend had backed out. The 15-year-old boy had been very hurt and asked Ler, "Why did you choose him when you knew me first? I can do the job. I'm better than him." And when, at the final moment, he had a change of mind, Ler sarcastically said, "It's not as easy as you think, is it?" Similarly, Aniza used the threat of asking her ex-lover to do the deed if Nasir "can't do it" knowing that the boy was very much in love with her and could not bear to lose her.

The tragedy in both these cases is that youths were employed by adults to commit murders. Ler was sentenced to death. He has been executed and I believe his last wish was to donate his organs, perhaps in atonement for what he did. In contrast, Aniza will be out in five to six years' time. But the prosecution has appealed against the sentence on Aniza. It is for the Court of Appeal to decide whether she'll get life or something else.

When Anthony Ler's mother came to see me, she was like most mothers—desperate to save her son in any way possible. I was not keen to take on the case. I had been following the investigations in the newspapers and was a little perturbed with the smile that appeared on every photo published by the press. It almost always seemed a permanent fixture on his face. But when I heard his mother's plea and saw the tears in her eyes, I just couldn't say no to her. I thought of my own mother and how she would have felt if something similar happened to me or my siblings. And so I agreed to defend him.

When I first went to see him at Queenstown Remand Prison, I really didn't know what to expect. He was already seated in an interview room waiting for me. As I entered the room, he politely stood up and shook my hand even though his other hand was handcuffed to a hook on the wall. The first thing I noticed was his smile. It was a smile that could be interpreted in so many ways. That smile could be a sneer, it could be a smile of confidence, or it could be one that belies some deep fear. For some reason, I have never related his smile to one of happiness. Throughout the trial, he wore that smile and he kept that smile even when giving evidence. Somehow, I felt it was his security blanket. Maybe I was right. I was not the only person who wondered about that enigmatic smile. Even the media mentioned it.

On the day of his execution and cremation, a crime reporter by the name of Vijayan called me to ask whether I would be attending Ler's funeral. Of course, I said no. It is not my practice to attend my clients' funerals. Later, Vijayan told me that only Ler's brother was at the funeral. Nobody else came.

A few days later, I had to go to the Condemned Prison to visit another client. When I was there, I asked the officer whether Anthony Ler was smiling when he was walking to the gallows. The officer did not reply. He just smiled at me.

TWENTY

TAN CHOR JIN
The One-Eyed Dragon

When you hear the words 'Las Vegas', your first thoughts would normally be of casinos, gambling, pretty girls and the United States. But Las Vegas in Singapore means something else; it refers to the well-known Las Vegas Nightclub KTV. I used to go there with my clients, and sometimes with my friends, to have a drink and some fun singing in our own private room so that no one will find out what fools we are all making of ourselves. Every time I'm there, the owner, Lim Hock Soon, who was fondly referred to as Lim Piggy because he was fat, would greet me with something like, "Hello lawyer, how are you?" I would return the greeting with, "Hello, how are you? How's your business?" He would reply it was good and would then ask me about my business. I would say, "Not too bad," and walk into the room to sing. Sometimes my friends and I would just sit in the hall to listen to a girl sing and we'd watch other people make fools of themselves.

One day I read in the papers that Lim Piggy had been shot dead by the notorious Tan Chor Jin aka One-eyed Dragon. I knew for a fact that Tan was one of the top hitmen for a very powerful gang in Singapore called Ang Soon Tong. Only able to see with one eye, he was known for his brutality and ruthlessness in his dealings with his enemies. The press reported that Lim was shot dead by One-eyed Dragon on the morning of February 15, 2006. Six shots had been fired into him and it was done at his home in front of his wife and maid. Singapore was rocked by this news because it is very rare to have cases of gun assassinations on the island. The punishment for possession of guns is very severe and the punishment for discharging a firearm is death.

One-eyed Dragon escaped to Malaysia but through the close cooperation of the Singapore and Malaysian police forces, he was apprehended in a five-star hotel in Kuala Lumpur. From what I gathered, the lead was given to the police in KL by Lim's own gang members who were also looking for One-eyed Dragon and had tipped off the police. One-eyed Dragon was extradited to Singapore and promptly charged with Lim's murder. His family engaged a lawyer to represent him in his defence. One-eyed Dragon was produced in Court 26 and charged with murder. He was held without bail because for a capital case like murder, no bail was allowed.

The prosecution subsequently found it easier to amend the murder charge to one of discharging a firearm. Under the Firearms Act, this also carries a sentence of death. It was easier to prove a case against One-eyed Dragon under the amended charge because in a murder charge, you have to prove an intention to kill among other things that you don't have to prove under the Firearms Act. In the latter charge, the prosecution only needed to show that One-eyed Dragon had discharged his firearm and the discharge had caused the death of a person.

One-eyed Dragon craved cigarettes. Each time he was charged and brought to court, he would make a request to the magistrate or judge for cigarettes. But his request was always turned down because in Singapore, prisoners are not allowed to have cigarettes. One-eyed Dragon suffered severe withdrawal symptoms and dismissed his lawyer because he said the lawyer didn't seem to be able to do anything for him—he couldn't get the cigarettes he wanted and he also wasn't able to prevent him from being held in the psychiatric ward at Changi Prison. One-eyed Dragon felt that he should be held in Queenstown Remand Prison.

His trial started in the High Court before Justice Tay Yong Kwang. When the judge asked him whether he wanted an assigned counsel, saying if he wanted one, he would be given one—in fact two, a senior lawyer and an assistant—he refused. He said that he would represent himself and that he was capable of defending himself. The trial went on for a few weeks and One-eyed Dragon, from what I read from the Notes of Evidence, did his best to cross-examine witnesses of the prosecution as well as the expert witnesses. He was allowed to call a psychiatrist to show that he was intoxicated and, as such, was not able to formulate any intention to kill or to shoot Lim. However, according to One-eyed Dragon, the psychiatrist played him out at the trial by giving evidence that he did not expect. One-eyed Dragon could have misunderstood him. The psychiatrist was well known and what he told One-eyed Dragon was that in a charge of murder, intoxication and other factors could help reduce it to one of culpable homicide, but these factors no longer counted when his charge was amended to one under the Firearms Act. One-eyed Dragon found it very difficult to accept that and called the psychiatrist all sorts of names. The poor psychiatrist may have regretted coming to court as his witness.

When the time came for the final submission, One-eyed Dragon told Justice Tay that he needed a lawyer. He said he was not capable of summing up as he didn't know how to. This request was turned down by the trial judge, which I thought was wrong and unfair. Just because One-eyed Dragon had decided that he didn't want a lawyer at the beginning of the trial did not mean that he should be denied one later. As expected, One-eyed Dragon was sentenced to death by the trial judge.

When One-eyed Dragon was taken to the condemned cell and asked to file his Notice of Appeal and Petition of Appeal, he realised again that he needed a lawyer. His wife and one of his gang members approached me and asked me to be his defence counsel. They told me that they did not have the money but would try to pay my fee somehow. I proposed that they request the government to assign me to the case so that they need not pay my fees. Since One-eyed Dragon had told his wife that he wanted only me to act for him in his appeal, I suggested he make this request to the registrar of the Supreme Court. He did and later that day I received a call from the registrar asking me if I would take on the case. I said I would and the case was assigned to me. I asked for my nephew, Sunil, to be the assisting counsel.

Usually, the assisting counsel should come from a different firm. This was a way of having senior counsels train a wider pool of young lawyers to handle criminal cases. However, in this case, the Registrar made an exception and allowed Sunil, who was from the same firm, to assist me. I asked for him to be appointed as it was a complicated case and I wanted to be able to choose who should assist me.

So I went with Sunil to see One-eyed Dragon in the condemned cell at Changi Prison. Before seeing him, we met with another client, Leong Siew Chor, the accused in the Kallang River body parts case, for a chat. He told me that he had spoken with One-eyed Dragon and found him an amusing person.

When Sunil and I met One-eyed Dragon, we were not able to shake his hand as we were separated from him by a security glass panel, but we exchanged nods by way of greeting. He thanked me for accepting his case and told me that he couldn't speak English very well but could speak a little Malay. I assured him that it was not a problem as Sunil could speak fluent Mandarin having taken the language in school. He was very surprised and glad he could express himself fully to Sunil. They started to talk and I intervened at times as I could understand a smattering of Mandarin.

The meeting was more to introduce ourselves and to assure him that we would be doing the best we could for him. At that stage, we did not have the Grounds of Decision and the Notes of Evidence. When we had all the documents ready and had gone through them, we would return to visit him. We asked him why he had shot Lim and he gave us his account of the incident. He also told us about how unfair he thought the system was and how the judge had not been fair to him. He felt that from the moment he was caught, he was not going to get a fair trial. I told him through Sunil that this was not true as we really do give everyone a fair trial under our system. It may appear to some as being unfair but the fact is that trials in Singapore follow the letter of the law.

When the Notes of Evidence and the Grounds of Decision were made available to us, we found that the evidence against One-eyed Dragon was overwhelming as the eyewitnesses were quite sure of what they had seen. From what we gathered from the Notes of Evidence, the prosecution witnesses, including the driver who had taken One-eyed Dragon to Lim's flat, were all reliable witnesses. However, we were disturbed by the fact that One-eyed Dragon had been denied a lawyer to help him with his final submission. We thought it was unconstitutional and as far as we were concerned, he had not been given a fair trial as his request for a counsel was not acceded to by the judge. We put as our first grounds of appeal: denial of a fair trial.

Another grounds of appeal we put forward concerned the judge's interpretation of the evidence given by the maid. Justice Tay had refused to visit the scene of the crime to verify One-eyed Dragon's statement but had chosen instead to rely on photographs and the maid's evidence. According to One-eyed Dragon, the maid was in the bedroom and could not see what was going on. The photographs could not show that the maid was lying. But the judge had refused his request to visit the crime scene, which we thought was a rather poor decision on his part. He should have gone to the scene to confirm the maid's evidence.

Why couldn't he when other judges have done so, like Justice V K Rajah, in the case of Constance Chee. According to Justice Rajah, going to the scene had helped him visualise what could really have happened. After observing the scene of the offence, he had asked the prosecution to create a mock HDB balcony so that the witnesses could enact the incident clearly. In another trial, Justice Woo Bih Li had gone to the crime scene to try and ascertain the truth. There have been occasions when judges felt it necessary to inspect the murder scene. It costs them nothing but One-eyed Dragon's judge decided not to which we thought was unfair.

Still, we knew deep inside that all these facts were not going to hold any weight. The only strong argument that we had was the fact that One-eyed Dragon had not been given a fair trial when he was denied counsel. I started the argument in the Court of Appeal before Justices of Appeal Andrew Pang, V K Rajah and Tan Lee Meng. It was a very good hearing. Although they complimented me on my arguments, they were not prepared to accept the fact that One-eyed Dragon had been denied a fair trial. In fact, they asked: "What could a counsel do if he was given counsel at that stage?" I argued that a counsel could have helped him sum up his case and given him pointers. That would have helped him in his closing submission which could have affected the verdict. Both Justices Pang and Rajah said: "Okay, you're the counsel now. Tell us what you could have said to help him in the lower court."

I replied: "If you ask me now, to be honest, I will not be able to, but the fact is that some other lawyer could have been able to put forward some arguments that may have helped him."

Justice Andrew Pang said: "Well, Mr Anandan, you are one of the most capable lawyers of the Criminal Bar and if you say that there is nothing much that can be said, then I think that's the end of the matter." He thanked me for being candid.

I lost the appeal and I think the Court of Appeal took the practical way out. They looked at the case and decided that there was so much evidence against One-eyed Dragon that it didn't matter. I think they thought it would be a waste of time to have a new trial because the evidence was not going to change much and there was enough to find One-eyed Dragon guilty. I suppose they were entitled to do that, but to me a re-trial would have been fair.

Before you give the supreme punishment to an accused person, namely the death sentence, I think you should give him every opportunity to have a different verdict. We live in a society where our judicial system is such that every man—no matter what his offence is, even if it is the most heinous offence under the law—should be given every opportunity possible to defend himself before being convicted and punished under the law. Only then can we say with a clear conscience when a man is hanged, that everything possible has been done for him and the law must take its course.

TWENTY-ONE

CHUA TIONG TIONG
Ah Long San

I first met Ah Long San in 1976 when we both were inmates at Queenstown Remand Prison. He was detained for various criminal activities. He was just an ordinary prisoner—that is, he was not considered a special prisoner by the other inmates as I was. In November that year, I was released from remand and went back to practise law. A few years later, I assisted my future mother-in-law in the sale of her land in Jalan Tua Kong, off Upper East Coast Road, to a group of my friends who were developing the land to build units of terrace and semi-detached houses. One day, Ah Long San walked into my office with a property agent to enquire about buying one of the semi-detached units. When the property agent tried to introduce us, we both started to laugh. The agent didn't know that we knew each other from our prison days and was completely puzzled.

I explained the contract to Ah Long San and told him that he had to pay a 10 per cent deposit on the selling price of $800,000. He simply took out from his pocket a wad of cash and gave me the full sum of $800,000. I was a little shocked at the amount of money in front of me. I told him that he did not have to pay the whole purchase price immediately and doing so would only attract the Inland Revenue Authority of Singapore. He was not perturbed and asked me whether I wanted to keep the money for him. I politely declined. When the sale was completed, he gave a cashier's order and took possession of the keys. He told me that he was buying the house for his mother. I believe his mother still lives there.

I would see Ah Long San occasionally in nightclubs, especially at the Lido Palace, a well-known expensive nightclub located on Havelock Road. He was a regular patron in most nightclubs. Every *mama-san* welcomed him as a customer because he was a big tipper. Even the valets would rush to park his car as he was known to tip them $50 every time. On one occasion, he tipped a valet $500 for parking his car.

Ah Long San was known as Singapore's No. 1 loan shark. His empire was vast, spread across Singapore. He was a pioneer in computerising his organisation and it was reputed that his income ran from six to seven figures annually. The richer he was, the more powerful he grew. His entertainment bill alone ran to thousands of dollars every month. But the bill included entertainment of police officers and that was the start of his downfall.

The Corrupt Practices Investigation Bureau (CPIB), who had no interest in investigating his alleged moneylending activities, became interested in Ah Long San because of his involvement with police officers. Investigations against Ah Long San ended with him being charged with a number of corruption charges. Even before he was charged, he was seeking me out for advice and so it came as no surprise when his men came to me one day to inform me that he was going to be charged the next day in Court 26.

I appeared in Court 26 and applied for him to be released on bail. Most of the charges were for corrupting police officers to obtain favours from them. Several police officers themselves were charged with showing Ah Long San favouritism, in exchange for being entertained at the Lido Palace. Others did them for a couple of drinks and sexual favours that Ah Long San or his men arranged for them. These police officers sold their careers very cheaply. They were found guilty and punished. They deserved it.

I started negotiations with the CPIB in the hope of getting the charges against Ah Long San reduced. The CPIB was prepared to strike a deal if Ah Long San testifed against the police officers and also provided more information that could be used against other police officers. The CPIB was sure that higher ranking police officers were involved. I thought the deal was reasonable but Ah Long San refused to accept it. He said that he would not testify against the police officers and he had no information to give the CPIB regarding other police officers. He told me that he could not betray the officers who had been charged and he was confident that they would not testify against him. He was mistaken. All the police officers gave statements against him and subsequently testified against him in court. I watched him as he sat in the dock, expressionless. Later I asked him what he thought of those policemen. He smiled and told me that nothing shocked him where the police was concerned, and I remembered what my clients used to tell me: "Don't trust a policeman."

His case was heard before District Judge Jasvinder Kaur, a stern but fair judge even though she had spent many years as a DPP. Most of the witnesses who testified were employees from Lido Palace. The *mama-san* described how she had served Ah Long San and his "police guests", the number of girls she had provided and who had settled the bills. The waiter testified to the number of policemen in the room and the drinks they had. In the course of the trial, it became evident that I too frequented the place. I told the judge that since all parties including the DPP had seen Lido Palace at night, maybe she should also visit the nightclub to get a real feel of it. She responded by saying that she was not going to allow me to take her to Lido Palace under any circumstances. The people in the court roared with laughter and some of the lawyers present told me it was a good try.

At the end of the trial, Ah Long San was convicted and sentenced to 18 months in jail. I wanted the remaining charges of similar moneylending and corruption of other people to be taken into consideration and to end the saga. Ah Long San refused. He gave me instructions to appeal against the conviction and the sentence, and I did accordingly. By the time the appeal came before Chief Justice Yong Pung How, I managed to convince Ah Long San to withdraw his appeal. A few days before the hearing date of the appeal, he came to my office and said that the CPIB must tell him how many charges they were going to proceed with out of the remaining charges. He felt he had to fight those charges. I told him: "First things first. Let us withdraw the appeal." He agreed.

In the Appellate Court, he produced a medical certificate stating that he was not fit to attend court because of a heart problem. Chief Justice Yong adjourned the case. The next time the case came up, I again produced a medical certificate stating that Ah Long San had undergone a heart by-pass operation. The case was adjourned. The third time the appeal case came up, Ah Long San did not turn up. Many of his men were there in court but he was not. I informed the Chief Justice that he was not in court and asked whether his case could be stood down to the afternoon. The Chief Justice agreed. He did not turn up that afternoon and a warrant of arrest was issued. The hunt for Ah Long San began.

I thought that with his various connections overseas, he would have escaped to Thailand or Hong Kong. That was not so. One of his friends told me that Ah Long San would be contacting him soon. Ah Long San called the friend to pass me a message: he wanted me to carry a mobile phone so that he could contact me whenever it was convenient for him. I told the friend to let him know that I was not going to carry a mobile phone and that he should surrender. I made it clear that I would talk to him only when he surrendered. He was upset with me and changed lawyers.

His new lawyer was Edmund Pereira. Ah Long San eventually surrendered and was produced before Chief Justice Yong. I was there to discharge myself. Edmund, who did not have much time to prepare for the case, asked my permission to use my submission as it had already been filed with the court. The Chief Justice, as usual, was polite throughout the proceedings. I was a bit surprised that no application to withdraw the appeal had been made. Obviously, Ah Long San had changed his mind again. Edmund argued the appeal with his usual eloquence but the Chief Justice was not one who is impressed with eloquence. He dealt with hard facts, being the hardnosed judge that he was. After listening patiently to Edmund, Chief Justice Yong asked him: "Mr Pereira, how long do you think your client should get?"

Edmund replied: "I leave it entirely to your Lordship (even though 'your Honour' was the term we used)."

Chief Justice Yong smiled and said: "I thank you for the faith you have in me, Mr Pereira. I am raising the term of imprisonment from 18 months to 48 months."

Everybody was stunned. I had expected an enhancement of the original sentence, which was why I wanted to withdraw the appeal, but 48 months was a bit too much. Subsequently, Ah Long San pleaded guilty to the remaining charges and was sentenced to 10 years imprisonment.

For a long time I thought Ah Long San was angry with me. So it came as a pleasant surprise when his daughter visited my office and said that he wanted to see me. I visited him in prison and things were the same as before. He wanted me to help him get out of prison earlier through the home detention scheme where offenders had to wear electronic tags to monitor their movements and curfew hours. I wrote to the Prisons director but he was not prepared to release Ah Long San early by electronic tagging. I felt that it was not a fair decision but that's the way it is.

Ah Long San was released in May 2008 and he visited me with his second wife. He instructed me to attend to some of his property matters. I introduced him to Sharon Tan, a legal assistant from the conveyancing department. She told me jokingly that he was her passport to the underworld!

TWENTY-TWO

PAL (MILK), THE BOOKIE

Pal was a young boy who delivered milk to my temple. *Pal* is the Tamil word for 'milk' and he got his nickname delivering milk in the Sembawang neighbourhood. When he became my client sometime in the 1990s, he confessed to me that he used to drink a little of the milk he was delivering to the temple. According to him, the Gods wouldn't mind missing a bit of milk. It made sense to me and it also revealed a little of his character.

Every Sunday after lunch, some of my friends and I would gather at the house of our friend, Dasa. It was a huge colonial bungalow which Dasa rented to house his dogs. It was an ideal place for poker games, especially on Sunday afternoons, and parties. We didn't play for big stakes and most times the winner only received IOUs which nobody cashed. We played for the fun of it and whoever won would pay for dinner that could cost more than the winnings. One of the players was my good friend and schoolmate Saivy. He was also known as Duck Legs because of his gait. An excellent flutist and a fantastic musician, he led the Indian band which provided music for Tamil talentime contests that were telecast on TV. Saivy died of a heart attack in May 1996 when I was away in Manila. I was not able to catch a flight back to Singapore to attend his funeral and spent a miserable day in my hotel reminiscing about him.

One Sunday, Saivy was late and we started the poker game without him. When he turned up, he looked worried and asked me to step outside for a chat. In the garden, he told me that his good friend and bookie, Pal, had been arrested by the CPIB. He also told me that he suspected Pal of fixing Malaysia Cup soccer matches. I asked him what he wanted me to do and he said that I should act for Pal and do the best for him. I had heard rumours about Pal which I didn't like and I told Saivy that he should perhaps look for another lawyer. Saivy was quiet for some time. He finally looked at me and said that as we have been friends for a long while, he was asking a favour of me and I should not refuse. Since it meant so much to Saivy, I decided to help.

The next day I called the CPIB and spoke to an officer, Mohammed Ali, who I knew from our university days. I said I was acting for Pal and asked if I could see him. Ali told me to come to his office for a chat. When we met, he told me that Pal was in a serious situation. The authorities had evidence of Pal fixing matches and betting millions of dollars on them. According to Ali, Pal could be locked away for a long time. Ali also told me that the director of the CPIB, Chua Cher Yak, wanted to see me. I knew Chua from my Raffles Institution days. He played soccer and I believed he played for the school. He was a hardworking student though not a good soccer player.

Ali escorted me to the director's room and left. Also in the room was the deputy director, Tan Ah Leck, with whom I had had several encounters. Ah Leck offered me coffee whilst I was chatting with the director about old times. After sipping the coffee (I had definitely tasted better), I asked the director what he wanted. He was frank and said that the choice was mine. He could send Pal away for a long spell in prison or I could save him. I asked him how I could help Pal and he said that if my client became a witness for the prosecution, he would consider reducing the number of charges against him.

I asked for permission to see Pal which was granted. We spoke for a long time and he agreed to be a prosecution witness. He was released with an order to return the next day. Pal met up with his associates to discuss the development and confirmed with me that he was prepared to be a prosecution witness. He added that he was leaving the negotiations to me and he would agree to whatever terms I negotiated with the CPIB. He was under the impression that he would still be charged but with fewer charges. The next day, I struck a bargain with the director and Ah Leck. There would be no charges against Pal if he testified against certain players and bookies.

An application was made before the hearing started to keep Pal's name and photograph out of the press for security reasons. The application was granted. Pal first testified against two persons: one Ong, an insurance broker and bookie, and one Kannan, a former Malaysia Cup player. Both were convicted and sent to jail. At one stage, the lawyer for Kannan asked Pal how he could have trusted Kannan with thousands of dollars. Pal answered that in this business, trust was the only way to go. When the lawyer asked Pal what would happen if he was cheated, the answer was that it would be the last time that that man would cheat him. It was a double-edged answer. Everybody in court understood its meaning and knew that Pal was a dangerous person. He next testified against Abbas Saad, a well-known player from Australia. Abbas was convicted, fined $50,000 and banned from playing soccer for life. Another player, Michael Vanna, was arrested and charged for accepting money from Pal to fix a match. Bail for Vanna was set at $500,000 but one of Pal's associates bailed him out and he absconded—$500,000 was nothing to the bookies.

After the saga was over in Singapore, the Malaysian police sent out a warrant for Pal's arrest and he was taken away to Malaysia. I drove to Kuala Lumpur to engage a lawyer for him and after many days in detention and after thousands of dollars had changed hands, Pal was charged in Penang for a minor offence. He pleaded guilty and was fined RM5,000 which he paid. He returned to Singapore. However, the matter didn't end there.

After Singapore pulled out of the Malaysia Cup in 1995 and started its own S-League, Pal's ugly head surfaced again. He tried to bribe players again and this time, when he was arrested, there was no bargaining. The director of the CPIB was furious and in the trial that followed, Pal and two players were convicted and sent to jail. In prison, Pal bribed a jail warden to get him a mobile phone which he used to place bets and contact his associates. He was caught and sentenced to a few more years in prison. The warden was jailed. If you ask me, Pal deserved it though I put up a mitigation for him.

You may wonder what made him so successful in fixing the Malaysia Cup matches. Every state in Malaysia had Indian players and Pal, as an Indian, used his connections to contact them. Many of the referees and linesmen were also Indian. Pal was a master in exploiting people's weaknesses. For those who wanted women, he provided the best and for those who wanted money, he gave cash. He wined and dined the players and officials. He was a generous host who could also be ruthless to people who played him out.

There was, however, a kinder side to Pal. He was known to help many people in Sembawang, especially those who needed money for hospitalisation, wedding and funeral expenses. But whatever money he made in the Malaysia Cup days (and that ran into the millions), he lost by gambling on the English Premier League matches. Somehow he had the impression that he was a genius in forecasting the outcome of football matches. A fool and his money are soon parted and I believe Pal is a pauper now. He still owes me money in fees.

Ah Long San was also a loan shark and bookie, and I couldn't help comparing the two of them. Both could be ruthless and kind at the same time. But while Ah Long San had the foresight to invest in properties and other business ventures, Pal was reckless, over-confident and had the misguided belief that he was a genius. He lost millions of dollars in betting and I still have the cheques he gave me which bounced. He avoids me nowadays, I suppose he is ashamed to face me. On the other hand, Ah Long San and I meet often and still maintain our friendship.

TWENTY-THREE

JOHNNY TAN
The Impersonator

When I first started my practice in Winchester House, I handled a variety of cases. Quite a number of them were cheating cases. My office was quite crummy at the time. One day sometime in the late 1970s, a man sporting a crew cut entered the office looking very agitated. He was about 1.5 m tall and weighed about 50 kg. He told the receptionist he wanted to see me very urgently and proceeded to enter my room. I asked him what his problem was.

"I'm going to be charged for cheating."

"Yes, cheating whom?" I asked.

"Cheating quite a lot of shopkeepers."

"And where are these shopkeepers?"

"They're all around Chinatown, near Smith Street. They deal in sharks' fins, amongst other Chinese delicacies."

"Alright. Who recommended you to me?" He gave the name of his former lawyer who I knew. "Why don't you use him because he handles crime cases and he has acted for you. Why are you not using him again?"

"Well, now that I have no more money, he has no more time for me. He also told me that you normally help people out. I'll be very grateful if you can help me."

I smiled to myself. Even at that early stage in my practice, I had a reputation for taking on hopeless cases or cases in which people didn't have money to pay my fees. I was curious. Because of his size and appearance, I wondered what sort of problem Johnny Tan was in. "Tell me, what is your problem?" I asked.

"It's a very serious one. If you want to know how I started my job (as he called it) as a conman, I will have to start from the beginning."

"Alright, tell me."

"Well, I was doing some sales at one time. I couldn't make money and I got into this bad habit of gambling. I needed money when I lost and had to borrow from loan sharks who would come after me when I couldn't pay them back. So I cooked up an idea to get some money. I decided to get a fire safety certificate that allowed me to inspect shops in Chinatown to see if they were adequately fitted with fire safety equipment, like extinguishers. I bribed someone in a certain department and got the certificate. I went around checking shops and telling the shopkeepers that their shops were a fire hazard as they were not well equipped. I told them they had to get a better type of fire extinguisher and that I would return in a week's time to check, and if I find no improvement, I would have to summon them to court. I also told them where to get the proper fire extinguishers."

In the meantime, according to Johnny, he set up a company selling fire extinguishers. Because of his earlier recommendation, there was a big rush of people buying fire extinguishers from his company. These people did not realise that the company was owned by Johnny Tan. He raised his prices but people still bought from him. He made quite a tidy profit. The other companies selling fire extinguishers were curious to know how Johnny, who could not read or write English properly, could be certified as a safety officer. They reported the matter to the CPIB.

Johnny was taken in by the CPIB and interrogated for a day. He refused to say how he got the certificate. When he was released, he contacted the people who issued the certificate and threatened them. "I will not be able to take any more torture from CPIB. You have to do something about it otherwise I may have to reveal your names." Johnny told me that the people who gave him the certificate found a scapegoat in someone who was going to be sacked over a disciplinary matter, and they managed to persuade that person to take the rap. The next time the CPIB caught up with Johnny, he revealed the man's name. When the man was pulled up by the CPIB, he accepted responsibility by saying he had taken money from Johnny in exchange for the certificate. He was subsequently charged in court and pleaded guilty. According to Johnny, he paid the man's legal fees and the fine. Johnny also gave the man a bonus and the whole matter was settled.

From these episodes, Johnny found that it was quite easy to make money by tricking people. Whenever he got into trouble, especially over his gambling debts, he would think of new ways to deceive people. The next time he got into trouble, he was caught impersonating an income tax officer.

One day, Johnny took a friend to a shop which he knew was doing very well. To the shopkeeper, he identified himself as an income tax officer, showed him a card and introduced his friend as his subordinate. He then screamed at the shopkeeper: "How long do you think you can keep cheating the government?" Johnny then turned around abruptly, looked at his 'subordinate' and ordered: "You stand here and guard the books while I go and call for transport to come."

You must remember that in those days, there were no mobile phones. When Johnny went out to make his phone call, his accomplice told the rattled shopkeeper, "My boss is actually quite a kind man but he lost a lot of money gambling at the racecourse last weekend. That's why he's in a bad mood. Actually, if you help him, this matter can be easily settled."

The shopkeeper replied, "Sure, sure, sure. I'd like to settle it. How much can I offer? Can I talk?"

Johnny's friend said, "Well, when my boss comes back, I'll put in a good word for you."

Five minutes later, when Johnny walked in, he said to Johnny, "Sir, this shopkeeper understands the situation. He doesn't want to go to court. He doesn't want to be charged. Can you help him?"

Johnny replied, "Oh, I see. So you know you've done wrong?"

The shopkeeper said, "Yes."

They went into a room to negotiate a deal. Johnny hit his first shopkeeper for a very large sum. "I want $200,000. I assure you that for the next two to three years you don't have to worry about any investigation into your company." The shopkeeper then took them to the bank in his Mercedes Benz, withdrew $200,000 in cash and gave the money to Johnny. After that, he drove them back to Johnny's 'office' in Fullerton Building; at that time, the Income Tax department was located in Fullerton Building which also housed the General Post Office. Johnny waved at the shopkeeper, went up the steps as if he was going back to work. After 10 minutes he came back out. He gave his partner in crime $2,000, which he seemed happy with, and pocketed the rest.

Johnny played this trick on many shopkeepers and was successful. All of them forked out equally large amounts. It was a scam that was going very well for Johnny but the law finally caught up with him. When the real income tax officers swooped on a shop which Johnny had 'raided' the previous day, the exasperated shopkeeper said, "What the hell are you trying to do? I just gave money to your senior officer, why are you coming back again? I don't have that sort of money to pay you all every day."

Of course the officers were puzzled and questioned him. "What do you mean? What are you talking about?"

The shopkeeper replied, "Yesterday, your boss raided my shop and he promised me that there won't be any more raids for two to three years. He has broken his word. I'm sick and tired of it."

The officers arrested the shopkeeper and took him in for interrogation, and there he found that he had been conned. He provided a description of Johnny, who was subsequently caught. But because of a technicality in identification, I managed to get Johnny's charge reduced. He pleaded guilty to a lesser charge and was given a short custodial sentence of a few months. While these things were happening, Johnny was making good money gambling. He became quite a good client in the sense that he paid me very well. In fact he paid more than what we had agreed upon. When I told his former lawyer how well Johnny was doing and how well he was paying me, I'm sure he regretted sending Johnny to me.

When Johnny was released from prison, he went back to being a conman. This time he impersonated an immigration officer. Somehow, based on his intelligence network, he knew who were overstaying in Singapore and who were doing businesses without the valid permits; these were situations that would get them into trouble. Roping in the same friend to assist him, he would target the rich overstayers like the Taiwanese and Malaysian Chinese. However, he didn't get much money from these scams, usually between $20,000 and $30,000, sometimes $50,000. He was eventually caught again. I managed to negotiate for a lesser charge, but because of his history of convictions, like the gun case in Genting Highlands, he was sentenced to five years of corrective training.

I was frustrated with him during this case. "You've made a lot of money, why are you doing this? I am sick of this. Enough is enough. You've been a good client but you've not been listening to me and this is goodbye to you."

"I'm sorry," was all he said and he shook hands with me. I still remember we had this conversation in Court 2 of the Subordinate Courts. The district judge who heard his case was Francis Remedios. Johnny was taken away.

After a few years, Johnny Tan hit the news once again. But he did not come to see me. I read in the newspapers that he was arrested for pretending to be an available bachelor. He had registered himself with marriage brokers, hitting on young women looking for life partners, sharing his sob stories with them and enticing them to release their savings to him. I think he was given the maximum preventive detention of 20 years.

When I read the report, I was quite sad because this was a man who was very intelligent, more intelligent than many other conmen I have defended. He came on as almost a simpleton but his schemes were so beautifully plotted and carried out. He made millions of dollars. He used to take me around in brand new Mercedes Benzes or Jaguars which he had paid for in cash. All the time his skinny, mousy-looking hyperactive wife would be at the wheel. When he picked me up, he would move to the back of the car and sit with me. I felt quite embarrassed and suggested that he should sit in front with her. He would just respond: "No, it's OK. I'd like to discuss matters with you. Let her drive." He also used to give money to my staff, in one instance he gave $500 for lunch. The latest I've heard about him is that he's in

Changi Prison and running a four-digit racket there. I do not know if this is true but knowing Johnny Tan, anything is possible.

The reason I've chosen to write about Johnny is because he is a unique character. He had the animal instinct to survive and the intelligence and courage to do things which others were not able to do. If he had used the same intelligence in a lawful business, I'm very sure he would have been a success. Unfortunately, his addiction to gambling stood in his way. If he wasn't obsessed with gambling, the money that he made out of his scams could have been used to set up a good business and he would have been a very wealthy man. But he never did it because he always had the urge to gamble.

That is why I always advise young lawyers never to get hooked on gambling. It's an addiction that can completely ruin a person. When you're addicted, you might be tempted to take your clients' money to gamble, just as my friend and colleague did. K S Ong was a high-flying lawyer in Drew & Napier. He left the firm and started his own company with some of his clients. But he was not satisfied with the money he was making and started to gamble in every way possible. He lost heavily and took money from his clients' accounts and gambled that away too. When he heard the police were looking for him, he told me that he would surrender but he never did. I was concerned and told him that if he did not surrender and the police caught him, the mitigating factor of surrendering would not hold any weight.

One day, he came to my office to discuss his case. I called Yeo Poh Teck of the Commercial Affairs Department. I told him that K S Ong was in my office and asked him to come and arrest him. Of course, K S Ong was upset with me.

"How can you do that to me?"

"Look, somebody's got to save you. I'm doing it for your own good." K S Ong realised that I meant well. The CAD officers, who were then in the CPF Building, came over to my office, which was then in International Plaza, to arrest and charge him. They charged him for criminal breach of trust and I pleaded guilty on his behalf in Court 26. It was a very sad moment. Many of his friends, mostly lawyers, came to the court to listen to my mitigation plea and to see the outcome. K S Ong had such a brilliant future but he wasted it. He was sentenced to jail and subsequently struck off the lawyer's registry.

I can provide similar stories about other lawyers but there's no point in doing so. I've chosen to write about K S Ong because I knew him as a friend and a colleague. I played mahjong with him. We were good friends. Loyal friends raised money for him but that was not enough to help him. He's out of prison now and I don't know what he's doing but I wish him well.

TWENTY-FOUR

UNIVERSITY MARTIN
The Public Prosecutor vs The Bomoh

Everybody during my university days knew Martin. He was once a boxer but became a security guard at the university library. When he married a Muslim girl, he converted to Islam and adopted the name, Abdul Razak. He had a reputation of having connections with the underworld. He was a likeable man and his job at the library was to make sure that students did not take out books they were not supposed to. He would be at the library's exit checking people's bags. Those whom he trusted, he would wave them on. There were some students, though, who abused the trust and arranged with him to take books out and return them a day or two later. It was not a racket but a small group of students benefited. I was quite close to Martin because some of my friends who knew him had asked him to keep an eye on me.

In 1970, when I was doing pupilage at Shook Lin & Bok under my master, Mr Chan Sek Kiong, the present Chief Justice, I had an urgent call from Martin. He said he was being investigated by the CPIB and would be charged in court under the Prevention of Corruption Act. He told me a student who was looking for a book had asked for his help to locate it. Martin asked him directly: "What are you going to give me as a reward for doing you this favour?" They agreed on a small sum. Later, the student reported the matter to the university authorities, who decided to inform the CPIB. The next thing we knew,

Martin was charged in court.

Since I was not called to the Bar yet, I had no choice but to ask Leo Fernando, a prominent criminal lawyer of the time, to defend him. I told Leo that I would assist him in the case and he was quite happy to do it. The case came up before District Judge K T Alexander, an elderly man known in the legal profession to have a kind heart and a lot of integrity. He was also partially deaf, I think. If I remember correctly, the trial was held in Court 3 of the old Subordinate Courts, which was then located on South Bridge Road. (The courts were affectionately referred to as cowsheds as there was hardly any air-conditioning. There were only fans, some wooden, and mostly creaking slowly in most parts of the building. I don't know why they had the audacity to call it the Subordinate Courts. Only Courts 1, 2, 3 and 4 on the top floor were air-conditioned.) Judge Alexander's court was quite large. Most of the gallery was occupied by university students who knew Martin personally at some point in time or other. Before the trial started at 9.00 am, Martin stopped me at the coffee shop downstairs and pleaded with me, "Please Subhas, make sure the case doesn't end today."

"Why?" I asked him. "I don't think the case will end today as it has been fixed for three days."

"Whatever it is, please, you must promise me that the case will not end today."

"Well, before I make such a promise, you must tell me why it is so important that it doesn't end today," I replied.

Martin spoke earnestly: "My *kampung bomoh* is only coming back from Malaysia tomorrow. I need him to be in court."

"What has he got to do with your case?" I asked.

He tried to explain. "You don't understand, Subhas. If he's in court, the situation would definitely favour us. Please, somehow, prolong the case. Make sure it won't be over today."

"There's no need to try very hard to prolong it. It will definitely not end today because there are too many witnesses, formal and informal, material and non-material."

He was pleased and looked relieved. We went up to Court 3. Leo was already there with some other lawyers. The case started around 9.30 am. The prosecutor, ASP M Amaladass, told Leo and I that we had a very bad case. "The complainant is a university student and there's no reason why the judge will not believe him. And your client is telling all sorts of stories," he told us. Leo, as brash as usual, said: "Just go on and do your work and I'll do mine." That ended the conversation.

The trial started and witnesses were called. Whenever Leo Fernando stood up to cross-examine a witness, Judge Alexander would get irritated and shout at him: "What's the purpose of asking this question? Why are you doing this? What's your defence after all?" From the time the case started till around 4.45 pm, Leo was getting hell from the judge. We all knew that Martin was going to be in very serious trouble.

However, when the case was adjourned, Martin held my hand and said: "Thank God it's not over and will be continued tomorrow. My *bomoh* will be there and he will know what to do. Please come early tomorrow morning around 8.30 am. I want you to meet him before he goes into the court." I agreed to the request but was feeling a little depressed as I thought for sure that Martin would be convicted. There was a possibility that he could even go to jail as I didn't think he had a clean record.

The next day, at the agreed time, I met Martin outside the Subordinate Courts. We walked to the coffee shop where he introduced me to a man who looked about 40 years of age. He was sitting alone and having a cup of coffee. He immediately stood up and shook my hand. "How are you?" he asked me.

"Okay," I replied.

He then asked me, "Would there be any problem if I sit at the back of the court and say a prayer while the hearing goes on? I will be holding a glass of water."

I replied that it should be alright as long as he did not make any noise. If his prayers were loud, it would definitely not be tolerated. "No, no, no. I'll be just praying to myself, holding the glass of water," he said.

"Then," I said, "I don't think it should be a problem. Anyway, what are you going to do?"

He assured me. "Don't worry about what I'm going to do. We will win this case today."

I was quite amused at his confidence and even more amused at the happiness on Martin's face. He had so much faith in the man. I laughed as we went to court. We went up earlier as we wanted the *bomoh* to get a good seat. As Martin and I walked off to our designated places, I asked him: "How old is he? He looks pretty young."

Martin replied: "You won't believe it but he's in his seventies!"

I was shocked and exclaimed: "What? He's in his seventies? He looks very young!"

"Do you remember the racial troubles in 1964?" Martin asked. "The Chinese tried to attack our *kampung* but retreated. When the situation settled down and there was peace and calm, I asked my Chinese friends why they came to attack but ran away instead. One of them said, 'I don't know what you all did, but we saw many people waiting to attack us'. I didn't believe it. But my friend said, 'Ya, really, giants. We could see giants. They were exceptionally tall people, 10 to

15 feet tall. We got frightened and ran away.'" According to Martin, the *bomoh* made a charm and threw this illusion into the minds of the attackers. "That seems to be a fantastic feat, whatever it was. This is law, you know," I reminded him, unconvinced.

Martin laughed. "Never mind, it's all the same."

As soon as the trial restarted that day, judge Alexander scolded Leo again and I thought that we were in for the same pattern of outbursts as the day before. But after about 20 minutes, we could see his attitude changing. The judge suddenly started picking on the prosecutor. What Leo got the previous day the prosecutor received worse that day. I was confused and wondered what was happening. All of a sudden, the prosecution closed its case. Leo Fernando got ready to make his submission: there was no prima facie case to answer because the prosecution had not established its case. But even before he could stand up, the judge asked him to sit down. He then turned to ASP Amaladass and asked, "Prosecutor, tell me, what is the offence that is being disclosed in this case?"

The prosecutor started to answer but the judge retorted: "No, no, no. Cut it out. The only offence that is committed in this case is the offence of you wasting the court's time. You have no case. You have no business to bring this matter to court. I don't know who advised you." He told the prosecutor to sit down and asked Martin to stand up. He told Martin, "I am discharging and acquitting you." The students in the gallery were overjoyed and started to applaud. I signalled to them to be quiet and sit down. Thank goodness K T Alexander, who was partially deaf, only stared at them and walked off.

Everybody congratulated Leo but he wasn't sure what had just happened. Neither was the prosecutor sure of what had just transpired. Martin and I looked at each other, both of us equally confused. Finally, when everybody had left, Martin and I walked over to the *bomoh* and I asked him, "What did you do?"

"Well, this judge is a good man. It took me a little longer to get through to him but in the end, everything is alright."

I really didn't know whether to believe him or not, but whatever it was, there was an acquittal for Martin who went back to work at the library. Even till today, Leo feels it was an unusual case. That was one of my first experiences with black magic, or whatever magic you can call it, being used in court.

Soon after, I was called to the Bar and was practising on my own in Winchester House. A man called Talib, an employee at Shook Lin & Bok where I did my pupilage, brought a drug trafficking case to me and asked if I could help. I agreed. Before the trial started, Talib came to see me and asked: "Can you do us a favour and let us know who is the most important prosecution witness? When he's giving his evidence, could you just turn around to signal to us that he's the one?"

Of course I was curious and said: "Why do you need me to do that?"

"Please, just do me a favour. Trust me. Just do it," he pleaded.

I agreed as it made my client and his family happy, but I think Talib felt I might be upset with him. He proceeded to explain that the family had a *bomoh* sitting there with them who they believed would help them win the case. "Whatever," I replied.

The most important witness for the prosecution was the arresting officer who had seen the accused throw away the drugs when he was being chased. As he came forward to give evidence, I turned around and signalled to the family. I remember cross-examining him for nearly two hours and managed to create doubt in the judge's mind as to whether he actually saw the accused throwing the drugs away.

When it came to my submission, I again submitted that the evidence of the arresting officer was not reliable because he had given so many versions under cross-examination. The judge agreed and acquitted the accused. I thought I had done an excellent job in cross-examining this witness and tearing him to pieces. But when I walked out, everybody was congratulating the *bomoh*. They all believed that the witness had broken down and given inconsistent versions only because of the man's magical powers. My cross-examination had nothing to do with it!

I wasn't very sure who did what, but there are many other instances of lawyers being approached by the families of the accused to do unusual things. For instance, they would ask the lawyer to pass a sweet to the accused to eat or they would ask the lawyer to give the accused a piece of thread to hold. We try to oblige them most of the time and more often than not, it appears to work, strange as it may seem. So much so that I really don't know whether it's my skill as a lawyer or the skill of the *bomoh* behind the acquittals I have obtained for some of my clients. For this reason, I will not come to any sort of conclusion about black magic. I have seen black magic working in my lifetime during my university days and while living in Kampung Wak Hassan. I will not say anything damning about black magic.

TWENTY-FIVE

PUBLIC PROSECUTOR vs HENG BOON CHAI

The last case that I want to include in this book is that of the Public Prosecutor vs Heng Boon Chai. It first hit the headlines in September 2007. *The Straits Times* reported that Heng Boon Chai was charged with the murder of his uncle, his father's brother. It was a violent murder that caught the public's attention because of the close relationship between the two men.

A few days later, while I was in my office, Sandra, my secretary, put a call through from a woman enquiring whether we were prepared to meet with her parents. She was the sister of the accused. She and her parents wanted to discuss the matter in the press report. One of the first things they said to me when they came to my office was that they had difficulty tracing me. They thought that I was still with Harry Elias Partnership. After some enquiries, they managed to track me down at KhattarWong. My nephew, Sunil, who assists me in my cases, was with me as usual when they eventually came to the office that day.

Heng's parents are illiterate and poor, and their story is a sad one. Their eldest son suffered from schizophrenia and committed suicide. Their younger son, the accused Heng, saw his brother jump from the flat and that triggered something in him. His parents said there was a drastic change in his character after that which became worse when his grandfather passed away shortly after. He had been very close to his grandfather, spending hours playing Chinese checkers with him. His parents had no idea why he killed his uncle. They said Heng had been mumbling to himself in the past few months. Heng had told them that he heard his grandfather's voice talking to him and asking him to do things. Heng also said that he could feel the weight of someone sitting on him when he was asleep. His parents tried to pacify him as much as they could. They also brought him to see a Chinese medium who gave them powders to mix in his drinks as well as a talisman for him to wear. But nothing helped and he killed his uncle. He was arrested, charged and taken for psychiatric evaluation which confirmed that he was a paranoid schizophrenic. As he was diagnosed with a mental disease, the prosecution reduced the charge from murder to one under Section 304a of the Penal Code, which is culpable homicide.

His parents told me they had no money to pay the legal fees. I assured them that as it was a capital case, the State would appoint two lawyers, a senior and a junior, to defend their son and that they didn't have to worry. Both of them started to cry in the meeting room. They did not want to lose their remaining son to the gallows and pleaded with me not to abandon them just because they were poor. At the time of our meeting, the charge had not yet been reduced. Sunil and I looked at each other. My nephew is a very compassionate young man and when I looked at his face, I knew he was hoping I would do the case pro bono. I could read his mind. After all, he is my nephew.

Heng's father reached into his pocket and took out a few $10 notes and a couple of $50 notes, totalling $200, and said, "This is all we've got. Please take this and help us."

I didn't want to take his money and told him, "Please keep your money. You need it more than I do. It's okay."

He insisted. "No, please. I will feel very happy if you take this money." He pressed the money into my hand. We opened a file with the $200 and worked on the case.

It was not difficult to get the charge reduced because of his mental condition. Heng appeared before Justice Woo Bih Li, who is very fair and reasonable and always prepared to listen. We made our mitigation plea based on the fact that Heng was being treated for his disorder and was on his way to recovery. We felt that he should get only four to six years. The DPP, however, said it should be nothing less than 10 years. In fact, he said he would prefer a life sentence. But Justice Woo was not happy with the psychiatric report as it did not state how long it would take for Heng to be cured. He asked for a further report as he wanted to assess Heng's latest psychiatric condition.

Heng seemed to suffer from many delusions, one of which was that he was the head of a gang of death comprising 30,000 to 40,000 members. The uncle he killed was said to belong to another gang which was trying to hurt Heng's gang and get rid of its leader. Heng also believed his uncle possessed a gun which he wanted to get hold of to commit a robbery. He said he needed money to marry a girl who was supposed to have lived with him. In another delusion, Heng said that he had a girlfriend who had aborted their baby and went off to live in Malaysia. However, she had called him to say that she didn't go through with the abortion and his child was alive. Heng was also convinced that his uncle was responsible for the death of his elder brother and his grandfather. He heard the voice of his grandfather telling him to kill his uncle. His was a classic case of paranoid schizophrenia.

Since the judge had asked for a further report, the psychiatrist treating Heng was produced in court. Dr Tan testified that it takes about a year for doctors to assess the optimum dosage of medication, and that Heng had been improving. She added that the next five years were crucial because that was when some 80 per cent of patients might go into a relapse. She stated that Changi Prison, where Heng was being kept, had better facilities for his needs and his parents would not have to monitor him. I asked Dr Tan if Heng had shown a marked improvement since he started treatment in October 2007. She replied that he had made a very great improvement. She also said that she did not see any reason why he should not continue to improve. Satisfied with her answers, I sat down and said "no further questions". The judge looked at me with a smile.

On hearing Dr Tan's testimony, the DPP stood up and said: "We are not asking for a life sentence, Your Honour. In this particular case, a deterrent sentence is not the objective because you never use mental illness as the basis for deterrence."

I responded. "Even retribution in this particular case is limited because of his mental illness. The two aspects of punishment the court has to take are rehabilitation and protection to society. There is a possibility that this mental illness may have a relapse in five years' time. We have to take it seriously because protection to society is very important. Not only is it protection to society, it is also protection for the accused because it is possible that he may commit suicide."

I told the judge that my earlier assessment where I said the sentence should be four to six years was incorrect and that it should be higher than six years. Once again, Justice Woo smiled at me.

When I was reading the authorities and the psychiatrist's report which had been given the night before hearing the case, I predicted that Heng should be sentenced to eight years in prison. In fact, I scribbled a calculation of how much time he had been remanded and noted that he should be there for another 54 months if he was given eight years. That was just my expectation and I did not dwell on it any further.

So when the judge sentenced him to eight years and backdated it to September 5, 2007, I was rather pleased. I turned to Sunil and showed him what I had hastily scribbled the night before. Then I showed it to the DPP and he remarked, "Not bad, you know, Subhas. You should be a judge!" We all laughed.

As he was escorted out of the courtroom, Heng shook our hands but showed no emotion. His family was very happy. His parents hugged Sunil and I and gave each of us a *hong bao* to show their gratitude. As we left in Sunil's car, I opened the red packets. In each packet was $100. I remarked to Sunil: "Look, as far as they are concerned, there is no such thing as lead counsel and assisting counsel. To them, the both of us are equally important and that should be the way." Many people do not understand that it is the assistant who carries the workload. He has the unenviable task of doing all the work including preparing the submission. The lead counsel merely presents the submission in court, for which he gets all the credit, but actually in many instances, most of the credit must go to the assistant and the team that worked together.

I think when Heng's parents gave us each $100, consciously or subconsciously they realised that Sunil had played an equally important part in their son's case, and I was quite happy that they recognised Sunil's efforts. I gave my share to Sunil and told him he deserved it. To me, it was the start of a good weekend. We managed to get what we wanted all because we had a judge who knew exactly what he should do and we had a prosecution team of Peter Koi and Winodan Vinesh who knew what to ask for and what their limitations were. They did not push for something they knew they would never get. If they had asked for life imprisonment, they would have been asking for trouble because this would have irritated the judge. So, they amended their request to 10 years. But I think eight years was a fair sentence.

THE NEW PAPER/Saturday, May 18, 2002

SINGAPORE

'Basher' finally gets S'pore IC

By TANYA FONG

FOR the last half a century, legal eagle Subhas Anandan (right) has been stateless, even though he has lived in Singapore almost all his life.

But after waiting 30 long years, Mr Subhas, 55, is finally a Singapore citizen.

Said Mr Subhas, chuckling: "I think my wife is even happier because now she does not have to fill in all those forms."

They have to fill in about four forms every time he needs to travel. He got so fed up with the tedium that he gave the task to his wife.

He said: "Just to go to Johor, I had to go to the Malaysian High Commission to get all the visa forms and entry permits." And he had to apply for the visa well in advance.

For his last working trip to Hongkong, he had to wait for two weeks for the visa.

In the early days, as a stateless person, he used to carry a card called "Certificate of Identity" (COI). Later, the COI looked more like a passport.

Nothing beats having the real red [...]

[...] he is looking forward to getting it Tuesday.

Subhas was born in Kerala, India, In 1948, when he was about five old, his father came to [...]

[grew] up in a kampung in [...] and attended Raffles [...].

applied for a citizen[ship] [...] ago. In 1982, he [...] his appli[cation] [...]

NO LONGER STATELESS: Mr Subhas Anandan holding up his provisional identity card as a citizen.

Picture/ KENNETH KOH

'THE BASHER'

A LAWYER with 30 years' experience, Mr Subhas is known as the "The Basher" in legal circles for his stinging courtroom attacks.

A consultant at Harry Elias Partnership, he has handled more than 1,000 criminal cases.

He has also appeared in court for a range of people — opposition leaders J B Jeyaretnam and Francis Seow, underworld figures "Ah Long San" Chua Tiong Tiong and "Bookie Pal" Rajendran.

Last year, he represented Anthony [...] the man who [...] his ins[...]

For a little while, I was wondering if I shou[ld] [...]

BANGKOK POST • OUTLOOK • THURSDAY, JUNE 6, 2002

features

Maverick lawyer

Singapore lawyer happily represents thieves and even terror suspects — but no dissidents, please

ALEXA OLESEN
Singapore, AP

Subhas Anandan, Singapore's top criminal lawyer, has defended a suspected Muslim extremist accused of plotting to blow up the US Embassy, a young German expatriate arrested for selling drugs, and a man charged with beating his maid to death. Anandan, 54, says he will take any kind of client, except dissidents. — AP

He's represented a German woman accused of selling drugs and a man charged with beating his maid to death. He took the case of a suspected Islamic extremist accused of plotting to blow up the US Embassy.

Subhas Anandan has become one of Singapore's best known criminal defense lawyers, building a reputation for his willingness to take on any kind of client.

"These are complex cases. Some would say 'no reprieve', but even people who commit the most heinous crimes must be given an even break." Anandan says when asked to describe his criteria for picking clients.

Yet there is one class he avoids — political activists. "Now I am married and I am a father, so I avoid politics," the 54-year-old lawyer says.

Opposition forces a firm grip on this Southeast Asian city-state by using the legal system to quash dissent, relying on big defamation suits to keep critics quiet. Those sued often complain they can't find a lawyer to defend their cases.

Anandan didn't always avoid political cases.

In the late 1980s he acted as junior counsel for Joshua Jeyaretnam, the godfather of Singapore's meagre political opposition corps. Jeyaretnam faced criminal charges concerning alleged irregularities in the collection of party funds.

Anandan's team lost the case in Singapore. But the verdict was appealed to London — at the time home to Singapore's highest court of appeal — and the ruling was overturned.

Anandan is not alone in his desire to avoid political cases.

"No lawyer in Singapore wants to do political cases," said Jeyaretnam, who calls Anandan a "very good friend."

"It's a very sad commentary. Lawyers here are too scared for their own livelihood." said Jeyaretnam, himself a lawyer who has been sued by the prime minister and other senior politicians.

Lawyers fear that they take on a political client, they may not have their licenses renewed, said Chee Soon Juan, an opposition leader who has had trouble finding local representation in a defamation suit levied against him by Prime Minister Goh Chok Tong.

Chee has had to look abroad for legal help. However, those lawyers — two from Australia and one from Hong Kong — have so far been denied Singapore government permission to represent him

in court. Whatever the reasons. Anandan focuses on criminal cases on this island of four million people.

His profile has grown internationally since he agreed to defend Julia Suzanne Bohl, a young German who narrowly escapes facing the gallows recently when she was arrested on drug trafficking charges. The charges were reduced to a non-capital offense when drugs found in her apartment were determined to be less than four [...]

The case cast the spotlight on Singapore's policy of executing drug traffickers, particularly in Bohl's home country of Germany, where the death penalty is banned.

Anandan currently has five other high-

profile cases on his plate, including the case of Ng Hua Chye, a 47-year-old tour guide who last year confessed to beating his 19-year-old Indonesian maid to death.

He also represents Lam Chen Fong, 25, who has been charged with stealing 9 million Singapore dollars (213 million baht) from hundreds of mainland

Chinese construction workers who thought they were sending their hard-earned savings home through his remittance business.

Anandan says he doesn't harbour religious or moral bias when it comes to defending affluent. He notes that while his firm's founder, Harry Elias, is Jewish and that he himself is an Orthodox

Hindu, the law [...] a suspected [...] this year

Mohamed Z [...] 27, was among [...] al-Qaeda ties [...] ember for alle [...] the US Emb [...] Singapore [...]

REFLECTIONS

J B Jeyaretnam
and the Queen's Counsel

Francis Seow and the Presidents
of the Law Society

David Marshall and the Jury System

Keeping a Promise

TWENTY-SIX

J B JEYARETNAM AND THE QUEEN'S COUNSEL

Defending J B Jeyaretnam (JBJ) brought me into contact with many Queen's Counsel. One of them was John Mortimer, the well-known playwright and author, whom I assisted in JBJ's first criminal case in 1982. JBJ was charged with depriving his creditors of the assets of the Workers' Party. It was a ridiculous charge and the case came up before Senior District Judge Michael Khoo, who was very well respected by the Bar for his righteousness and fairness. Leading the prosecution was Senior State Counsel Glenn Knight. Assisting him was Cambridge-educated John Koh, a very capable deputy public prosecutor.

Glenn Knight and I were classmates at university. We studied law together. Unlike me, he was a brilliant student. He worked very hard and got into the legal service. He was, at the time, an up and coming star in the Attorney-General's Chambers. He was a very good prosecutor but an arrogant twit who thought he was better than he actually was. However, I must say that he was one of the rare prosecutors who had the courage to make decisions that were fair. When he was a DPP at the Subordinate Courts, many lawyers who had made representations to him came out happy because he had either reduced a charge or withdrawn it. He was one who would reduce a charge or even withdraw it if he thought it merited a withdrawal. In that sense, he was a very good DPP.

John Koh and Glenn Knight were the deputy director and director of the Commercial Affairs Department respectively. The fact that they were both capable and intelligent didn't faze me because however good you are, you must have a good case to win. They say a lawyer is as good as his case.

JBJ's trial was a very high profile case because he was then the only opposition member of parliament. The court was always crowded with local and foreign press. When I arrived at Court 1 at the start of the trial with John Mortimer, I asked Glenn Knight and John Koh if we could all see Michael Khoo in his chambers as I had something to discuss with him. They said that they themselves had tried to ask for an appearance in chambers but was told by the district judge that whatever they wanted to say could be said in open court. But I still insisted on seeing him. I went up to Miss Kong, Michael Khoo's personal assistant, and told her the reason why I would like to see him in chambers: I wanted to introduce John Mortimer to him. It was a normal courtesy call.

Michael Khoo agreed to see us and the four of us walked into his chambers. Glenn Knight was peeved as his application to see the judge in chambers had been turned down. I introduced John Mortimer to Michael Khoo. They shook hands. Michael Khoo said: "Mr Mortimer, I've read your books and I find them very interesting. It's a pleasure to meet you in person." They exchanged pleasantries and then we left.

There were a total of four charges against JBJ, the Workers' Party's secretary-general, and Wong Hong Toy, the party's chairman. Glenn Knight and John Koh were very meticulous in their work, but the evidence they produced was shabby. At the end of the prosecution's case, Glenn Knight made a very strange application in court. He wanted to amend the charges without giving any notice of his intention to do so. I immediately asked John Mortimer to object. He stood up and objected very strenuously to the prosecution's last minute amendment which he said was unfair, unreasonable and caught the defence by surprise. He said that this shouldn't be the way things ought to be done. Senior District Judge Michael Khoo nodded his head and said: "Mr Mortimer, can you tell me what are your reasons? Give me the authorities."

Without any hesitation, the QC replied, "Sir, I was told to object by my learned junior and I did. Will you allow me to give you the reasons after lunch?" The whole court laughed.

Michael Khoo just smiled and said, "Well, I'll adjourn it to the afternoon and by that time you should give me the reasons." John Mortimer agreed. He then told me that he was having lunch with our client and asked me to find the reasons why we were objecting. I immediately went to the Subordinate Courts library, took the precedents and authorities, and prepared the arguments. I only had a sandwich for lunch in the Bar Room that day. After his lunch, he came to the Bar Room and I gave him the authorities. He read it and said, "Well, it looks sensible, it looks reasonable. I think the judge will have to uphold our objection." I smiled in agreement. He then added, "Do you know what's funny about this whole thing, Subhas?"

"What, John?"

He laughed. "If our objection is upheld, people are going to say I'm a damn good QC but if it is not, they are going to say that his assistant is incompetent and didn't furnish me with the sufficient materials." I laughed nervously.

Back in court, we argued our objection and Glenn Knight was asked to reply. He was very upset with our objection and the way the case was proceeding. He stood up and said: "I do not know why Your

Honour is asking me to reply. We have been doing it this way all the time. We have been amending charges whenever we feel like it, even at the end of the prosecution. If I'm not mistaken, even you, Sir, when you were a DPP, also amended charges at this stage. So, what is the problem?"

Michael Khoo simply looked at him and said: "Maybe I too did it when I was a DPP, but now I am being told by counsel for the defence that what we did was wrong. Instead of giving me the reasons why it is not wrong, you choose to talk about what I did when I was a DPP. As an officer of the court, I expect you to be of assistance."

I could see that the judge was quite annoyed. Glenn Knight knew he had gone too far. He promptly apologised and assured Michael Khoo that he would return with arguments to counter our objections. But the arguments he brought forward were weak and did not throw any light on the matter. The judge rejected his reasons and disallowed his application to amend the charge. In fact, he dismissed one charge without calling for the defence which angered Glenn Knight even more. However, it was decided that JBJ could choose whether he wanted to give evidence in his defence. He said he would.

I have to say that I've never seen as vicious a cross-examination of anyone as I saw Glenn Knight cross-examine JBJ. Some of the questions were unwarranted. A lawyer himself, JBJ told Glenn Knight that the implications of the questions were very vicious and should not be asked. Michael Khoo was silent and stared at Glenn Knight. Halfway through the case, John Mortimer left for California where his book *Rumpole of the Bailey* was being launched as a TV programme. He told the judge: "Your Honour, I have to take leave at this stage because I have an important engagement in the States. I'm leaving the defence in the capable hands of my learned junior. I have complete faith in him. I wish Your Honour well." Michael Khoo also bade him farewell. I was left alone to face Glenn Knight and John Koh.

When the evidence was completed, both sides made their submissions. Michael Khoo acquitted JBJ on all charges except one where he was fined $400. We came out of the court feeling very happy about the whole matter. Waiting outside the court were party supporters who garlanded JBJ, Wong Hong Toy and I. There was a big celebration, but I was not feeling very comfortable with it as I felt it would just make a lot of people angry.

True enough, the prosecution appealed against the acquittal and the case came up before then Chief Justice Wee Chong Jin. In the Petition of Appeal, the prosecution raised the point that Michael Khoo was wrong not to allow them to amend the charge. But strangely enough when it came to arguments, the appeal was argued by the head of crime, Tan Teow Yeow, because Glenn Knight had left for London for further studies. Tan was assisted by John Koh. Frankly, I did not understand what they were saying in support of the appeal. They were beating about the bush. They abandoned the ground about Michael Khoo not allowing the amendment.

I was arguing the case for JBJ, who in turn was arguing for Wong Hong Toy. We knew from the outset, from the way the Chief Justice was reacting to our arguments, that we were going to get a tough time. True enough, he gave us a difficult time. I remember particularly one instance in the appeal when I told him that it was very difficult to prove common intention between JBJ and Wong Hong Toy and the person who gave a particular cheque, which was the subject matter of the charge. The evidence was that both Wong Hong Toy and the donor of the cheque were speaking in Mandarin. It has never been proven that JBJ could understand or speak Mandarin. So we were out to prove that definitely he could not understand what the conversation was all about and as such his mere presence while Wong Hong Toy was talking to the donor could not make him guilty of the common intention charge.

Chief Justice Wee stopped me and asked, "Weren't you counsel for the defendants in the lower court? Weren't you present when evidence was given that they were speaking in Mandarin?"

To both these questions I said, "Yes."

"Why didn't you ask the witnesses whether JBJ could understand Mandarin or not? You could have clarified the situation then," the Chief Justice said.

It was one of those rare times when I really lost my cool in court. I replied, "Is it my job to prove the prosecution's case? Isn't it their duty to prove that JBJ understood Mandarin? Why should I do the work for them?"

There was silence from the Chief Justice. After a while he raised his voice and said nastily, "Carry on."

The trial went on. In the end, Chief Justice Wee gave judgment that the case should be sent back to the Subordinate Courts and that defence should be called for the charges where defence was not called originally and for the case to be heard again. Our appeal against one conviction was dismissed. The cases were transferred back to the Subordinate Courts. Normally, the judge who heard the case earlier on would continue to hear the case and call for the defence as ruled by the Appellate Court. But in this instance, that could not be done because Michael Khoo, the judge who had originally heard the case, was transferred to the Attorney-General's Chambers as deputy public prosecutor. He was no longer a judge and his transfer was actually a demotion. JBJ commented about the transfer and hinted that it was most probably due to the fact that Michael Khoo had acquitted him. JBJ also said that there was public disquiet. For making those statements, there was a parliamentary inquiry which got JBJ into further trouble. But that's another story.

When the case came before the Subordinate Courts again, the next district judge to hear it would have been Chandra Mohan, who was the Second District Judge. Out of the blue, a day or two before the hearing, we were told the case would be heard by Errol Foenander, who had just been transferred to the Subordinate Courts as the Senior District Judge. We found this strange because Errol Foenander was the head of crime in the Attorney-General's Chambers when JBJ was originally charged with the offences. It would not have been fair for him to hear the case as the judge. So when the trial commenced, I stood up and made a preliminary objection that he should not hear the case because of the previous position he held in the Attorney-General's Chambers. I said that justice should not only be done but must be seen to be done fairly. I gave him the authorities and asked him to disqualify himself and transfer the case back to Chandra Mohan.

Errol Foenander overruled my objection very rudely, I must say. He did not approve of my objection in the first place because every journalist in the court was scribbling very furiously about the reason for my objection. He remarked: "I'll continue to hear the case and we'll now proceed."

Again JBJ was defending Wong Hong Toy and I was defending JBJ. Glenn Knight returned from London to prosecute and again was assisted by John Koh. As expected, (it was expected simply because of the Appellate Court's decision), both JBJ and Wong Hong Toy were convicted.

After listening to mitigation, Errol Foenander decided to sentence

JBJ and Wong Hong Toy to three months imprisonment for the offences. We lodged an appeal immediately and got both of them out on bail. I remember telling JBJ at one meeting while waiting for the Grounds of Decision that the three months imprisonment would not disqualify him as a member of parliament. I suggested that he should abandon the appeal against sentence and just argue on conviction. In fact, it would have been better if he had gone in and served the sentence right then. By the time the appeal could be heard, he would have served his sentence and we could just argue on conviction.

JBJ was very angry with me. "Why do you insist on me going to jail, Subhas? I don't want to go to jail. I don't think I should go to jail. I think we should fight the case."

"Well, this is just my opinion because after serving the sentence and getting the one-third remission, you would be out in two months and you can be back in parliament, you know." I added, "Politicians all over the world go to jail. That is why I suggested it."

JBJ was not interested in my advice.

To argue the appeal we engaged Lord Emlyn Hooson, QC, who belonged to the same Chambers as John Mortimer. I assisted Lord Hooson in the appeal. Lord Hooson was a very dignified and well-respected man. We made our introductions and had a drink with JBJ in a room in the Raffles Hotel where Lord Hooson was staying. While JBJ was attending to a phone call, I turned to the QC and said: "My Lord, I feel that we should not appeal against the sentence because it is only three months and would not disqualify him as a member of parliament. I am afraid that if we proceed with the appeal against sentence, his jail sentence may be removed and replaced with a fine. If it is a fine of $2,000 or more, he would be disqualified from parliament. This is what I'm worried about. It can happen in the Appellate Court especially when we are appealing against sentence. So I think we should abandon the appeal against sentence."

Lord Hooson replied: "You are absolutely right. I think it's silly for us to appeal against sentence especially if he is going to run the risk of losing his seat in parliament."

When JBJ joined us after his phone conversation, the QC told him: "I've been listening to Subhas and I think what he says makes sense. We should abandon the appeal against sentence and if the appeal against conviction is dismissed, you would go to jail. You can still continue to be a member of parliament on your release."

JBJ was annoyed. "Emlyn, don't listen to Subhas. He has all sorts of ideas. I don't think I'll be going to jail. I don't think I'll be disqualified. I don't want to go to jail. Just follow what we had discussed earlier. We're going to appeal against conviction and sentence."

I remember Lord Hooson telling JBJ: "You might regret this decision. You are the client and if you want to go on, we will go on." He looked at me and shrugged his shoulders.

The appeal went before Justice Lai Kew Chai. We argued for the whole day and Justice Lai was very polite. Tan Teow Yeow represented the State again with DPP Loke Yoon Kee. Again we felt that we had a good case because Tan Teow Yeow did not have much to say. At the end of the arguments, Justice Lai reserved his judgment. I remember Lord Hooson saying: "In the event the appeal is dismissed, my Lord, can I file some questions for public interest because I am leaving for London. I can't wait indefinitely in Singapore. I thought I would like to file these questions."

Justice Lai shook his head. "You know I can't do that, Lord Hooson. I can't allow you to put the carriage before the horse. I've not even given my decision. It has to wait."

Before Lord Hooson left Singapore, he provided me with a draft of some of the questions of public interest that we could raise if the judgment went against us.

A week or two later, Justice Lai delivered his judgment in which he dismissed our appeal against conviction. But what he did with the appeal against sentence was very unusual. He converted the three months' imprisonment to one month's imprisonment and imposed a fine of $10,000 against each of the two accused, JBJ and Wong Hong Toy. On my application, Justice Lai allowed them bail for one day to file the questions of public interest.

After the sentence was passed, I returned to the Subordinate Courts library to research some facts. In my discussions with some members of the Bar in the Bar Room and upon my research, I learnt that Justice Lai could not impose a sentence of $10,000 because at the time when JBJ was found guilty and sentenced in the Subordinate Courts, Errol Foenander had the power only to impose a maximum fine of $5,000 if he wanted to. The power to impose $10,000 only came about after JBJ's case ended. So, Justice Lai was wrong to set the fine at $10,000. I immediately rushed to JBJ's office, which was at the old Colombo Court building near the High Court, to discuss the matter with him.

I said to JBJ, "I believe Lai Kew Chai was wrong in imposing his $10,000 fine as he didn't have the authority."

JBJ looked at me and remarked, "My God, you're right! What do you think we should do?"

"There are two schools of thought, Ben," I replied. "Some of my friends tell me that we should file this question of public interest on whether he had the jurisdiction to impose the fine of $10,000 only tomorrow morning, just before our hearing commences. But this means we aren't giving him a chance to alter his sentence because he would have risen for the day. The law states that if he's risen for the day, he cannot alter his sentence. If we do this, we won't give him a chance to rectify his mistake and he will be caught flat-footed the next day."

"What is the other school of thought? What are your thoughts?" JBJ asked impatiently.

"Ben, to me, if he has passed his sentence, he has already risen for the day. It doesn't matter whether it's 2 o'clock, 3 o'clock or 5 o'clock. That's my interpretation of risen for the day. But most importantly, I think we should file it today simply because we are both officers of the court and if we have discovered an error made by the judge, we should not capitalise on the error. We should file it straight away. If he wants to alter it, that's his problem but we should object to his alteration. It's not fair or legal. I think we should file it today. That's my opinion."

JBJ looked at me intently for the longest moment. "You know something, my friend, you are absolutely right. We will file it now."

I gained a lot of respect for the man when he agreed with me even though the move may have been detrimental to him. We immediately called in his secretary, Wendy, to type out another question, basically asking whether the Appellate Court had the right to exceed the jurisdiction of the lower court in imposing a sentence, or something to the effect which indirectly stated that Justice Lai had exceeded his right. We filed it at about 3.00 pm with copies sent to the Attorney-General's Chambers. I thought that was the end of the matter for the day but Low Wee Ping, the registrar, was frantically looking for me about an hour later. He left word at my office to return his call urgently.

I learnt that the registrar was looking for me urgently only at about 5.00 pm. I returned his call and his first question was to find out where I was. I said I was in the Bar Room of the High Court having a cup of coffee. Quite assertively he told me to stay right where I was. The next thing I knew, Low was next to me. He said, "I want you to appear before Justice Lai Kew Chai now."

I was confused. "Whatever for?"

"It has something to do with what you've filed and he would like to see you now. So please finish your coffee and go immediately."

"Look, I don't even have my jacket here with me," I said, feeling a bit flustered.

He insisted. "Never mind that, just borrow somebody's jacket now and go. Can you get your client, Jeyaretnam, to come along as well?"

I told him that I didn't know where JBJ was as I knew that he had left his office earlier. The registrar was more anxious that I should appear before Justice Lai immediately. He escorted me to Justice Lai's chambers. Tan Teow Yeow and DPP Loke were already seated outside. As soon as I arrived, Justice Lai's personal assistant, Eugene, invited all parties into the chambers.

Justice Lai said to me, "Subhas, I'm so glad that you have filed this latest question of public interest. I have checked it and I realised that I've made a mistake. I shouldn't have imposed a fine of $10,000. I am altering it to $5,000 instead."

I said to him, "I do not know whether Your Honour could do it now especially after you've risen for the day. The accused is not even here, you know. Can you just do it like that?"

"Well you're here and that's more than enough," he said with conviction. "I do not know if you want to go on with the argument with the question of public interest now that I've rectified it."

I said I was unable to reply until I took my client's instructions. I told him that I would probably be arguing it anyway. Justice Lai said, "I'll leave it to you." He walked out of the room.

I managed to contact JBJ later that evening and update him on what had just transpired with Justice Lai. He just said: "Never mind."

We went back to court the next morning and I argued the alteration from $10,000 to $5,000. I told Justice Lai that firstly, he was wrong to impose the $10,000 fine and secondly, he made it worse by altering the sentence after he had risen for the day in the absence of the accused person and without giving sufficient notice. I raised all the points that had to be raised and there was an exchange of words and arguments between us. Justice Lai took it very well. He was always a very friendly judge and I had a lot of time for him. Finally, he dismissed all the questions of public interest and said that JBJ had to go to jail. JBJ promptly asked permission for him to give a press statement before being taken to the prison. Justice Lai apologised and said that he was not able to allow him to give a press statement in his court. Before he was escorted away to prison, he instructed me to call for a press conference on his behalf. I told the reporters who had gathered around that I would be holding a press conference on behalf of my client in his office at 2.30 pm. JBJ was taken to prison at around noon. I went for lunch.

When the press conference started, I told everyone present that it had been called under the instructions of my client, JBJ, and that what I was going to say were not my words but the words of my client as instructed. JBJ wanted me to tell the people of Singapore, and specifically the people of Anson constituency, not to worry and that he would return. I think he said, "Don't worry, I shall return" or words to that effect. I kept emphasising to the press that the words were JBJ's and not mine. Of course, the newspapers were full of news about JBJ the next day and reported what I had said.

The next thing I knew, the Attorney-General Tan Boon Teik had reported me to the Law Society for conduct unbecoming of a lawyer, that is, for calling the press conference and saying what I had said. I was a bit shocked but I thought it was a knee-jerk reaction from the Attorney-General. Anyway, I went before the Inquiry Committee comprising District Judge Chandra Mohan, a lawyer called Lee Han Yang and two other members. Out of a number of complaints, they thought that there were two or three concerning my calling for a press conference that had to be decided by the Disciplinary Committee.

The Disciplinary Committee was chaired by retired Justice Choor Singh with lawyer Woo Tchi Chiu and two others as members. As soon as I appeared before the committee, I told Justice Singh that I objected to Woo Tchi Chiu sitting as a member of the panel as it was a well-known fact that he was a very close friend of the Attorney-General.

Justice Singh said, "So you think that Woo Tchi Chiu will be able to influence all of us and get the verdict against you? Is that what you think?"

I replied, "No, that's not what I think. In my mind, I would be starting with one vote down and so I'm objecting."

Justice Singh then said, "What if I overruled your objection? Do you know that if I overrule your objection, you'll have to write to the Chief Justice and he may not agree with your views? So what are you going to do?"

"Well, Mr Chairman, I'm prepared to write to the Chief Justice, putting my objection forward, if you are going to overrule my objection," I replied. "I will tell the Chief Justice that Woo Tchi Chiu should be removed from the Disciplinary Committee Panel. If the Chief Justice decides not to listen to me, I'll go further. This matter will not rest here."

Justice Singh glared at me and I glared back at him. I was told to leave the room and return in 15 minutes. On my return, I was told that Woo Tchi Chiu had disqualified himself. Replacing him was T P B Menon, a former Law Society president. I said that I had no objection to him.

In the meantime, before my inquiry, I had written to John Mortimer, Lord Emlyn Hooson and another QC, Martin Thomas, informing them about the Attorney-General's complaint against me. I told them I did not know what the motivation behind it was and that it was not fair. They all responded saying that, to them, I had done nothing wrong. In fact, if I had not adhered to my client's instructions, I could have faced disciplinary proceedings for disobeying his instructions. They advised me not to worry and said that if I needed their help, they would come at their own expense to defend me. I was very touched by their gestures of goodwill. I thanked them for their offers but assured them that I should be able to handle the matter myself.

When I appeared before the Disciplinary Committee, I had with me as my defence counsel, Francis Seow, who was the ex-Solicitor General of Singapore and an ex-president of the Law Society. Anthony Godwin appeared for the Law Society.

Anthony Godwin told Justice Singh, "Mr Chairman, my clients, the Law Society, has instructed me not to offer any evidence against the defendant, Mr Subhas Anandan."

There was absolute silence. Justice Singh looked shocked. "What are you saying?"

Godwin reiterated: "The Law Society does not want to proceed or produce any evidence. In other words, they do not support these charges against the defendant."

Justice Singh said, "Maybe he's not guilty of this particular clause but look at the Legal Profession Act. There are so many offences.

Doesn't the Law Society feel that some of his misconduct could fit into some of these offences?"

Choor Singh was dying to get me charged under some of those sections but Godwin stood up and said, "Mr Chairman, the Law Society has taken advice from the highest authority in this particular case and they are of the view that Mr Anandan has not committed any offence at all."

Choor Singh replied, "Well, in that case I can do nothing."

Francis Seow retorted: "Of course you can do something, Mr Chairman. You can write to the Attorney-General Tan Boon Teik and tell him how stupid his allegations are. There is no basis for all these things." Francis Seow continued rattling on, condemning the Attorney-General.

Choor Singh interjected, "I don't write to anyone except the Chief Justice."

Francis Seow said, "Well you said you could do nothing and I was merely suggesting that you could do something if you wanted to."

I smiled to myself at the exchange of words and walked out of the hearing with Francis Seow.

In the Bar Room, I met Jeffrey Chan, a state counsel in the Attorney-General's Chambers. I told him: "Jeffrey, tell your boss Tan Boon Teik that since the Disciplinary Committee has thrown out my case because of the Law Society's position, he now has the option to take the complaint against me all by himself to the High Court. Tell him I am looking forward to it."

Jeffrey Chan did not respond. The Attorney-General never appealed because I think deep inside he knew that the allegation he made against me was unfounded.

We thought that the saga would end there but it did not. Based on JBJ's conviction, the Law Society took disciplinary action against him and the court of three judges struck him off. The law is such that they can do that if you're convicted. At that time, Singapore had not abolished the Privy Council, and thank God for that. JBJ appealed to the Privy Council and Martin Thomas, who was engaged to be his counsel, invited me to assist him. As the Worker's Party had no money to pay for my services and was unable to fly me to London for the purpose, I did not go. Besides, I was getting a little tired of the whole exercise.

At the hearing of the Privy Council, the Lords informed Goh Joon Seng, who appeared for the Law Society at the time and who subsequently went on to become a High Court judge, that they were looking into the legality of JBJ's conviction because the striking off of JBJ was based on his conviction. They found that the conviction was unreasonable and could not be sustained. The Privy Council gave a beautiful judgment. They criticised Errol Foenander, the Court of Appeal, Chief Justice Wee Chong Jin, Justice Lai Kew Chai and some others who made certain orders. The whole judgment vindicated JBJ and I was very happy for that decision because I had received hell from the Chief Justice. The arguments that I had put forward were dismissed by him with total disregard. The same arguments, however, were accepted by the Privy Council as reasonable arguments. In some ways, I found that I was vindicated too.

JBJ was reinstated as a member of the Bar. But even though the Privy Council decided his conviction was bad in law, he was not given a pardon by the government and he remained disqualified as a member of parliament. Subsequently, he got sued again for defamation and became a bankrupt. He could not take part in elections and only managed to discharge himself as a bankrupt in 2008. He went back to practice and started a new political party called the Reform Party. He said he would stand in the next general election as a candidate. I wish him luck.

On September 29, 2008, I was in the High Court to defend a bus driver who allegedly murdered his 15-year-old stepdaughter. It was my usual practice to go to the Bar Room to have a coffee and chat with Choo, the caretaker. He has been there long before I was called to the Bar in 1971. While having my coffee, JBJ walked in and greeted me. He looked very tired. Since I was with my interns discussing my case, he sat at a table all by himself. He was in a very melancholic mood and appeared deep in thought.

As I was leaving the Bar Room, I walked past him and asked him how he was. He said he was alright and told me that he had been instructed to act as lead counsel in a civil case before Justice Kang Ting Chiu. I remarked that the judge was my former classmate. JBJ smiled. Then he said, "I presume you're here to defend someone for murder." I laughed and said, "Yes."

After lunch that same day, I saw him in the Bar Room again. He was having a nap. He woke up suddenly and asked Choo for a cup of tea. While sipping his tea, he asked me how long my case was scheduled for. I told him that it was for eight days. He finished his tea and left for court.

The next morning, as I was about to have my breakfast, my wife asked me if I had heard the news. I enquired, "What news?" She gently informed me that JBJ had passed away that morning. I was shocked and saddened to hear that. I couldn't believe it as he was with me just the day before. Though he looked tired, I never expected him to die the next day. At that moment, so many memories came flashing back.

I remember the first time I was introduced to JBJ and how I looked at him with awe. My mind also went back to the time when we were embroiled in cases together. I remember the joy of winning and the anguish of losing cases. The anguish was far more than the joy. Most of all, I remember a courageous man who sacrificed so much for Singapore because of the principles he believed in. In my sorrow, I forgot that this man can be stubborn, obnoxious and pig-headed. I could only remember his toothy grin and the way he wept when I saw him in prison. It was so sad.

I will remember JBJ for all the good things—his courage, tenacity and the will to fight on against all odds. He did not see the fruits of his struggle during his lifetime but I am sure that some time in the future, a new generation of Singaporeans will.

TWENTY-SEVEN

FRANCIS SEOW AND THE PRESIDENTS OF THE LAW SOCIETY

I consider the Law Society Council's decision not to adduce evidence against me when the complainant was none other than the Attorney-General to be a very courageous act. The Law Society stood by a member to ensure that he was not bullied. I look upon this as its finest moment. I believe the reason the Law Society Council took that stand was partly due to the calibre of its members, with the likes of Teo Soh Lung, a lawyer who was later detained for what she believed in as a member of the council. There were many others like her who had very strong principles, who believed in fair play and that no one should be bullied.

The other time the Law Society stood out, when lawyers walked with pride, was when Francis Seow was its president. It would subsequently be proven though that many of his actions were fuelled by deep-seated motives or what one would consider as personal desires. Whatever his motives may have been, the way he conducted himself as president and the speeches he made had lawyers walking with their heads held up high. We had the feeling that we could not be trampled upon. We had a leader who would stand by us. Little did we know that the same leader would some day pack up his things and slink away from Singapore leaving behind a lot of disillusioned people who believed in him. There were also those who gave him money. He still owes me $25,000. I suppose I should say goodbye to it. Most of all, there were many who thought that he would open up a new chapter in Singapore politics.

But he was a disappointment and a disaster. He didn't have the moral courage to return to Singapore to face income tax charges. Even if he was convicted of those charges, it would have only amounted to a fine but he was not prepared to take the risk. In the final analysis, he was after all, nothing. A man who spoke well—his eloquence was often very charming—but other than that he did not have what it took to be a leader. He was not prepared to go through the test of fire which all politicians must face. Whatever you may say about Lee Kuan Yew, Goh Keng Swee and the other first-generation PAP leaders, they all went through their "baptisms of fire" and came out stronger. It is a pity that Francis Seow was not made of sterner stuff.

Francis Seow was the reason behind the 1986 amendment to the Legal Profession Act. Section 38(1) was introduced to prevent the Law Society from commenting on any legislation that was passed by the government. Francis Seow was making use of the Law Society as a sort of political platform to attack the government and to make political in-roads with the Singapore public. Lee Kuan Yew, the Prime Minister then, did not like it at all. In fact, there was a Parliament Select Committee hearing for which I was subpoenaed along with many council members including Francis Seow, who was then president of the Law Society. Those who were there at the hearing will remember the confrontation between Francis Seow and Lee Kuan Yew. Most of them said that Francis Seow had the upper hand. When the hearing was over, I remember asking him about what I had heard. He told me: "Well, when I was solicitor-general, there were many instances when it was only between me and the PM. So, when I said these things happened, and if they didn't, there was nothing he could do because it is his word against mine." I honestly thought that when you lie so glibly like Francis Seow, it must have astonished Lee Kuan Yew that a man can lie that well. I think in an interview Lee himself asked how can one handle somebody who tells lies.

It is very difficult to confront a man who is lying when only he and the other person know the truth. I don't think Lee was in a position to go into details because some of the conversations they had must have been quite serious and he was not prepared to discuss the circumstances. Francis Seow took full advantage of Lee's difficulty, lied through his teeth and came out victorious. But his victory was short-lived because in the end the statute was amended. He was statutorily terminated and had to cease being the president because he had been suspended before and the new amendment will not allow him to hold office in the Law Society.

When we were going through this turmoil in the Law Society, the trouble and confrontation with the government, and changes in the law, I couldn't help but think of what my good friend Chelvarajah, a person whom I have a lot of respect for, told me a long time ago. He said: "Subhas, you do not know Francis Seow. He can be a dangerous person." How true his words were.

After Francis Seow stepped down, Giam Chin Toon took over. He had lost to Francis Seow the previous year. Giam was a very unassuming person and not very eloquent or demanding. But he had the knack of getting the right people to do the right things and he would get the job done. In that sense, he was an effective leader. Of course, he paled in comparison with Francis Seow, who was flamboyant and outgoing. Giam was the opposite. He was quiet and was not interested in publicity. He just wanted to be left alone to do his work.

I still remember the time when Giam met with an accident during his tenure. He was driving his Porsche when he knocked down a cyclist who was going against the flow of traffic. The cyclist, an old man, was riding up a slope and Giam couldn't see him in time to avoid him. The cyclist died. Giam was badly shaken up but he still attended the council meeting and was re-elected president of the Law Society for a second year. I recall the man's family was threatening him. In fact during the coroner's inquiry, word went around that the family was going to create a scene and possibly harm Giam. I was asked by some council members to show support for him in court and I roped in some lawyers to join me. We hung around there to make sure that nothing happened to Giam. He was a friend and our president. We felt that it was our duty to ensure that nothing happened to him. Finally, the matter was settled. Giam was not charged because he was simply not responsible for the accident.

After his term was over, Chelvarajah, who was his vice-president, took over as president of the Law Society. Chelva is remembered for his courage in speaking out over Chief Justice Yong Pung How's demands to get things done quickly. The Chief Justice wanted backlogs cleared quickly. He did not want justice to be delayed, all the time emphasising that justice delayed is justice denied. He was always rushing everyone. He wanted the law to be swift but in his enthusiasm, he did not take into consideration the practical problems lawyers faced, for instance, when bringing in foreign witnesses in time for trials. No quarters were given. The registrar was given instructions to issue early dates and to clear the cases quickly. If people could not accept the dates given, the registrar was told to strike off the court action. It was getting to be a very serious problem.

At an annual dinner held during his term as president between 1990 and 1992, where the Guest-of-Honour was then Prime Minister Goh Chok Tong, Chelva made his speech. He took a dig at the Chief Justice, who was present at the dinner, when he said: "When we talk about justice delayed being justice denied, we must also remember that justice hurried is justice buried." There was practically a standing ovation for him because he had put it so aptly at the appropriate time. I think it took a lot of guts for the Law Society president to stand up and say that. Though enthusiastically received, his speech did not have any effect on the judicial administration. Cases were still being rushed but I feel Chelva made his point that evening.

After Chelva, we had Peter Low as president for two years. He was a very insipid president, not noted for anything good or bad. He did not make any changes and there was no effect on the Law Society or on the lawyers. He just plodded along. How he managed to remain president for two years, no one knows. That's all I can say about him. After Peter Low, came another friend of mine, Chandra Mohan. He used to clash with Chief Justice Yong on policies, the Legal Profession Act and many other matters. He was quite bold and spoke his mind. The next president was the late R Palakrishnan. During his three-year tenure, there wasn't much dispute between him and the judiciary. In fact, we called him a "yes" man because practically everything the Chief Justice wanted, he gave. I suppose that was the best way out. There was no point fighting if you were not going to win anyway. You might as well give in gracefully and reap the ensuing rewards.

Arafat Selvam took over from Palakrishnan. She was a disaster. She did not read the minds of the lawyers. There was an attempt to pass a vote of no-confidence against her and her council by the general body of lawyers. I think it's the first time in the history of the Law Society that such a motion was tabled. After two hours of serious debate, my good friend, Lee Tow Kiat, wisely suggested that the meeting be adjourned. That motion was carried and the meeting was never reconvened again. After the incident, I think she decided that she had enough after being president for one year. She stood down. She blamed me amongst others for making her life as president miserable and blamed us for all the problems she had. In some ways what she said was true.

We also had Philip Jeyaretnam, another effective president. During his time, we set up the Association of Criminal Lawyers of Singapore. He misunderstood the motive behind its formation and clashed with us. We hit back at him. There were some antagonistic exchanges between the both of us. Finally, during his last few months as president, we met for lunch and managed to resolve our differences. We realised that it was all a case of miscommunication. After Jeyaretnam, we had Michael Hwang, who is the current president. To me, he seems to be doing well and making the right moves, but others say "a new broom sweeps clean". We'll have to wait and see how his tenure progresses.

I am not in a position to say much about other Law Society presidents. I know Harry Elias very well. He was president before Francis Seow. I worked with Harry in some of his sub-committees. I know T P B Menon who was president for four years. He managed to run the Law Society with a small secretariat. People like him did not have the luxury of the type of secretariat the current president has.

TWENTY-EIGHT

DAVID MARSHALL AND THE JURY SYSTEM

As mentioned early in this book, David Marshall was my counsel when I was detained in Queenstown Remand Prison, along with prominent lawyer Leo Fernando and my classmate, Mak Kok Weng. After I was released from prison, I used to call David Marshall occasionally to say hello. We would chat even when we met in the courts.

A childhood friend of mine, an engineer, was one day charged for corruption. We engaged David Marshall and I briefed him. After a few days, he suggested that my friend should plead guilty. I said that if he wanted to plead guilty, we would not have engaged him in the first place. He said, "Well, that's all I can suggest." We parted amicably enough. Of course, the deposit I paid to him was not refunded and my friend rebuked me for going to see him in the first place. My friend then asked that I should defend him on my own, which I did. He was acquitted by District Judge Ibrahim Burhan without his defence being called. The case appeared in the newspapers the following morning. I ran into David Marshall in Court 26 and he congratulated me on my victory.

A few days later, I saw David Marshall again in the same court. By this time, we already knew that he had been appointed ambassador to France. Many of us were a little disappointed because we thought that he would be the one who would lead the opposition against the ruling party. He had the calibre, the charisma and the experience to be a good opposition leader. When I met him in Court 26, I said to him, "Congratulations, Mr Marshall. But how do you like Mr Rajaratnam as your new boss?" Some of the other lawyers present laughed.

He replied, "Come on, lad. Don't talk like that. I just want to serve my country."

"That's great, Mr Marshall, that you like to serve your country but it's also true that Mr Rajaratnam is also your boss. You shouldn't get upset about that," I persisted. At that time, S Rajaratnam, a pioneer founding leader in the ruling PAP, was Singapore's foreign minister. David Marshall remained silent.

Years later, I had a call from Harry Elias. I had not joined his firm yet, but he telephoned to invite me to a dinner that he was hosting for David Marshall who was back in Singapore to celebrate his 80th birthday. He had asked that I be invited and I was quite happy to attend. The dinner was held at La Brasserie at the Marco Polo Hotel. I met quite a few of my good friends that evening, about 20 of them. When David Marshall saw me, we exchanged greetings. He said, "How are you, my lad? I hear good things about you." I thanked him and gave him my contact details because he said he wanted to invite me for his birthday party. We all sat down to dinner.

The dinner conversation was surprising. David Marshall was very sarcastic, very critical of the government and the ministers. He even cracked political jokes. I felt that what he said could be considered derogatory. I was feeling uncomfortable and uptight. It was not because I loved the government or the ministers. I just could not accept any criticism of them from an ambassador. How could he be talking about his leaders in this manner? I remained silent. I could sense some others were also feeling a little uneasy.

It came to a stage when he said, "Come on, we're all here. We're all Singaporeans. Tell me who has the guts to take the PAP on? Put your hands up." There was no show of hands.

I said, "Mr Marshall, you did not put your hand up. So what's your complaint? What's your beef?"

He responded, "My lad, I can't put my hand up. I'm going blind and I can't even read documents. So how can I oppose the PAP?"

"If you can do an ambassador's job when you're going blind, you can lead the opposition because there are enough people who would gladly be your eyes," I replied. "There'll be enough opposition support for you. You don't raise your hand but you expect us to do so?"

Most of the people at the table agreed with me. I think David Marshall felt a little awkward and did not comment further. It was a good dinner other than that embarrassing moment.

The next day I had a call from Teo Soh Lung, a practising lawyer and friend. She said she had had breakfast with David Marshall and he was practically on the verge of tears, and had commented that I was very insulting at the dinner. I explained to her what had transpired at the dinner. She understood that I did not have any ill intentions when I pointed out that Mr Marshall did not raise his hand too. I told her that it was up to him if he wanted to read anything into that statement. I did not go out of my way to be unpleasant to him. She remarked that he could be sensitive to what I had said. Whatever it was, I did not receive an invitation to his birthday celebrations. I suppose that was fair enough.

David Marshall was a very good lawyer, there's no doubt about that. The best of his time, I felt. He could get acquittals quite easily because the jury system was still in place. If you're eloquent and dramatic enough, you can sway a jury to your point of view. The next thing you know, the jury has come to a verdict in your client's favour. The poor judge can only sit there looking and feeling helpless knowing that the accused was guilty based on the evidence and the law. The judge's hands are tied and there is nothing he could do.

If David Marshall had practised after the jury system was abolished, he would be in the same position as we, the defence counsels, are in now. He would also be very fortunate to get some acquittals. Why was the jury system abolished? I believe one of the factors could have been that he was getting too many acquittals. I think it was becoming quite apparent to the government that the jury system was not a fair system because decisions were made through emotions and not on facts and law.

The last case Singapore had under a jury was that of the Public Prosecutor vs Freddie Tan. Freddie was accused of the murder of his friend, Gene Koh, whose father was a big contractor in the public works sector. He had befriended Gene since their days in London. When they were back in Singapore, he kidnapped Gene and murdered him. David Marshall was holding a watching brief for the family of the deceased. Another well-known criminal lawyer, S K Lee, was defending Freddie Tan. The presiding judge was Justice Choor Singh. When the prosecution and the defence had made their case, S K Lee was able to convince the jury, among other arguments, that it was not murder but culpable homicide because of diminished responsibility. The jury agreed with the defence that Freddie Tan was guilty of culpable homicide and not murder. The judge sentenced Freddie to life imprisonment. We were told that when Justice Choor Singh was asked what had happened, he had to say that his hands were tied as the jury had found the accused guilty of culpable homicide. So, he did the next best thing and sent him in for life.

Strangely enough, in 1976 when I was sent to the psychiatric ward of Changi Prison, I met Freddie Tan. He came to see me, having heard that I was there. He was serving out his life sentence. He wore a green ribbon on his uniform. He said that it allowed him to move around the prison freely with no restrictions. The wardens gave him a lot of freedom and he could choose to visit me with cigarettes whenever he felt like it. Looking at him, you would never know that he had killed somebody and that he had narrowly escaped the death sentence. He was cheerful and looked strong as he said he had been working out.

Freddie Tan's case was the last held with a jury. The law was amended thereafter and it was determined that all capital cases—cases where the death sentence is mandatory—would be heard by two judges, who would decide based on facts and the law. After some time, it was decided that there was no need for two judges to hear capital cases. For many years now, a single judge hears such cases. It was a gradual process—from the jury being abolished to the setting up of a two-judge court and finally to a single judge hearing capital cases. Let us hope that one day we will not reach the situation where capital cases will be heard in the Subordinate Courts. Looking at the calibre of some of the judges there, that would be a real tragedy.

TWENTY-NINE

KEEPING A PROMISE

I will end this book by going back full circle to my early days in Naval Base. But before I do that, I would like to relate an episode in my life that has affected me greatly. I think it's important that I tell you this story because it always reminds me to keep my promises. It also reminds me of the intrinsic goodness in people. You just have to show that you care and people will respond in ways that pleasantly surprise you.

I think I was in my third or final year at university. Before heading for classes in the morning, I would drive my elder sister to the Singapore General Hospital where she was a houseman. I would then head to the university canteen and have my breakfast of usually coffee and toast. I had different groups of friends at university. One of the groups I used to move around with consisted of Sunny Chew, who was at one time president of the Socialist Club; Conrad Raj, who is today a well-known journalist; Francis Yeo, a business administration graduate; Sim Yong Chan, the present vice-president of the Association of Criminal Lawyers of Singapore; and Linda Neo, a very close and dear friend with whom I still keep in touch. She now lives in Germany where she has settled down with a German doctor. There were other ladies in the group like food columnist Violet Oon; Laura Tan, who really wasn't part of the core group but used to hang around us; and also Jill,

Sue and Ruth Kuok, the daughters of the Malaysian sugar magnate, Robert Kuok.

Sunny Chew had this wild idea of making money from the Turf Club. He said that he studied the horses and knew how to read the tracks and that we could make a lot of money betting on the horses. My friends would go to the Turf Club on weekends but I seldom joined them as Saturday was football day and Sunday was "stay-at-home" day for me.

One Saturday, after collecting my sister's salary from her, I went to the Union House and met my friends. There was an excited discussion among the group about the race day. Sunny Chew said he had picked some sure winners and they were going to the Turf Club that afternoon. They persuaded me to join them. I agreed and went with them, still holding on to my sister's salary. I also had with me my university fees which I was supposed to pay.

At the Turf Club, off Dunearn Road in those days, we started betting. Sunny Chew had this habit of changing his mind at the last minute, saying that even though his research showed a particular horse should win, his instinct told him that another horse would be the one to win. Laura never followed Sunny's tips. Instead, she relied on her grandmother, who would give her one or two tips. She would share the tips with us but we did not take her seriously because we thought Sunny was the expert. We should have known better because every time they attended the races, Sunny would lose and Laura would make some money. It was no different that day.

With each bet, we slowly lost more of our money. I lost the money for my fees and finally, in desperation, with my friends urging me on with "sure bet, sure bet", I lost my sister's salary too. I was miserable and in my frustration, shouted out loud at Sunny and Conrad, "What the hell!" I could always delay paying the fees as good old Reginald Quahe, deputy vice-chancellor at the university, was always sympathetic to sad stories. But my sister's salary of $650—it had to be given to my mother as she was expecting it. "What am I going to do?" I exclaimed. It was too late to borrow money from anyone. My friends tried to calm me by saying that they would try to recover some of the losses on Monday by borrowing from other friends. They told me that somehow I had to bear with it the best I could.

It was easier said than done for them and I wondered what I was going to tell my mother. Out of desperation, I drove my car to one of those places where regular people would not go, as it was infested with triad members. I knew a few of the members, having grown up with them. I went into a den, found some of them building up their bodies with weights, and asked, "Where's the boss?" I was told that he was in one of the rooms and I proceeded to enter.

A game of mahjong was being played, and I stood and watched for a while before the boss spoke to me: "I've not seen you for a long time. How are your studies? What made you come here?"

I replied that I needed to talk with him.

We went into one of the inner chambers and he asked, "What's wrong? You look worried? What's happening?" I explained that I needed money to buy some textbooks and added that I would be able to return the loan later. He told me that even though he was illiterate, he was well aware that it was not the time of year to buy books. Besides, I was asking for quite a lot of money, almost $1,000. I had thought that since I was asking for an amount equivalent to my sister's salary, I might as well ask for my university fees too. I tried to convince him that I would be able to return the loan in a few months time.

Somewhat affectionately he asked me: "*Keling kiah*, are you telling me the truth? Don't bluff me. I hate it when people bluff me. Tell me what happened. Why do you really need the money?"

I looked at him sheepishly and decided that it was better to come clean. "I went to the Turf Club today with my friends. My friend thought it was a sure bet and I betted my sister's salary and my university fees. I lost everything. I have to go home now and my mother is waiting for my sister's salary to pay for household expenses as my father's salary is not enough."

He was shocked that I had gone to the Turf Club and reprimanded me. "You gambled with money that didn't belong to you! What are you trying to do? You're already showing signs that you can be irresponsible with other people's money. Tomorrow you will be a lawyer. Then what will you do? Take other people's money and gamble it away in the Turf Club? Pay it back and take more money to gamble again?"

He went on. "Your parents are so proud that you're going to be a lawyer. We too are proud that you're going to be a lawyer and this is what you do. You're such a disappointing bastard. Actually I don't know why I should be talking to you. I should just kick you out of this place."

I just kept quiet. Feeling miserable and remorseful, I asked him softly: "Are you going to help me?"

After calling me all sorts of undesirable names, he said: "Well, what has happened, has happened." He opened a drawer and took out $1,000 and gave it to me. He said: "This should cover your sister's salary and your fees. Let me say one thing. This money is not given to you for nothing. You promise me today, give me your word that you will never ever return to the Turf Club and do what you did today." I made the promise on the spot.

He added: "You'd better keep your promise, Subhas. You see, I'm going to tell our people in the Turf Club to look out for you. If you're there, they are going to pick you up and throw you out and I will definitely not interfere. So, you'd better not go."

I assured him. "I've promised you that I will not go. So I will not."

As I was walking away, he called me back, put his arms on my shoulders, gave me a hug and said: "Don't get angry with me for being so tough on you just now but I'm worried. You're the hope of so many people. I hope you realise that."

I nodded. "Yes, I realise that. I realise what a fool I've been. I'll keep my promise."

He then went back to the same drawer, took out another $500 and shoved it into my pocket. "Take your girlfriend out for dinner. Do what you like but don't gamble." I thanked him. He ruffled my hair like an uncle would and walked me to my car.

That was in 1968. Ever since that day, I have not stepped into the Turf Club. My friends have invited me, especially Harry Elias, who is a member of the committee at the Turf Club, and Edward D'Souza, who is a steward. I've also been invited by the chairman, Herman Hochstadt, but I have always made excuses to avoid going there.

One day, when I was having lunch at the Singapore Cricket Club with Harry, Eddie, Joe Grimberg, who is my good neighbour, and a few others, Harry asked, "Why don't you want to come? Just come and have a good time." Then I said, "Harry, I must tell you a story." I narrated the events of 1968 and the promise I made to the man. Harry looked at me and said: "What a beautiful story this is, Subhas, and of course, you must keep your promise. I am so proud that you're still keeping it even though the man is dead and gone as you said. If ever you write a book, you must include this part of your life."

Gambling got people of the likes of Johnny Tan into trouble. It could easily have gotten me into a lot of trouble if not for a wise old man. He may have been a gangster but he cared enough to give me sound advice. I will forever be grateful to him.

When I think about the Turf Club incident and the promise I made, I'm reminded of another encounter I had when I was still in university. The encounter was with a young Indian boy I met while in a coffee shop with some friends in Naval Base. I noticed the boy, who was perhaps 11 or 12 years old, coming into the coffee shop smoking a cigarette. He sat at a corner table and ordered a cup of coffee. I turned around and asked him, "Hey, don't you think you're a bit too young to smoke?" He looked at me arrogantly and replied, "Well, it's my money and if I want to smoke, I'll smoke. Just because you're older than me gives you the right to smoke and I can't?"

I looked at him and since he made some sense to me, I agreed. My friends were upset with his rudeness but I felt that he showed some spunk and I suggested that we should leave him alone.

After about 10 minutes, he finished his coffee and came over and tapped me on the shoulder. He said, "Can I speak with you alone outside?" This further irritated my friends and one of them retorted, "Hey, young punk, what are you trying to do?" I calmed them down and agreed to leave the coffee shop with the boy. Once we were outside, he asked me if I could lend him $50. I was shocked.

"Fifty dollars! What the hell do you want $50 for? To buy more cigarettes, is it?"

The air of arrogance left his face and he said rather humbly, "Please, I need the money to pay for school fees for myself and my sister and for some household expenses."

"What about your father? Don't you have a father?"

"Don't talk about my father," he replied. "He's always drunk and he doesn't care much about the family. He frequently beats up my mother and that's all he does."

I was curious. "How have you been managing all this while then?"

He told me his story. In those days at the Base, lunch for the workers was prepared by the wives. The families would pay someone to collect tiffin carriers containing food from the homes and deliver them to the workers at lunchtime. The boy assisted the deliveryman and he was paid every day. The man, however, had gone back to India for a long break. The boy did not have the same arrangement with the new deliveryman.

I told the boy: "If your story is true, of course, I'll help you. Not that I've got money but I'll raise it from somewhere. If you're telling me some bullshit, boy, you're in big trouble." He assured me that he wasn't lying and that he knew who I was. I suggested that we meet in a day or two at the same coffee shop.

I discussed the matter with my friends and we decided to find out who his father was. We discovered that his father worked at the Base and drew a regular income. But he was a drunk who had a bad habit of frequenting a strip of 50 to 60 bars called The Sembawang Patio. It was normally patronised by sailors, amongst others. Like the boy's father, most of the customers would get drunk at the bars and beat up their wives when they got home. For some of these Indian men drunk on alcohol, the climax of their night would be to beat up their wives.

When we knew that his story was true, I collected $50 with the help of some friends and gave it to the boy. I said to him: "Here, take your time to pay it back. Study hard and do well. I have one condition when I hand this money to you. You must stop smoking. It's bad for you." He said that he appreciated my help and would definitely agree to quit smoking. He said that he was not addicted to it and it was not difficult to give it up.

Meanwhile, my friends and I decided that his father should stop visiting the bars. We made sure that whichever bar he went to, he would be beaten up when he left and warned not to go there again. Soon we learnt that he had stopped going there and was just enjoying a beer or two at home. His neighbours also confirmed that he had stopped beating up his wife because he was not that drunk anymore.

About a month or two later, the boy returned the $50. I asked him, "How are things at home now?" He said that he could now focus on his studies and didn't need to assist the deliveryman anymore as his father had stopped going to the bars and would give the family money. Things were much better at home. The boy said that his father claimed that he had been beaten up many times and had lodged police reports but nothing had come out of them. So he decided to stay at home.

I smiled and said, "You mean he has changed for the better?"

"Something like that," the boy replied. He gave me a funny look as though he knew that I must have had something to do with the change in his father but he didn't say anything. He was very grateful, thanked me for the loan and walked off.

Many years later, when I was staying at Kampung Wak Hassan, I had to drive past The Sembawang Patio every day. One night on my way home, I stopped there to buy a packet of Dunhill cigarettes. I parked my car, bought my cigarettes and as I was returning to my car, I heard this voice call out, "Mr Subhas, Mr Subhas." A young man came running and caught me by my hand and asked, "Do you know who I am?"

Obviously, I didn't and said to him, "The way you caught hold of me, I thought you were going to beat me up."

He laughed. "Who would want to beat you up, Mr Subhas? Not in this area."

He led me to a group of people who were having supper there. He introduced me to his wife and a few other couples. He quickly grabbed a stool for me and insisted that I joined them. He said, "You don't remember me, do you? Remember, a very long time ago, I borrowed $50 from you and after a month or two, I returned the loan?" As he was narrating the story of our meeting, it all came rushing back to me.

I looked at his wife and asked, "Does your husband smoke?"

She smiled warmly and replied, "No, he doesn't smoke. He told me the whole story and how he gave you his word that he would not smoke and he has not since then. I've not seen him smoke."

I looked at him and said, "You don't smoke, huh?"

"No, Mr Subhas. A promise is a promise."

We talked for a while and I learnt he was working as an engineer. At that time, he had one child. As I got up to leave, his wife held my hand and said, "There's nothing we can do to repay the kindness you showed my husband then but we always pray for you."

I said, "That's the greatest thing anyone can do for me. Thank you."

"Look after your health," she called out as I left.

On August 14, 2008, as I neared the end of writing this book, I went to the Women's Prison in Changi to see three people: two ladies who were charged with capital offences for drug trafficking, and another who was charged for murdering her husband's brother and stabbing the brother's wife and mother. The husband of the accused is an opposition politician in Singapore. As the woman is a Chinese citizen, I was briefed to handle the case by the Chinese embassy. The prison has not given me permission to see her yet and I still do not know why she murdered her brother-in-law. She is going through a psychiatric evaluation.

After seeing the other two alleged drug traffickers, I visited One-eyed Dragon in his condemned cell. I had just prepared his clemency petition and wanted him to sign it. When I gave the petition to him, he looked at it, turned to me and said, "Lawyer, is there any use in sending this to the President? You know and I know that I'm not going to get any clemency from the President. So why are we going through this rigmarole?"

"It is your last avenue of appeal asking for clemency and as your lawyer, I have to advise you to do it. Of course, if you don't want to do it, I can't force you."

"What is your advice?" he asked.

"My advice obviously is that you should sign the petition and we should send it to the Istana. If not, I would not have bothered to prepare one and come to see you."

One-eyed Dragon thought for a moment. "You know, I want to defer my execution for as long as I can."

"Why? Are you afraid to die?" I asked

"No, no, no. I'm not afraid to die. In fact, it would be quite good to die."

"Then why do you want to delay the execution?"

"When I was arrested and charged, my son was only a few months old. Now he is almost two years old. When he comes to see me, he calls me 'papa'. I spend time with him even though I'm in this condemned cell. I love that boy and love even more to hear him call me 'papa'. I just want to hear him call me that for a few months more. That's why I hope to have the execution delayed."

I told him that when I send the petition to the President, I could include a note stating his wish. It could give him a little more time. He instructed me to do that.

"The people here say that one way to get more time is to change lawyers. They said I should tell the Superintendent that I don't like my present lawyers and that I want to replace them and that would give me some time," One-eyed Dragon said.

I agreed with this. "There you are. They've given you a way to get your extension. Why don't you just replace me? Get another lawyer."

He smiled at me. "You know I thought about it but I don't want to do that. When my wife came to see you to appear for me in the Court of Appeal, you agreed to do so. I know you've been a good counsel and you've done the best you could for me. I can follow all the arguments you put forward in my defence because the interpreter was there. I don't think it's right for me to replace you because people will think that you've done something wrong and that you had to be replaced. Nobody would know the real reason and I don't want to do that to you because, you see, I respect you quite a lot."

I was really moved and thanked him for his compliment. But I assured him that I wouldn't mind if he replaced me with another lawyer just to get his extension. He reiterated that he did not think it was right or fair to me. We could not even shake hands. I just placed my palm against the glass panel and he put his palm against mine on the other side.

As I walked away, I saw Sunil approaching me. He had just come from interviewing another client in the prison. As we walked together to the prison's main exit, I told Sunil what One-eyed Dragon and I talked about. He just smiled. Even though my nephew has been in practice only for three years, he has proven to be a man with a lot of passion for criminal law. He defends the accused very passionately and he does everything he can for them. He is very conscientious.

"Well, at least One-eyed Dragon feels that we have done the best for him," he said.

"Yes, it looks as though our best is not good enough. It looks as though *so* often our best is not good enough."

Sunil remained quiet.

He looked at me and asked, "Are you very tired?"

"Why do you ask?"

"You sound very tired," he replied.

I told him I was a little tired and frustrated. Sometimes I wish I can retire and forget about criminal law and all these accused persons and their problems. I told Sunil I may retire sometime at the end of 2009.

He said: "*Valiachan* ('big father' in Malayalam), you've been saying this from the time I've been your assistant but every year something comes up and you've gone on to fight."

"I suppose so."

At the exit gate, we retrieved our identity cards and returned the prison entry cards. Sunil asked me to wait there while he fetched the car which was parked quite a distance away. We've always had to park a long distance away. It's not often that lawyers for the accused get to park within the prison compound, which is mainly reserved for civil servants. A police sergeant who is there to take a statement from an accused person will be given a choice parking lot. People like me, who can't walk long distances due to ill health and who go there for official reasons, are treated like third-class citizens and do not get the same privilege of parking inside.

As I was waiting for Sunil, a guard, an Indian woman, came out and asked me, "Mr Subhas, are you waiting for someone?"

"Yes, I can't walk. So my nephew has gone to get the car. I'm waiting for him."

"If he has gone outside to get the car, he's going to take a while, sir. Please come inside and take a seat in the air-conditioned room while you wait."

I explained that I had already returned the prison entry card but she insisted that I should wait in the comfort of the air-conditioned room. I was very grateful to her. Another guard showed his hospitality by adjusting the temperature of the air-conditioning as I was still feeling a little hot. Many of the prison wardens greeted me and enquired after my health as they walked past. Some even offered to get me a drink which I politely refused.

As I looked around, I thought to myself: "Years have passed and I really appreciate that at least some people recognise some of the good things I have done. I have in my twilight years become some sort of celebrity but I wonder how long that will last. People have short memories and very easily you can become yesterday's hero."

EXCERPTS FROM "IT'S EASY TO CRY"

When I was released from prison in 1976, I wanted to write a book about my experiences in prison. When that was reported in the press, David Marshall, who was my lawyer then, rang me up and said to me, "Be careful, my lad. You don't want to look for trouble. You may state issues that are protected by the Official Secrets Act. I suggest that you hold on." I took his advice and held on for a very long time — until 2008 when I wrote my first book, which became an instant hit and stayed on the bestsellers chart for a long time. I had initially thought to title it "It's Easy to Cry" but instead titled it "The Best I Could".

I decided that my second book would be called "It's Easy to Cry" because it is dedicated to cases that bring humanity and emotions to the forefront and there are cases where people have pleaded guilty just to save somebody else or to ensure that somebody else does not get into trouble.

In August 2013, I was beginning to feel unwell, but I was still working. I was in my office when my assistant, Diana Ngiam, brought one of the Submissions that she had prepared. I looked at the Submission and said that there were missing points. She had failed to mention some of the facts that happened in court. She said, "You know, Uncle, I've gone through the notes very carefully." I said, "Go and look at it once more." She went back to her room and later realised that I was right. She approached my nephew, Sunil, who was working with me, and said, "Uncle may be getting older but he is still very sharp. His memory is so good." Sunil laughed. She came back with the amended Submission, and this time I said, 'Yes, this is what I wanted." Diana is a very intelligent girl, very compassionate to all, including the accused persons. Sometimes she feels too much and that is not good, but I am glad that she's part of my team. After reading the Submission and approving it, I told her, "Diana, I've got a funny feeling that I will not be accompanying you and Sunil to court anymore. I somehow feel that my career is going to be over soon." She looked at me and said, "You may be a little under the weather but you are not going to die. Don't talk like that." She was very upset. I said that there was no point being upset for this was what I felt. She came nearer and looked at me and said, "No, Uncle, you are going to be with us for many more years." I laughed.

In September that year, I fell ill and was taken to hospital. I was diagnosed with heart failure, and after some rest in the hospital I was discharged. Soon after, I resumed work but realised that I was not able to cope with full work. I was going in and out of hospital over the next couple of months, and finally fell gravely ill in mid December 2013. Doctors were at their wits' end as to what they could do for me and several propositions were put to me, all of which I had initially rejected. By the year end, one of the doctors gently explained to my wife and my elder sister that my sole kidney was failing and there was nothing more they could do other than dialysis, and even that was risky due to my failing heart. He offered palliative support if my family so needed and indirectly suggested that there was nothing more they could do for me. On hearing this, both my wife and sister decided that they were not giving up on me and with their faith in God, they believed that I would be well again. My wife explained the circumstances to me and insisted that I should fight on. Gently, I told her, "Ask Dr. Ching to see me."

Associate Professor Ching Chi Keong is my cardiac electrophysiologist. He had recommended the insertion of a Cardiac Resynchronisation Therapy Device (CRTD), which I had initially rejected. As it was the least invasive, I finally decided that I should give it a shot. I should not go without putting up a fight.

The procedure was a success but sadly, by then, my kidney had been impaired. I was required to go for dialysis three times a week. This altered my lifestyle significantly. I found it hard to cope emotionally and I would get upset with myself, depressed and frustrated with what I had to deal with — three times a week, being pricked twice on the arm at each session and being confined to an uncomfortable chair for four hours to dialyse my blood. It was during the long and weary four hours that I decided I should start dictating my second book to keep myself occupied.

It has been an emotionally and physically tormenting experience coping with my poor health. I was previously racing through my life, but suddenly, that lifestyle has come to a grinding halt. It was hard to bear. The positive thoughts that got me through these low points were my wish to see my son graduate; my niece, Sunita, get married; and to attend my nephew, Naresh's, wedding. Inevitably, there were moments of depression when I forgot these desires and allowed myself to dwell on negative thoughts.

My wife, Vimi, would always tell me, "Be brave, think of positive things, know that your glass is not half empty, it's half full. We are here with you and I will never leave you. We will always take care of you. Don't be afraid." Sometimes when I am down, I feel like no one understands me. When I am alone in my room, or alone attempting to read a book, negative thoughts would creep into my mind and that whole day is ruined.

I find that dictating while doing dialysis is not as easy as I thought. You are with other patients, and nurses are walking up and down monitoring you. Suddenly, you realise that you are totally dependent on the dialysis machine for your life. Then, depression hits and you wonder why you have to go through this stage, and there are even times when you curse God. But, there are also times when you pray to Him. It's all a confused state of mind. Sometimes, you even question the existence of God and wonder whether you are actually going to some place that does or doesn't exist. But deep inside, with my religious upbringing and the fact that I am the Chairman of the Board of Trustees of a temple, there lies a conviction within me that there is a God and God works in mysterious ways. You really do not understand some of the things He does, but again you must learn to accept it. The process of accepting is difficult but slowly I am getting the knack of it.

They say that in any incident, there will always be a silver lining. To me, my illness made me a more realistic person, one who realises that in the past, I got all my priorities wrong. It was my career first, my career second, and my career third. I didn't make time for my wife and son. I didn't make time for my siblings and I didn't make time for my very close friends. These are the people who are now with me through my difficult times. It is in the time of crises that you know who your friends truly are.

I have reached the age of sixty-seven years and they have been very eventful sixty-seven years. There are many things that I have done that I regret but then a life without any regrets is really not a life, is it?

Subhas passed away on January 7, 2015. These are excerpts from It's Easy To Cry, *which Subhas dictated while on dialysis. The book is scheduled for publication in 2016.*